WHEN?

The Biblical Timing for Prophetic Fulfillment

RON J. BIGALKE

DISPENSATIONAL
PUBLISHING HOUSE, INC.

In honor of the legacy of
Dr. John & Mrs. Norma Whitcomb.

Table of Contents

ENDORSEMENTS

Dr. Ron Bigalke's book, *The Biblical Timing for Prophetic Fulfillment*, presents a thorough examination of prophetic Scripture, highlighting many important issues such as Israel, the church, the rapture and the millennium. This work addresses the varied views on prophecy that have confused many, such as preterism and amillennialism, with scholarly detail. Ron's excellent research contributes to a much clearer understanding of the times in which we live and, in particular, the future that is to come. This book deserves a large distribution among those who concern themselves with prophetic Scripture.

— **Arno Froese**
Executive Director, Midnight Call Ministry
Editor-in-Chief, *Midnight Call* and *News From Israel*

Ron J. Bigalke has produced a clear and substantive examination of one of the major areas of debate when it comes to eschatology—timing. Bigalke deftly weaves together exegesis, history and critique as he evaluates the four major schools (as well as variations within each) of prophetic interpretation. The book begins with a clear discussion of terms and then guides the reader through a unique analysis of how each of the four major views sees the timing of the millennium and the rapture. The author's evidence provides compelling evidence for a premillennial and pretribulational position driven by a consistent hermeneutic. I found this volume to be Biblically and logically satisfying. Highly recommended!

— **Dr. Jerry Hullinger**
Professor of Bible, Piedmont International University

When? is not a book for superficial Bible readers. If you are serious about Scripture and want a deep dive into eschatology, this book is a must read. While the doctrine of future things has lost its popularity, it is foundational to our faith and as basic as this statement by Bigalke: "The primary difference between premillennial and non-premillennial systems is hermeneutical." Your entire approach to Scripture will be demonstrated by your position on prophecy.

— **Paul Seger**
General Director, Biblical Ministries Worldwide

Within Evangelical Christianity, the study of eschatology, or what the Bible reveals about the end, can be one of the most divisive and polarizing of subjects. The reason for such a sharp difference of opinion typically relates not to the *what* question but rather to the *when* question. For example, while most Christians believe in a rapture of some kind, the debate concerns the timing of the rapture. Will it be before, in the middle of, or at the end of the tribulation period? Moreover, while most Christians believe in the manifestation of the kingdom of Christ, the debate concerns when this kingdom will materialize. In other words, will it occur before or after Christ's second advent? Furthermore, while most Christians accept as true the prophetic contents of the book of Revelation (Rev. 4—22), the debate concerns when these prophetic details will be fulfilled. For example, have they been fulfilled in the past, are they being fulfilled today, or will they be fulfilled in the future? All of these hot-button topics relate not to the question of *what* but rather to the question of *when*. If you have ever been perplexed concerning *when* key prophetic events will take place related to the kingdom, the rapture and the fulfillment of the book of Revelation, then this book is for you. In the present volume, Dr. Ron Bigalke painstakingly sets forth a compelling case concerning the prophetic timing related to these vital subjects. He convincingly demonstrates to the reader that the futurist, pretribulational and premillennial understanding of eschatological events is the proper Biblical understanding. He also takes his readers a step further by explaining why this proper timing sequence is important and how it relates to their personal lives. This work receives my highest recommendation.

— **Dr. Andy Woods**
Pastor-Teacher of Sugar Land Bible Church
President of Chafer Theological Seminary

FOREWORD

If memory serves me correctly, I first met Dr. Ron J. Bigalke more than a decade ago at a conference on Biblical eschatology in which we were both making presentations. We were certainly aware of each other prior to this, as we were both active in trying to impact our respective communities for Biblical truth. We both were involved in academic service and pastoral ministries, and we both shared a passion for focusing our listeners and readers on the importance of methodology in handling the Bible, drawing theological conclusions from the Bible and applying the Bible in everyday life. I remember being appreciative even then of the thoroughness, objectivity and precision with which he spoke. We quickly developed a friendship and became co-laborers in several contexts. We collaborated on a number of writing projects, shared editing responsibilities for an academic journal and were involved together in teaching and administration of a seminary. Through this time, I have observed that Bigalke has remained consistently committed and true to the simplicity of the Bible and the method it prescribes for developing theological conclusions and practical applications. He has done so in a way that reflects a high value of depth and rigor of scholarship. His personal commitment to study and growth is reflected in his quality credentials and academic experience and influence, but more importantly he puts all that to use in the simple service of others. His is not simply an academic pursuit; it is intensely practical, and is reflected in his ongoing service to real people in real contexts. Thus, the quality of his present work is no surprise to me— nor is the tone in which he presents it.

As I recall, it was Mark Twain who once said, "If a man doesn't believe as we do, we say he is a crank, and that settles it." Twain's lament was a general one and broadly applicable, but it could have been said to characterize much of the mood in theological discussion. So often in theological matters issues are "settled" by *ad hominem* attacks rather than by evenhanded considerations of the issues and fair representations of those who hold to differing views. In the 20th century, due in part to globalization, advances in technology, the narrative of two world wars and the general trajectory of history, eschatology captured the attention of the evangelical world in ways it had not previously, and theologians worked to address specific questions that had previously gone unexamined. Resulting views were diverse, and while there were many respectful and gracious thinkers holding to these diverse views, the general mood of the broader discussion seemed less than cordial and more deserving of Twain's description.

In a 21st-century approach, Dr. Bigalke addresses key eschatological questions with scholarly evenhandedness, and a charitable approach, representing the diverse views he encounters with respect, clarity and technical precision. He emphasizes accurately the centrality of hermeneutic method as the primary catalyst for diversity of views in the areas covered. The disagreements he discusses here are not generally rooted in ill motivations or ignorance, but are largely the result of sincerely held beliefs that are theologically derived. Bigalke's work here is important, as it is careful not to attack differing thinkers, but rather to focus on the derivations of the diverse views themselves. Bigalke encourages readers to examine things from an exegetical perspective—recognizing what even those who disagree with his (premillennial, dispensational) conclusions will acknowledge: If we consistently apply literal, grammatical, historical hermeneutics to the Biblical text, we will draw premillennial and dispensational conclusions (even if there are nuanced differences here or there).

Bigalke's is a timely methodological discussion, focusing appropriately on ... timing. He provides here a straightforward catalog—a handbook of sorts—of major distinctions between dispensational and non-dispensational views, but the uniqueness of this work is in its organization by chronology of events. This structure underscores a thoroughness, as the catalogued events are not handled in isolation, but rather in their appropriate chronological context. This allows Bigalke to be comprehensive without being voluminous, and the approach further fosters good representation of the differing methodologies for handling eschatology and the contexts they encompass.

As Bigalke articulates the reasons certain conclusions are to be preferred, the practical implications are not lost here. He appeals to Christians that the prophetic Word of Scripture matters to each of us in our lives. Through the record of Biblical prophecy, we ought to gain even greater confidence in our Lord as we engage the path He has prepared for us. Further, Bigalke appeals to Christians that Biblical prophecy, rightly understood, provides a tremendous urgency and tool for reaching those who do not know Christ.

Brothers and sisters, we have much work to do. Let us take our next steps with the knowledge and confidence of Biblical prophecy and its implications for life.

Christopher Cone, Th.D., Ph.D., Ph.D.

August 2017

PREFACE

One dynamic of godly living is "looking for the blessed hope and the appearing of the glory of our great God and Savior, Christ Jesus" (Tit. 2:13). As the Greek verb translated "looking for" is in the present tense, it signifies a characteristic attitude: being always ready to meet the returning Lord. Therefore, with this hope in mind, Scripture reminds believers (in v. 14) that the Lord Jesus, who will be met someday, is the one who redeemed his people from all wickedness. The reason for this redemption is to purify a people who are "zealous for good deeds." The doctrine of the Lord's return, which is woven throughout the New Testament, addresses the motivation for godliness.

There is not a single Bible verse that reveals precisely when the Lord will return for his church in relation to the tribulation or the second coming (in a manner that would satisfy everyone). However, this does not imply that the Bible does not straightforwardly reveal the timing of the Lord's return.

Many Biblical doctrines are not derived from a solitary verse of Scripture; rather, those teachings are developed into systematic conclusions by harmonizing several passages.

Some truths are revealed explicitly in the Bible, such as the deity of Christ (Isa. 9:6; John 1:1; Heb. 1:1-8) or salvation by grace through faith in Christ alone (Hab. 2:4; Gal. 3:10-12; Eph. 2:8-10). Other doctrines, such as the Biblical revelation of God as triune, are affirmed by harmonizing the many passages that relate to such teaching. The most inexplicable and mysterious revelation concerning the Biblical description of God is that, though the Bible is unequivocal in its declaration that there is one God, there are three distinct personalities to whom deity is ascribed. Consequently, the only teaching that is faithful to all the Biblical evidence is what is known as the Trinity (or tri-unity) of God. Similarly, a literal, systematic interpretation of all New Testament passages relating to the Lord's return will lead to the pretribulational assertion that Jesus will translate all living believers and resurrect all dead believers at least seven years prior to his coming to establish his 1,000-year reign upon the earth.

Similar to the doctrine of the Trinity, the timing of the Lord's return must be developed from a literal interpretation, in addition to the harmonization of many Biblical passages. Consequently, pretribulationism is best understood by considering the doctrine according to three aspects: (1) foundational issues; (2) specific Biblical texts; and, (3) practical implications. Foundational issues involve the role of timing in prophetic fulfillment. For instance, one must answer when will a Biblical prophecy be fulfilled historically. The four classical answers to that question are preterism, historicism, idealism and futurism, which are addressed in chapters 1-5.

Understanding there are only four possibilities in relation to the time of prophetic fulfillment helps to provide a Biblical foundation for understanding the pretribulational rapture. Throughout chapters 1-5, it will be evident that premillennialism is foundational to the doctrine of the rapture, and one's understanding of prophetic timing directly affects whether to embrace amillennialism, postmillennialism or premillennialism. The doctrine of the rapture is a premillennial consideration, and thus if one embraces preterism or idealism, that person will not be concerned with the Lord's coming for his church in relation to the future tribulation. (Due to the particularities of historicism, one could only affirm midtribulationism or posttribulationism in that perspective). Chapter 6 addresses other foundational issues, such as literal interpretation and the distinction between Israel and the church. Chapters 7-13 consider the specific Biblical texts concerning the doctrine of the rapture, in addition to considering the practical implications in the defense of pretribulationism (chs. 11-13). Finally, in an age in which many neglect the study of Biblical prophecy, a concluding application of the doctrine's importance is the subject of chapter 14.

A word of appreciation is due *Midnight Call* for gracious permission to reproduce in revised form much of the material that already appeared in a series of articles. Dr. Randy White, founder and CEO, and Paul Scharf, editor in chief, for the Dispensational Publishing House also deserve indebtedness for their encouragement and support to publish this work. The work herein is commended to God and to students of the Word of God in the hope that it will provide greater clarity of the prophetic Scriptures.

CHAPTER 1

THE INTERPRETATION
OF BIBLICAL PROPHECY

The word eschatology is derived from two Greek words, eschatos ("last") and logos ("discourse"), meaning the doctrine of last things. Biblical eschatology can be divided into two categories: personal eschatology and general eschatology. Personal eschatology addresses the subjects of death, hell and resurrection. General eschatology addresses the timing of events such as the tribulation and millennium. Whereas there is slight disagreement among evangelicals in regards to personal eschatology, there is significant disagreement among evangelicals in regards to general eschatology. The main reason for such disagreements has to do with one's usage or disregard of a consistent and literal interpretation of Biblical prophecy. Of course, interpretative differences are certainly true in regard to the timing of prophetic fulfillment and the meaning of the millennium. Knowledge of the various theological systems of prophetic timing fulfillment provides understanding of the logic and tenets of the various views regarding the meaning of the millennium. If the basic characteristics of preterism, historicism, idealism and futurism are understood, then it is not difficult to understand a particular position regarding the millennium. Furthermore, the views of prophetic timing are more foundational as to what a person believes Scripture to reveal concerning the millennium.

THE TIMING OF
PROPHETIC FULFILLMENT

Prior to proceeding further, one should understand what is meant by the terms "tribulation" and "millennium." For instance, the word "tribulation" is not a technical term; it can refer to general suffering (John 16:33; Acts 14:22; Rom. 5:3; 12:12), to the seven years of Daniel's 70th week (Jer. 30:7-9; Dan. 9:24-27; 12:1), or to the second half of that week: the "great tribulation" (cf. Matt. 24:21 which refers to the last half of Daniel's 70th week as the great tribulation, while Matt. 24:8 uses "beginning of sorrows" in reference to the first half).[1]

The word millennium is derived from the Latin *mille* ("thousand") and *annum* ("year") in reference to the statement in Revelation 20:4 ("and they came to life and reigned with Christ for a thousand years"). The early church referred to the millennium by the Greek term, *chiliasm*. Throughout the history of the church, there have been three primary views concerning the nature of the 1,000 years: (1) amillennialism; (2) postmillennialism; and (3) premillennialism. Interpretative differences are the reason for the

---

1   Daniel's 70th week does not relate to God's purpose for the church. The tribulation will come upon a world that is in rebellion against God (Rev. 15:1; 16:1-21; 19:15) and will reveal Satan's nature (12:7-12). During the tribulation, national Israel will be brought to faith and repentance in the Messiah, which is in preparation for the millennial kingdom (Jer. 30:7-9; Zech. 12:9—14:5; Rev. 19:1-6); it will also be a time of profound evangelism (Matt. 24:14; Rev. 6:9-11; 7:1-17; 11:2-14; 12:13-17; 13:7; 14:1-5, 12-13).

three views, such as whether to understand "thousand" in Revelation 20 as literal or symbolic. How one understands the millennium will also influence views concerning the details of eschatology. Directly influencing one's view of the millennial kingdom is how one understands the fulfillment of Biblical prophecies to occur.

There are four possible views concerning the timing of prophetic events: preterism (past), historicism (present), idealism (timeless), and futurism (future). Preterism is the view that the majority of prophetic events have already been fulfilled. Historicism equates the current church age with the time of the tribulation; therefore, prophetic events are regarded as being fulfilled throughout the church age. Idealism is the view that the Bible does not specify a time (chronology) for the fulfillment of prophetic events. Recognizing that approximately 300 prophecies were fulfilled literally in regard to the first coming of Christ, futurism believes that the remaining prophecies associated with the Lord's second coming will also be fulfilled literally in an eschatological period.

As already stated, unfortunately, significant disagreement exists among evangelicals in regard to general eschatology. However, the interpretative differences are certainly not due to lack of clarity in Scripture, but they exist mainly because of one's usage or disregard of a consistent and literal interpretation of Bible prophecy. The most natural interpretation of unfulfilled Biblical prophecies leads to a pretribulational and premillennial expectation. Disagreements exist due to inconsistency in Biblical interpretation (of course, this could be said about so many doctrines of the Bible). How one understands the timing of prophetic fulfillment also influences an understanding of the meaning of the millennium. Throughout this work, the reader will understand how one's understanding of prophetic fulfillment relates to an understanding of the meaning of the millennium (and why all the views on the timing of prophetic fulfillment could be consistent with postmillennialism, but not with amillennialism and premillennialism).

Preterism

Preterism is a term from the Latin *praeter* meaning "past." The preterist view is that most, if not all, of prophetic fulfillment has already occurred.[2] Preterists believe that they have already identified the beast of Revelation. The first beast of Revelation 13 is understood to be Nero and the second beast is understood to be Domitian. Moreover, preterists believe that everything in Revelation has been fulfilled centuries ago and has no meaning in the 21st century (apart from an apologetic purpose of proving the Bible is authentic). The preterist view limits the majority of eschatological references to salvation and judgment in the first century of the church.

---

2   The dating of the book of Revelation is a recurring argument in regards to preterism. Whereas the majority of Bible scholars date Revelation during the reign of Domitian (A.D. 81–96), the preterist *must* date Revelation during the reign of Nero (A.D. 54–68). Generally, preterism offers five basic arguments for an early dating of the book of Revelation. *First*, preterists connect descriptions of the Antichrist with the reign of Nero as emperor (e.g., Rev. 6:2; 13:1–18; 17:1–13). Assuming his conclusion before proving it, David Chilton wrote,

> As we will see throughout the commentary, the Book of Revelation is primarily a prophecy of the destruction of Jerusalem by the Romans. This fact alone places St. John's authorship somewhere before September of A.D. 70. Further, as we shall see, St. John speaks of Nero Caesar as still on the throne—and Nero died in June 68." Second, preterists regard the letters to the seven churches in Revelation 2–3 as dealing with Jewish persecution of Christians that would result in the destruction of Jerusalem. Third, preterists believe that the Apostle's intimate knowledge of the Temple in Revelation 11 indicates that he wrote Revelation while it still stood. Fourth, preterists say the testimony of Irenaeus is "somewhat ambiguous; and regardless of what he was talking about, he could have been mistaken." Lastly, preterists connect the closing of the canon of Scripture with the destruction of Jerusalem and believe the canon to be in complete form by A.D. 70 (e.g., Daniel 9:24–27). Therefore, the major prophetic events in the New Testament have fulfillment at that time. The preterist viewpoint believes that the Titus and the Roman armies fulfilled these major prophetic events, such as the Olivet Discourse and Book of Revelation, when they destroyed Jerusalem in A.D. 70. (*The Days of Vengeance: An Exposition of the Book of Revelation* [Fort Worth: Dominion Press, 1987], p. 4).

Certainly persecution of Christians during the reign of Nero and the reign of Domitian was monstrous. As revenge for the burning of Rome (an event for which he claimed Christians were responsible), Nero began the first persecution of Christians. However, the majority of evidence favors a date in the reign of Domitian. Hobbs wrote, "Eusebius quotes Irenaeus as saying that the Book of Revelation was written during the closing period of Domitian's reign. Many other early Christian writers (cf. Clement of Alexandria, Origen, Jerome) support this. The words 'shortly come to pass' in 1:1 suggest an event which would bring relief to the suffering saints. This could well refer to Domitian's death in A.D. 96 suggesting a date late in his reign. So A.D. 95 is probably the date of the writing of Revelation" (Herschel H. Hobbs, *The Cosmic Drama: An Exposition of the Book of Revelation* [Waco, TX: Word Publishing, 1971], p. 11).

Historicism

Historicists agree that Biblical prophecy is a panorama of both church and secular history beginning with the apostolic church until the perfection of the age. Historicists typically will envision the history of the world as prewritten in apocalyptic language that overflows with symbols and visions. The majority of the Protestant Reformers were historicists.[3] The Reformers believed that major prophetic writings, such as the book of Daniel, the Olivet Discourse and the book of Revelation revealed the rise of the Roman Catholic Church and God's destruction of that entity. The major prophetic writings were also believed to give exhortation to the church that would be purified during the time of the Reformation.

Within historicism, majority agreement regarding the prophetic fulfillment of the beginning and ending of historical movements cannot be ascertained; rather, Biblical prophecy provides the panorama of historical movements throughout the various ages. Historicism thus equates the current church age with the tribulation based upon the day-age theory. Historicists interpret literal numbers like 2,300 days (Dan. 8:14) and 1,290 days (Dan. 12:11) as years. They also view Biblical prophecy as finding continual fulfillment in the present age. The minority view among historicists is that the destruction of Jerusalem in A.D. 70 was consistent with the breaking of the seals of Revelation.[4] The majority view is that the breaking of the first seal is consistent with the death of Domitian in A.D. 96. The other six seals are associated with the rise and fall of the Western Roman Empire, which would include the invasion

3 The majority of the cults appear to be historicists (there are reasons why this is true, which is another subject for another time, which are different than the reasons why most of the Protestant Reformers were historicists).

4 See Adam Clarke, *Clarke's Commentary on The New Testament, Volume 5: Matthew through Luke* [CD-ROM] ("The Master Christian Library," v. 6, AGES Software, 1998), pp. 451–72; Clarke, *Volume 8: 1 Thessalonians through Revelation* (AGES Software), pp. 1083–89; Matthew Henry, *Commentary on the New Testament* (AGES Software), pp. 81–3, 719–21.

WHEN? *The Biblical Timing for Prophetic Fulfillment*

by the German barbarians (Ostrogoths, Visigoths and Vandals) around the middle of the fifth century.[5]

Whenever historicism is dominant, it is characteristic to witness the portrayal of many time schemes that relate primarily to the end of the world and to the Lord's second coming. Although it may seem that date-setting is a common practice in current times, the truth is that there are fewer time schemes today. The media can give the appearance that date-setting is more common because stories of that variety appeal to both secular and religious persons. Indeed, if one desires to write a bestseller in the field of prophecy, one need simply do something as sinister as name the Antichrist and set a date for the Lord's return. There have been hundreds, if not thousands, of date-setting (or date-hinting) schemes from the time of the early church until the present, yet all those schemes are proven to be false prophecies.

Idealism (Spiritual or Timeless View)

Idealists interpret Biblical prophecy not as an indication of eschato-logical events to be fulfilled (historicism and futurism) or that have been fulfilled (preterism); they interpret prophecy texts as representative of the conflict—recorded in symbolic and metaphoric language—between good and evil. Therefore, Biblical prophecy is not an actual record of historical events or future events, which means there is no single historical fulfillment. As it merely sets forth great principles that are common throughout the age of the world, Biblical prophecy is applicable to believers in any age, and history is almost completely separate from its fulfillment.

Idealism stresses great ethical principles—hidden in symbols and metaphors—with regard to world events that occur. The conflict between good and evil continues, but the triumph of the ages will be the victory of the good. In the idealist view, time and history for Biblical prophecy are

---

5   See Albert Barnes, *Barnes' Notes on the Old and New Testaments* (Grand Rapids: Baker/Revell, 1983); E. B. Elliott, *Horae Apocalyptica* (London: Seeley, Burnside, and Seeley, 1847).

meaningless. Biblical prophecy is an allegory of the spiritual conflict between good and evil. Idealism, therefore, does not affirm belief in an eschatological rapture, tribulation, Antichrist or literal 1,000-year millennium.

A refinement within idealism may be termed "eclecticism." Eclectics attempt to amalgamate what they perceive as the strengths from each of the other interpretive views. Osborne explained, "The solution is to allow the preterist, idealist, and futurist methods to interact in such a way that the strengths are maximized and the weaknesses minimized."[6] Thomas identified the problem with the eclectic approach.

> The combination approach is deficient on another ground: it leaves to human judgment the determination of where the details of a text end and its general picture begins. Allowing this liberty for subjective opinion cannot qualify as objective interpretation. In other words, it cannot satisfy the criteria of a grammatical-historical system of hermeneutics such as has characterized an evangelical Christian understanding of Scripture. . . . No provision can be made for elasticity of interpretation that allows for a change in meaning from generation to generation and from place to place.[7]

The error of the eclectic approach is the tendency of the interpreter to ascribe different meanings to the same vision, which results in the words of a prophetic text meaning almost anything. Different interpreters will make decisions regarding a text in various manners resulting in interpretations that are just as diverse as the eclectic approach, and obviously negates the reality that God's Word has one primary meaning. Beale is an example of such confusion arising from the eclectic approach.

> Accordingly, no specific prophesied historical events are described in the book [Revelation], except for the final coming of

---

6 Grant R. Osborne, *Revelation* (Grand Rapids: Baker, 2002), p. 21.
7 Robert L. Thomas, *Revelation 1-7* (Chicago: Moody Press, 1992), p. 35.

Christ to deliver and judge and to establish the final form of the kingdom in a consummated new creation – though there are a few exceptions to this rule[8] [E.g., 2:10, 22 and 3:9-10, which are unconditional prophecies to be fulfilled imminently in the specific local churches of Smyrna, Thyatira, and Philadelphia.[9]].

The arbitrary nature of the eclectic approach is evident in the assertion that "no specific prophesied historical events are described" and yet the eclectic can make reference to "unconditional prophecies to be fulfilled imminently." The increasing popularity of eclecticism is certainly consistent with the spirit of postmodernism.

Futurism

Futurists believe that prophetic fulfillment regarding the rapture, tribulation, second coming and millennium is in an eschatological period. Consistent futurism teaches that the tribulation, second coming and millennium are all future events pertaining to national Israel. Consistent futurists should never fluctuate between historicism and futurism. Some futurists do interpret current events as fulfilling prophecy; however, when futurists interpret in this manner they are being inconsistent in their interpretation of Scripture. Any date-setting scheme is inconsistent with the principles of futurism that recognize a distinction between Israel and the church.

Biblical prophecy cannot be fulfilled in the present age *if it is prophesied to occur during the tribulation.* Current events cannot be claimed as the fulfillment of prophecy; neither can they be claimed as the sign of Christ's coming. The legitimacy of this assertion is true no matter how many false christs, wars and rumors of wars, famines and earthquakes are present today. History is replete with those who thought they had identified the sign of Christ's coming only to express commiseration for their great

---

8 G. K. Beale, *The Book of Revelation* (Carlisle, UK: The Paternoster Press, 1999), p. 48.
9 Ibid. fn. 16.

disappointment (the most famous in United States history being the Baptist preacher William Miller). The reason is that the prophecies concerning the tribulation, second coming and millennium have specific relation to Israel. In the current age, the only prophecy for the church is the rapture.

To clarify, asserting that consistent futurists do not commingle future events with the present is not to imply that current events are not significant in relation to God's plans for the future. Walvoord explained, "Instead they could be a setting of the stage for the final drama leading to the Second Coming."[10] To prevent misunderstanding,[11] the doctrine of "stage setting" does acknowledge that God is preparing national Israel for the eschatological fulfillment of His covenantal prophecies with them. God began regathering Israel—in unbelief (commencing in 1844) —culminating in her rebirth as a nation in 1948, which is in fulfillment of Ezekiel 37, and "in preparation, namely the judgment of the tribulation" ("followed by a second world-wide regathering in faith in preparation for blessing, namely the blessings of the messianic age").[12] The majority, if not all, of the Biblical prophecies concerning the regathering and restoration of Israel in the latter days is in relation to the future tribulation or the millennial kingdom, and thus specifically indicates that Biblical prophecy is not being fulfilled today (with Ezek. 37 as the only exception), yet this does not mean that the doctrine of "stage setting" depreciates the significance of current events nor is it to assert a lack of relation to prophetic fulfillment.[13]

The modern nation of Israel is significant, for Isaiah 11:11 refers to God recovering "the second time with His hand the remnant of His people." The "second time" refers to the regathering—in belief (her future state) —at

---

10   John F. Walvoord, *The Final Drama: 14 Keys to Understanding the Prophetic Scriptures* (Grand Rapids: Kregel Academic, 1993), p. 1.

11   See, for instance, David R. Reagan, "The Future Has Arrived!", *The Lamplighter* 30 (November-December 2009): 10.

12   Arnold G. Fruchtenbaum, *The Footsteps of the Messiah* (Tustin, CA: Ariel Ministries Press, 1983), p. 65.

13   See, for example, Reagan, "Future Has Arrived," 11.

the conclusion of the tribulation (Matt. 24:31). The present Middle East peace crisis will culminate in the nations staggering and stumbling with Jerusalem, the "cup that causes reeling" (Zech. 12:2).[14] The fact that Israel is reestablished as a nation and also controls the entirety of Jerusalem (since the Six Day War in 1967) is a general indication that God is bringing the church age to completion, yet as there are no chronological details in Scripture regarding the time of preparation, believers cannot know with certainty whether theirs is the final generation prior to the Lord's gathering of His church. In contrast to either historicism (as a whole or in partial expression), "the prophetic timetable ha[s] been interrupted at the founding of the church and . . . the unfulfilled biblical prophecies must all wait upon the rapture of the church. The church was a great parenthesis which Old Testament prophets had not revealed." Consequently, "none of the events foretold in the [book of] Revelation ha[ve] yet occurred nor could they be expected until after the . . . rapture of the church."[15]

Consequently, it is consistent with futurism to affirm that God is stage-setting through current events that will lead to the fulfillment of prophesied events for Israel in the tribulation, yet typically Biblical prophecies are not being fulfilled in the present age because they have reference to events subsequent to the Lord's return for His church and the events that occur thereafter. "Just as history was prepared for Christ's first coming, in a similar way history is preparing for the events leading up to His Second Coming."[16] While Biblical prophecies are not being fulfilled currently, it is possible to discern a general direction in which God's plans for the tribulation are developing. Moreover, it is important to recall how the book of Acts serves as a transition from Israel (and the Old Testament economy) to

---

14 Eugene H. Merrill, *Haggai, Zechariah, Malachi* (Dallas: Biblical Studies Press, 2003), p. 274.

15 Ernest R. Sandeen, *The Roots of Fundamentalism* (Chicago: The University of Chicago, 1970; reprint, Grand Rapids: Baker, 1978), p. 63.

16 John F. Walvoord, *Armageddon, Oil and the Middle East Crisis* (1974, 1976; reprint, Grand Rapids: Zondervan, 1990), p. 217.

the church as God's vessel through whom He commissioned to proliferate the gospel message, and thus, in a similar manner, will there be a process of change at the end of the present age as the Lord prepares the world for events that will resume His unfulfilled prophecies with Israel.

To say that consistent futurism means not asserting that a prophetic event of a future time of tribulation is currently being fulfilled is not to assert that present developments could not be indications of Christ's return. "There is not scriptural ground for setting dates for the Lord's return or the end of the world;" nevertheless, "As students of the Bible observe proper interpretation principles, they are becoming increasingly aware of a remark-able correspondence between the obvious trend of world events and what the Bible predicted centuries ago."[17] God is certainly preparing Israel for the fulfillment of His covenantal promises with the believing remnant. "In the present world scene there are many indications pointing to the conclusion that the end of the age may soon be upon us. These prophecies relating to Israel's coming day of suffering and ultimate restoration may be destined for fulfillment in the present generation."[18]

The nation of Israel was given signs for the Lord's coming, specifically relating to Christ's plans for the Jewish people as the only elect nation. In contrast to Israel, the church is instructed to be ready for an imminent return of the Lord. Paul wrote, "For indeed Jews ask for signs and Greeks search for wisdom" (1 Cor. 1:22). Acts 1:6 reads, "So when they had come together, they were asking Him, saying, 'Lord, is it at this time You are restoring the kingdom to Israel?'" When the disciples asked the resurrected Lord to explain His earthly plans for Israel, He said to them, "'It is not for you to know times or epochs which the Father has fixed by His own authority'" (1:7). The history of the Old Testament illustrates the times or epochs related to God's covenantal purposes for Israel. During the current

---

17 Ibid., pp. 21-22.
18 John F. Walvoord, *Israel in Prophecy* (Grand Rapids: Zondervan, 1962), p. 129.

dispensation of the church, God has postponed fulfillment of prophetic events, and Biblical prophecies await fulfillment until after the rapture of the church.

As a consequence of national (ethnic) Israel's rejection of Messiah, the fulfillment of the Messianic promises to Israel has been postponed. The current dispensation of the church is the interval between the announcement and proffer of the Messianic kingdom to Israel at Messiah's first coming, and the future fulfillment of the Messianic promises. The technical expression for the concept of postponement is derived from the Greek verb *apotelō*, meaning "to complete" or "to be perfected." Randall Price explained, "The *apotelesmatic* interpretation recognizes in Old Testament texts that present the messianic program as a single event, a near and far historical fulfillment is intended, separated by an indeterminate period of time." The "indeterminate period of time" can be termed a "gap" or "intercalation;" however, the term "prophetic postponement" would better express the concept.

The church as the body of Christ was a mystery in the Old Testament (Eph. 3:1-10; Col. 1:24-27), and thus remained unrevealed until the New Testament. Since the Old Testament prophets did not have the current dispensation of the church revealed to them, God did make the mystery of the church known in the New Testament. Postponement is an intercalation (gap) in fulfillment, which leads to the conclusion that the delay is only temporary and, hence, prophetic since there is a "purposeful, preordained act in the divine program." In several Old Testament texts, God implied a parenthesis in His Messianic program with Israel, which includes her hardening (Isa. 6:9-13; Zech. 7:11-12) and judicial exile (Deut. 4:27-30; 28:36-37, 49-50, 64-68); however, this postponement in the Divine program was not revealed entirely until the New Testament (John 12:37-40; Acts 28:25-28; Rom. 11:25-26).[19]

---

19   Randall Price, "Prophetic Postponement in Daniel 9:24-27," in *Progressive Dispensationalism: An*

To avoid misunderstanding,[20] to speak of the church as a parenthesis does not mean she is "simply a temporary aside in God's plan." From the human perspective, the church is an interlude (to some extent) in God's revelation. However, from the Divine viewpoint, the church is a foundational and primary entity in God's comprehensive and eternal decree. For instance, the Hebrew people were not a reality prior to Abraham and thus Israel (Jacob) did not exist, yet God's choice of Israel as His chosen people and elect nation was not "a temporary aside" from His previous work. Both the church and Israel must be understood within the comprehensive disposition of God's plans in world history.

Concerning the issue of eschatological events, futurists (if they are consistent in their hermeneutic) should believe it is possible to witness signs prior to God resuming His eternal program with Israel in the tribulation and the millennium. Consistent futurism recognizes that current world events set the stage for eschatological events in relation to Israel. The only prophetic event for the church in the future is the rapture, which is imminent, and without any signs. Even though the tribulational events will not occur during the present church age, this is not to imply that world events are not significant. If there are present signs of events that are setting the stage for the fulfillment of prophesies that relate to the tribulation, then it is appropriate to believe in the soon coming of the rapture of the church since that blessed event will come prior to the beginning of the tribulation. Thomas Ice remarked:

> A good interpreter keeps the future in the future. If an event in a passage is to occur during the Tribulation, then it cannot happen during the current church age. It is wrong to say that something is being fulfilled in our day when in fact, the biblical context sets it within the future time of Tribulation. . . .

Analysis of the Movement and Defense of Traditional Dispensationalism, ed. Ron J. Bigalke Jr. (Lanham, MD: University Press of America, 2005), p. 218-19.

20 Robert L. Reymond, "95 Theses," #47 [article online] (Against Dispensationalism), <http://againstdispensationalism.com/95-theses>; Internet; accessed 10 May 2017.

Having emphasized the point that we are not to commingle the future with the present, it does not mean that current events have no future meaning in the present. The issue is how they relate and have meaning. After all, as a futurist, I do expect that God will one day fulfill His plan for the last days.[21]

Tribulational events do not find fulfillment in the current church age. Consistent pretribulationism will not adopt a historicist interpretation of world events by quoting, as fulfillment, passages that clearly refer to eschatological events in relation to the nation of Israel. Chafer reminded his readers:

> . . . distinction must be made between the "last days" for Israel— the days of her kingdom glory in the earth (cf. Isa. 2:1–5)—and the "last days" for the Church, which are days of evil and apostasy (cf. 2 Tim. 3:1–5). Likewise, discrimination is called for between the "last days" for Israel and for the Church and "the last day," which, as related to the Church, is the day of the resurrection of those who have died in Christ (cf. John 6:39–40, 44, 54).[22]

Expositors must relate Biblical passages to the appropriate period in time (either the church or Israel). Commingling eschatological events for the church and Israel confuses the prophetic message that God has revealed.

THE MEANING OF THE MILLENNIUM

The theological term *millennium* is derived from the combination of two Latin words, *mille* ("thousand") and *annum* ("year"). The early church referred to the millennium by the Greek term, *chiliasm*. Throughout the history of the church, there have been three primary views concerning the nature of the 1,000 years: (1) amillennialism; (2) postmillennialism; and,

---

21 Thomas Ice, "Stage-Setting of the Last Days," in *Revelation Hoofbeats*, ed. Ron J. Bigalke Jr. (Longwood, FL: Xulon Press, 2003), pp. 284-85.

22 Lewis Sperry Chafer, *Systematic Theology*, 8 vols. (Dallas: Dallas Seminary Press, 1947; reprint, Grand Rapids: Kregel, 1993), 4:374–75.

(3) premillennialism. Interpretative (hermeneutical) differences are the reason for the three views, such as whether to understand "thousand" in Revelation 20 as literal or symbolic. How one understands the millennium will also influence views concerning the details of eschatology.

Premillennialism

Premillennialism is the doctrine that Jesus Christ will return to Earth prior to the inauguration of the millennium. Premillennialists believe that the establishment of the millennium will be preceded by cataclysmic events that are unleashed through the sovereignty of God. Premillennialism is (generally) characterized by a literal interpretation of all 66 books of Scripture. A distinct feature of premillennialism is the belief in a literal 1,000-year reign of Jesus Christ on Earth.

Two different schools of thought prevail among premillennialists: "historic" premillennialism and "dispensational" premillennialism. The historic school is characterized by the beliefs of the early church fathers. Due to the influence and acceptance of progressive dispensationalism in some dispensational schools, it is not uncommon to hear professors at such institutions say that although the church fathers gave much attention to Israel's future role, they applied most of the Old Testament promises to the church in a figurative way that was not entirely different from the amillennial view. Crutchfield provided substantial research to support the blatant falsity of such assertions.

> Only under the combined impact of the allegorizing tendencies of the Alexandrian theologians (notably Origen, ca. 185-ca. 254), the union of church and state under Constantine (Roman emperor, 306-337), and the influence of the great African bishop and theologian Augustine (354-430), did the doctrine eventually fall into disrepute. . . .
>
> . . . the early church fathers maintained distinctions among the people of God throughout the ages.

In this, the fathers are in disagreement with covenant amillennialists and covenant (or historic) premillennialists. The church was never confused with national Israel nor was it assumed to have existed in the Old Testament. The church, according to the fathers, began after the First Advent of Christ, not with Adam or Abraham. . . .[23]

The dispensational school interprets eschatological passages more literally than the historic school. Dispensational premillennialists believe that the Old Testament promises to Israel will be fulfilled literally by a future national Israel.

Generally speaking, premillennialism views history as generally declining toward a culmination in the tribulation period, yet there is a hopeful and living reality to the premillennial outlook. Belief in the imminent return of the Lord "sanctifies life to its highest service in the mission field," as premillennial truth "steadfastly believed and maintained by God's servants," equips them "while they are journeying through this heathen land, not toward darkness but the sunrising." When difficult times arise, "the promise of the glorious appearing of Jesus is steadily discerned, [and] it determines not only the direction of the journey but also its character."[24]

Postmillennialism

Postmillennialism is the view that Christ will not return to earth until after a golden age wherein the church is reigning on Earth as the vicar (governmental representative) of Christ. The term postmillennial, therefore, refers to the time when Christ returns to earth: subsequent to the 1,000 years. Postmillennialists do believe in an earthly kingdom that will occur sometime in the future; however, they do not believe that it will be a

---

23 Larry V. Crutchfield, "Millennial Views of the Church Fathers" in *Dictionary of Premillennial Theology*, ed. Mal Couch (Grand Rapids: Kregel, 1996), pp. 255-56.

24 W. H. Griffith Thomas, "Is Premillennialism Pessimistic?", *Moody Bible Institute Monthly* 22 (January 1922): 756.

theocratic kingdom with Christ reigning on David's throne from Jerusalem. Postmillennialists interpret the 1,000 years as a long period of time that is perhaps longer than a literal 1,000 years. Regarding postmillennialism, Ice made the following comments:

> While many of the basic elements of postmillennialism remain the same, distinction should be made between liberals who promote a postmillennialism through humanism (i.e., the so-cial Gospel of the past) and evangelical postmillennialism that promote progress through the church's preaching of the gospel and application of Mosaic Law. Both adhere to a gospel combined with social change as the agency of change and progress. Thus, in a sense, evangelical postmillennialists believe that many nineteenth-century postmillennialists went astray by adopting humanistic liberalism; instead, they should have relied upon a more traditional, conservative approach.[25]

The distinctive feature of postmillennialism is that the church will institute the conditions of the millennium through world evangelism and these changes will constitute a "millennium" of righteousness, as the world is converted to Jesus Christ. The majority of postmillennialists are quite optimistic in regards to the future (in the sense of not believing in cataclysmic events before the establishment of the millennium). They believe that Christian principles will have an increasing impact on the world and society will keep getting better and better.

Amillennialism

Since the term amillennialism means "no millennium," the designation is somewhat misleading. Anthony Hoekema commented, "It suggests that amillennialists either do not believe in any millennium or that they simply ignore the first six verses of Revelation 20, which speaks of a millennial

---

25 Thomas D. Ice, "Postmillennialism," *Dictionary of Premillennial Theology*, p. 307.

reign. Neither of these statements is true."[26] To avoid confusion, amillennialists are favoring the terms *realized eschatology* or *realized millennialism*.

Amillennialists interpret the 1,000 years of Revelation 20 figuratively, as an indefinite period of time. During this period, a spiritual millennium occurs between the first and second comings of Christ. Amillennialism teaches the kingdom is present currently, with Christ ruling from heaven. The kingdom entails present realities from the time of Christ's ascension until He returns again. Throughout the present kingdom, there will be a growth of good and evil in the world, as the kingdom of God battles the kingdom of Satan (i.e., Augustine's notion of the city of God and city of Satan). Amillennialists do not believe that history will necessarily get much better or that world evangelism will be entirely successful.

Models of World History

How does an understanding of the return of Christ relate to the future? History can be divided into one of two models: cyclical or linear. The majority of Eastern worldviews believe history is cyclical, whereas the majority of Western worldviews represent history as linear. Although the cyclical model is not characterized by apocalyptic thinking, this does not mean that such thinking is entirely absent. The Eastern worldview regards the timing of prophecies as timeless (e.g., idealism). German philosopher Friedrich Nietzsche is an example of how Western philosophy can promote a cyclical view of history since his "*over*man" (or "superman") returns historically ("eternal recurrence").[27]

The Hebrews and their surrounding neighbors disseminated the linear model of history. Although this model primarily views history as progressing in one direction, it also views history as somewhat repetitive.

---

26 Anthony A. Hoekema, "Amillennialism," in *The Meaning of the Millennium: Four Views*, ed. Robert G. Clouse (Downers Grove, IL: InterVarsity Press, 1977), p. 155.

27 Walter Kaufman, ed., *The Portable Nietzsche* (Princeton: Princeton University Press, 1968), p. 441.

"The present is not a replay of the past. Rather, history moves from one event to the next until it reaches its final goal."[28] Therefore, the apocalyptic will present history as progressing linearly. In other words, history itself is progressing toward a climatic end of time that will be preceded by cataclysmic judgments. Although amillennialists and postmillennialists may believe that the end of the world will be climactic, they would not necessarily affirm the premillennial view of cataclysmic judgments preceding the return of Jesus Christ and the establishment of His kingdom. The linear view of history may appear to be entirely pessimistic since there will be a definite judgment in the apocalypse, but it is actually optimistic in the end since cataclysmic events will be followed by victory. The cyclical view of history only pictures things as worsening since there is no intervention within history.

THE DOCTRINE OF THE KINGDOM

How one understands the millennium will also influence views concerning the details of eschatology. Currently, amillennialism and premillennialism are the dominant views of the millennium (postmillennialism was dominant among early liberalism; however, today it is dominant only among Reconstructionists, leaders within the Word of Faith Movement, and the cults). Hermeneutics is the reason for the differences, such as whether to understand "thousand" in Revelation 20 as literal or symbolic.[29] The purpose herein is not to examine these differences *per se*, but to explain the doctrine of the kingdom and its relationship to the church. When appropriate, premillennial doctrine will be regarded as the Biblical teaching.

---

28   Richard Kyle, *The Last Days Are Here Again* (Grand Rapids: Baker, 1998), p. 22.

29   Since the text mentions the term "thousand" six times, a plain reading would deduce that the duration is one thousand years.

The millennium is the kingdom of the Lord Jesus Christ, and includes not only spiritual blessings but also glorious expectation. Specifically, the term premillennialism refers to the future literal reign of Jesus Christ on David's throne in Jerusalem. Premillennialism is in contrast to amillennialism and postmillennialism. Amillennialism does not deny the literal return of Jesus Christ (which is taught to occur at the consummation of the church age), but it does communicate falsely that the church age is presently the kingdom of God; therefore (according to the amillennial view) there will not be a future literal reign of Jesus Christ on the Earth. Postmillennialism also does not deny the literal return of Jesus Christ (which is taught to occur after the millennium), but it does communicate that the church will inaugurate the kingdom of God (which is not a literal 1,000 years but rather consisting of a long indefinite duration) through the moral and spiritual influence of gospel preaching and teaching.

Kingdoms of Scripture

Premillennialism is the Biblical teaching that when Jesus Christ returns to Earth, He will inaugurate His kingdom for a literal 1,000 years. The teaching that Christ will reign personally and visibly during the millennium is an important distinction because many conservative evangelicals believe there is only one general, inclusive rule of God in the hearts of all His people. According to such an understanding, the kingdom of God is essentially soteriological (soteriology is the doctrine of salvation). For instance, John Walvoord explained the amillennial view.

> Amillennial interpreters combine various forms of "kingdom" into one concept, namely, a kingdom of God. . . . In keeping with this general conclusion that all the kingdoms are phases of one kingdom idea, many hold that soteriology is the one factor that binds them all together. . . . Salvation is obviously a major part

of this revelation, but not the totality. The whole theory that all kingdoms should be reduced to the soteriological equivalent is not what the Bible teaches in its doctrine of the various kingdoms.[30]

As Walvoord noted, the concept of the kingdom cannot be reduced to soteriology alone. There are other aspects of the kingdom in Scripture. The concept of the kingdom of God is the major theme or purpose of Divine election. The entirety of world history—from Genesis to Revelation—concerns the progression of the kingdom of God. The concept of the kingdom includes more than one aspect.

The definition of a kingdom would include the following: (1) the ruler; (2) the ruled; and, (3) the realm. Walvoord noted the importance of observing "that the Scriptures themselves give a detailed description of various spheres [aspects] of kingdom." Therefore, to ignore the Biblical distinctions will result in "erroneous conclusions in the doctrine of the kingdom" and confusion in regard to an "understanding of God's promises."[31] The various aspects of the kingdom include: (1) the universal kingdom; (2) the millennial (Davidic/Messianic) kingdom; (3) the mystery form of the kingdom; (4) the spiritual kingdom; and, (5) the kingdom of man.

The universal kingdom is God's sovereign rule of history from creation throughout eternity (1 Chron. 29:11; Ps. 96:13; 103:19; 145:9-13; Dan. 2:37). The ruler of the universal kingdom is the triune God. The ruled is all creation (including heaven and earth). The realm is all time and eternity. It is God's inclusive sovereign rule of history from creation throughout eternity.

The millennial (Davidic/Messianic) kingdom is according to God's promise to Israel (2 Sam. 7:5-16; 1 Chron. 17:3-15; Rev. 20:1-10). The ruler of the millennial kingdom will be the King, Jesus Christ (as King David

---

30 John F. Walvoord, "Biblical Kingdoms Compared and Contrasted," in *Issues in Dispensationalism*, eds. Wesley R. Willis and John R. Master (Chicago: Moody Press, 1994), pp. 84-85.

31 Ibid., p. 74.

ruled in history). The ruled is the Earth and its inhabitants. The realm is during the 1,000 years following the second coming of Jesus Christ. This kingdom could also be called the single, unified, mediatorial kingdom that existed historically under the Mosaic Covenant and was prophesied by the Old Testament prophets to be restored in its former glory at the second coming. It is the same kingdom John the Baptist preached and Jesus offered to Israel at His first coming; it is, therefore, the same kingdom that Israel rejected in the first century. The kingdom is historic, prophetic, offered and rejected.

The mystery form of the kingdom is the church age, which encompasses the period between the comings of Christ (Matt. 13). The ruler of the mystery form of the kingdom is Jesus Christ. The ruled is Christendom. The realm is the period between the comings of Christ.

The spiritual kingdom is God's rule over His people at all times in history (John 3:3; Col. 1:13; Heb. 1:4-14; 2 Pet. 1:11). The ruler is the triune God. The ruled includes the elect of humanity and the angels. The realm is from eternity past to eternity future.

The kingdom of man includes humanity as ruler (Gen. 10—11; 11:31—12:9; Rev. 17—18). The ruled, of course, is mankind. The realm began at the Tower of Babel and will culminate at the beginning of the millennial kingdom. God's blessed provision to end the kingdom of man began in history with the calling of Abram for the purpose of establishing His kingdom through the nation of Israel.

The Church and the Kingdom

One should recognize a distinction between the Greek terms *ekklesia* ("church") and *basileia* ("kingdom"). Enns noted, "The terms *church* and *kingdom* are never used interchangeably in Scripture. Of the 114 occurrences of the word church (Gk. *Ekklesia*), it is never equated with the kingdom."[32]

---

32   Paul Enns, *The Moody Handbook of Theology* (Chicago: Moody Press, 1989), p. 352.

The usages of the terms in the New Testament indicate distinctions. Radmacher clarified, "Thus, this entire advancing change of emphasis from *basileia* to *ekklesia* and back to the *basileia* yet to come may not be overlooked . . . it serves to emphasize the fact that the *ekklesia* and the *basileia* are two distinct entities in the eternal program of God."[33] Consequently, the millennial (Davidic/Messianic) kingdom will be different from the church age.

There is, however, a relationship of the church to the kingdom. Ryrie explained, "If one were to try to summarize the relationship of the church to the kingdom, he would have to say that it is related but not equivalent to certain concepts of the kingdom; it is unrelated to another concept; and is equivalent to another. The concept of kingdom must be defined before one can determine the relationship of the church to it."[34] The church age can be understood as a component of the universal kingdom. Since God created the church, she exists in the world as a component of the universal kingdom. God "designed it, brought it into being, and rules over it, as He does all aspects of His universe."[35]

The church age, however, is not a component of the millennial (Davidic/Messianic) kingdom, which national Israel rejected at the Lord's first coming, and it will not be fulfilled until after the second coming. The millennial kingdom is a political dominion, whose ruler is the Lord Jesus Christ; it will commence subsequent to the second coming and will bring Gentile world domination over the nation of Israel to a conclusion. The millennial kingdom will remove all previous earthly kingdoms. The fulfillment of all God's promises in the Biblical covenants will be realized in the millennial kingdom. "When this kingdom is established the church will have been resurrected and will reign with Christ over the millennial kingdom."[36]

---

33 Earl D. Radmacher, *The Nature of the Church* (Hayesville, NC: Schoettle, 1996), p. 172.

34 Charles C. Ryrie, *Basic Theology* (Colorado Springs: Victor Books, 1986), p. 399.

35 Ibid., p. 398.

36 Ibid., p. 399.

The church is now a component of the mystery form of the kingdom. The "mystery" aspect is concerning the unrevealed nature of this kingdom in the Old Testament. The unknown aspect of the kingdom "does not correspond precisely to any of the other kingdoms. It is not specifically the kingdom of God (though it includes the kingdom of God) because there are some in it who apparently are not saved."[37] Therefore, the relationship of the church to the concept of the kingdom cannot be regarded as a component of other aspects of the kingdom (i.e. the millennial—Davidic/Messianic—kingdom). Ryrie clarified, "If one were to try to summarize the relationship of the church to the kingdom, he would have to say that it is related but not equivalent to certain concepts of the kingdom; it is unrelated to another concept; and it is equivalent to another. The concept of kingdom must be defined before one can determine the relationship of the church to it."[38]

To define the doctrine of the kingdom necessitates that one observe all the various aspects that are revealed in Scripture. The various aspects of the kingdom include the universal kingdom, the millennial (Davidic/Messianic) kingdom, the mystery form of the kingdom, the spiritual kingdom and the kingdom of man. Each of these aspects of the kingdom is described distinctly in Scripture. Understanding the relationship of the church to the kingdom necessitates discernment regarding what aspect of the kingdom is being referenced in Scripture. The millennial kingdom is clearly distinct from the present church age, that is, the mystery form of the kingdom. However, the church will have been resurrected prior to the inauguration of the millennial kingdom and will reign with Christ in that aspect of the kingdom, as it is God's intent to rule personally and visibly upon the Earth. Presently, the church is a component of the kingdom of God in the mystery form (interadvent period) of the kingdom.

---

37 Walvoord, "Biblical Kingdoms," p. 81.
38 Ryrie, *Basic Theology*, p. 399.

CONCLUSION

Significant disagreements exist among evangelicals in regards to general eschatology. However, the disagreements are not due to lack of clarity in Scripture; rather they exist mainly because of one's usage or disregard of a consistent and literal interpretation of Bible prophecy. The most natural interpretation of unfulfilled Biblical prophecies leads to a pretribulational and premillennial expectation. Disagreements exist due to inconsistency in Biblical interpretation (of course, this could be said with regard to so many doctrines of the Bible). How one understands the timing of prophetic fulfillment also influences an understanding of the meaning of the millennium. Throughout the subsequent chapters, the reader will understand how one's understanding of prophetic fulfillment relates to an understanding of the meaning of the millennium (and why all the views on the timing of prophetic fulfillment could be consistent with postmillennialism, but not with amillennialism and premillennialism).

CHAPTER 2

PROPHETIC TIMING AND THE MILLENNIUM: PRETERISM

Failure to maintain a consistent and literal interpretation is the reason for significant disagreement among evangelicals regarding Biblical eschatology, which is especially true in regards to the timing of prophetic fulfillment and the meaning of the millennium. Preterism (Latin for "past" in regard to time) is the view that the majority (sometimes all) of Bible prophecy has already been fulfilled. The preterist viewpoint affirms that Titus and the Roman armies already fulfilled major prophetic events, such as the Olivet Discourse and the book of Revelation, when they destroyed Jerusalem in A.D. 70.[39]

---

39 Kenneth L. Gentry Jr., a preterist, wrote: "Revelation has two fundamental purposes relative to its original hearers. In the first, place it was designed to steel the first century Church against the gathering storm of persecution, which was reaching an unnerving crescendo of theretofore unknown proportions and intensity. A new and major feature of that persecution was the entrance of imperial Rome onto the scene. The first historical persecution of the Church by imperial Rome was by Nero Caesar from A.D. 64 to A.D. 68. In the second place, it was to brace the Church from a major and fundamental re-orientation in the course of redemptive history, a re-orientation necessitating the destruction of Jerusalem (the center not only of Old Covenant Israel, but of

Preterist expressions with regard to the timing of prophetic fulfill-ment allow for both amillennial preterism and postmillennial preterism. Due to the particulars of preterism, one could not affirm the preterist posi-tion and still believe in a literal return of Christ to earth followed by the millennial kingdom. Full preterists (John Bray, Walt Hibbard, Max King, J. Stuart Russell and Ed Stevens) find it especially difficult to embrace premillennialism since they believe the second coming of Christ occurred in A.D. 70, and obviously a literal millennial reign did not occur thereafter.

Of course, if advocates of preterism did believe in a literal millennial reign then the current age would be more than 1,000 years postmillennially into eternity. *Theoretically*, at least, it is possible for mild preterists (Isbon T. Beckwith) and middle preterists (R. C. Sproul, reconstructionists) to be premillennial; however, because of an inconsistent hermeneutic, the pret-erist position is more consistent with the amillennial and postmillennial view. The majority of contemporary preterists seem to be postmillennialists. However, it could be said that these preterists are actually transmillennial since a large majority teach the church is already in the new heavens and new earth (full preterism is entirely transmillennial).[40]

There are many similarities between amillennialism and postmillen-nialism, which is the reason why one can easily affirm the preterist viewpoint and consider themselves either amillennial or postmillennial. The most popular amillennial preterist today is R. C. Sproul. The dominant arguments for post-millennial preterism are from reconstructionists (a neopostmillennial view[41]) such as Gary DeMar, Kenneth Gentry, Gary North and Greg Bahnsen.

Apostolic Christianity [cp. Acts 1:8; 2:1ff; 15:2] and the Temple [cp. Matt. 24:1-34 with Rev. 11]" (*Before Jerusalem Fell: Dating the Book of Revelation* [Atlanta: American Vision, 1998], pp. 15-16). In order to make Nero's name the numerical equivalent of 666, preterists use the Greek form, "Neron Caesar" written in Hebrew characters as follows: N=50, R=200, W=6, N=50, Q=100, S=60, and R=200.

40 Kenneth L. Gentry Jr., "A Preterist View of Revelation," in *Four Views on the Book of Revelation*, ed. C. Marvin Pate (Grand Rapids: Zondervan, 1998), pp. 87-90.

41 For more information regarding this viewpoint, see Ron J. Bigalke Jr., "Reconstructionism," in *The Encyclopedia of Christian Civilization*, 4 vols., ed. George Thomas Kurian (Chichester, UK: Wiley-Blackwell, 2012), 3:1934-36.

PROPHETIC TIMING	MILD PRETERISM		PARTIAL PRETERISM		FULL PRETERISM	
	A.D. 70–400	FUTURE	A.D. 70	FUTURE	A.D. 70	FUTURE
Coming of Christ	Yes	Yes	Yes	Yes	Yes	No
Resurrection	No	Yes	No	Yes	Yes	No
Last Days	Yes	No	Yes	No	Yes	No

PRETERIST INTERPRETATION

Preterists believe they are adequately interpreting the historical background by relating the fulfillment of major prophetic events to the time period of the original audience. For instance, the preterist viewpoint is thought to best interpret Christ's words in Matthew 24:34 ("Truly I say to you, this generation will not pass away until all these things take place"), and other references to the coming of Christ as "quickly" or "at hand" (Matt. 4:17; 10:7; Mark 10:15; Luke 21:30-31; Rev. 2:5, 16; 3:11; 22:7, 12, 20).[42] Since the events of the Olivet Discourse and the book of Revelation parallel each other, which is true,[43] then these passages are understood to refer only to events that occurred in the first century, which is false. The following chart indicates the different types of preterism.

---

42 Matthew 24:34 and the Revelation passages, are indicating "the manner in which tribulational events will occur, and not their timing" (Ron J. Bigalke Jr., "The Olivet Discourse: A Resolution of Time," *Chafer Theological Seminary Journal* 9 [Spring 2003]: 125-26).

43 Ron J. Bigalke Jr., "A Comparison of the Synoptic Eschatological Discourses and Revelation 6-20," *Chafer Theological Seminary Journal* 13 (Spring 2008): 60-78.

Mild preterism interprets the book of Revelation as fulfilled in both the first century with the fall of Jerusalem and the fifth century with the fall of Rome. The first half of Revelation refers to A.D. 70 when the Romans destroyed Jerusalem and the second half refers to the judgment upon Rome. Therefore, the majority of Bible prophecy has already been fulfilled when God brought His wrath upon Israel and Rome. Partial preterists understand the majority of Bible prophecy as fulfilled in the destruction of Jerusalem, but they still anticipate a future second coming and resurrection/judgment. Full preterism believes that all eschatological prophecies were fulfilled in A.D. 70 and that there will only be a spiritual resurrection rather than a bodily resurrection. Consequently, full preterism is heretical. The preterist view teaches the destruction of God's enemy, Israel, is indisputable proof for the Divine establishment of Christianity.

In a manner similar to dispensationalists, preterism places substantial emphasis upon the context of the Olivet Discourse. Jesus' words in Matthew 23:38 ("Behold, your house is being left to you desolate!") are said to be fulfilled in the destruction of the Temple, as prophesied in Matthew 24:1-3. Matthew 24:34 prophesies "this generation will not pass away until all these things" (false christs, wars, famines, earthquakes in vv. 4-14) occur and the preterist believes this has to be fulfilled in the days preceding A.D. 70 for the prophecy to be true. The abomination of desolation would then be fulfilled in the siege of Jerusalem, and the coming of the Son of Man is in the judgment upon Jerusalem.

Citing Matthew 23:36 ("Truly I say to you, all these things will come upon this generation"), Kenneth Gentry commented,

> It seems totally clear that He is speaking to the religious rule of that day, to the religious center of Israel, to the culture of His time, and He is pointing out sin in them. And He says, "Woe unto you." Why? Because these great tribulational

things will be coming upon them: those who betrayed Him, those who had Him crucified, and those who persecute Jesus' followers from city to city—the first century Jews here being confronted in their leadership. It is important to recognize that "that generation" was objectively the most wicked generation of history for "that generation" committed the worst crime and the worst sin of universal history. It crucified the Son of the living God by rejecting Him though He did many wonderful deeds in their presence.[44]

Matthew 23:36 does indicate the imminence of judgment upon the nations, in addition to the religious leaders, for all their violence against the prophets. Consequently, the generation will be rejected and the King will not establish His proffered kingdom among them (23:37-39). However, the rejection of the nation is not permanent as the "until" in Matthew 23:39 indicates. Christ will establish the prophesied kingdom when the Jewish nation repents in faith. Indeed, one of the purposes of the tribulation is to bring Israel into a state of repentance whereby they confess belief that Jesus is Messiah. At the conclusion of the tribulation period, all living Jews will acknowledge Jesus as Messiah, and Romans 11:25-27 will be fulfilled when "all Israel will be saved."

Gentry then attempted to connect the indictment upon the nation in Matthew 23 with the phrase "this generation" in Matthew 24:34, meaning that the prophesied events in the Olivet Discourse have already been fulfilled. J. Marcellus Kik indicated the same reasoning.

Since, then, the obvious sense of the word *generation* must be taken, then the obvious sense of the sentence in which it appears must also be taken, which is, that all the things which Christ mentioned previously occurred before the passing away of the generation living at the time when Jesus spoke. And this would

---

44 Kenneth L. Gentry Jr., "Postmillennialism and Preterism: Great Tribulation is Past" (Nacogdoches, TX: Covenant Media Foundation, n.d.), audiotape.

mean that it has found fulfillment in the destruction of Jerusalem in the year A.D. 70.[45]

The generation of Jesus' day was being left with her house desolate
as the Messiah indicated by His judgment upon the Temple (Matt. 23:38;
24:2). The questioning of the disciples in Matthew 24:3 was in response
to this judgment. Jesus answered by warning the disciples against false
Christs who would come in His name. In contrast, Jesus stated that when
they hear of many claiming to be the Messiah and see "wars and rumors
of wars . . . *that* is not yet the end" (24:4-6). Matthew 24:7-14 indicates
why the false messiahs and wars are not "the end" because it is only when
the cataclysmic events and preaching of the gospel of the kingdom occur
together that "then the end will come" (24:14).

Partial preterists will interpret Matthew 24:36 variously. For instance,
Gentry interpreted the pronoun "this" in 24:34 as a different period than
indicated by the pronoun "that" in 24:36. In other words, 24:36 refers to a
time when the second coming occurs.

> [B]y all appearance Matthew 24:34 seems to function as a
> concluding statement, having specific reference to the pre-
> ceding events. If *all* of Matthew 24 were for the first century,
> why would not the Lord hold off on the concluding statement
> until the end of His discourse? The following events (Matt.
> 24:36-51) relate to some other event that was not to occur
> in "this generation[.]" Thus, all events before verse 34 are
> to occur to "this generation[.]" [T]here seems to be an in-
> tended contrast between that which is *near* (in verse 34) and
> that which is *far* (in verse 36): *this* generation vs. *that* day.
> [I]t would seem more appropriate for Christ to have spoken
> of "this day" rather than "that day" if He had meant to refer
> to the time of "this generation." Of course, this argument is
> wholly contextual: by themselves the words "this"/"that" do

---

45   J. Marcellus Kik, *An Eschatology of Victory* (Phillipsburg, NJ: Presbyterian and Reformed, 1971), p.
     31.

not have to point to wholly different things. But in this context their juxtaposition strongly suggests such. . . .[46]

Conversely, DeMar interpreted "that" in 24:36 to refer also to the destruction of Jerusalem. He interpreted 24:36—25:30 as referring "to events leading up to and including the destruction of Jerusalem in A.D. 70." Therefore, in DeMar's view, the parable of the householder was fulfilled within the time of the faithful and unfaithful servants, which would be no longer than 40 years after the ascension of Christ.[47] For example, DeMar wrote:

> There is no indication that Matthew 25:31-46 describes a single event. Rather, the passage describes a judgment over time, related to Jesus' dominion as an "everlasting dominion" (Daniel 7:14). . . . The King of glory is continually judging and reigning among the nations, and He will not cease from this work until "He has abolished all rule and all authority and power" (1 Corinthians 15:24).[48]

In light of the contrasts with other more moderate preterists, it is important to understand why there is such a necessity in the mind of preterists to date the events of the Olivet Discourse in A.D. 70. R. C. Sproul explained the preterist view concerning literal interpretation.

> The cataclysmic events surrounding the parousia as predicted in the Olivet Discourse obviously did not occur "literally" in A.D. 70. Some elements of the discourse did take place "literally," but others obviously did not.
>
> This problem of literal fulfillment leaves us with three basic solutions to interpreting the Olivet Discourse:

---

46 Kenneth L. Gentry Jr., "An Encore to Matthew 24," *Dispensationalism in Transition* 6 (May 1993): 1.

47 Gary DeMar, *End Times Fiction: A Biblical Consideration of the Left Behind Theology* (Nashville: Thomas Nelson, 2001), pp. 68-69, 111-12, 114.

48 Gary DeMar, *Last Days Madness: Obsession of the Modern Church*, 3rd ed. (Atlanta: American Vision, 1997), pp. 190-91.

1. We can interpret the entire discourse literally. In this we must conclude that some elements of Jesus' prophecy failed to come to pass, as advocates of "consistent eschatology" maintain.

2. We can interpret the events surrounding the predicted parousia literally and interpret the time-frame references figuratively. This method is employed chiefly by those who do not restrict the phrase "this generation will not pass away . . . " to the life span of Jesus' contemporaries.

3. We can interpret the time-frame references literally and the events surrounding the parousia figuratively. In this view, all of Jesus' prophecies in the Olivet Discourse were fulfilled during the period between the discourse itself and the destruction of Jerusalem in A.D. 70.[49]

False accusations were made toward "advocates of 'consistent eschatology'" (viz. dispensationalists) because while they do interpret the Olivet Discourse literally, no dispensationalist would say, "some elements of Jesus' prophecy failed to come to pass." While preterists give extensive emphasis to the demonstrative pronouns in verses 34 and 36 of Matthew 24, only a futurist interpretation seeks to understand those pronouns within the context.

Demonstrative pronouns help locate and identify nouns or other pronouns. Pronouns substitute for nouns when the nouns they replace can be understood from the context. They also indicate whether they are replacing a singular or plural tense and identify in what location (near/far) the speaker references self in relation to the object. The following chart identifies whether the pronoun indicates substitution of a singular or plural word, and if the pronoun gives a location as either near the speaker or at a distance from the speaker.

---

49   R. C. Sproul, *The Last Days According to Jesus* (Grand Rapids: Baker, 1998), p. 66.

English Demonstrative Pronouns

PRONOUN	TENSE	LOCATION
this	singular	near
that	singular	far
these	plural	near
those	plural	far

As an example, if a speaker wishes to refer to books that are at a distance from him, he would say, "You take these books and I will take those." As another example, if a speaker wants to refer to a singular book that is near him, and is able to be understood readily in the context of his speech, then he would say, "I bought this last year."

In Greek, there are two demonstrative pronouns. Frequently, these demonstratives will be used independent of a noun and carry the intensity of a substantive. The most common use of the demonstrative pronoun is with a noun and it carries the strength of an adjective. In other words, the noun will contain the article and the demonstrative pronoun can be found in the predicate position but never in the attributive position (e.g., οὗτος ὁ υἱος or ὁ υἱος οὗτος would be translated "this the son").[50]

Greek Demonstrative Pronouns

PRONOUN	TENSE	LOCATION
οὗτος	singular	near
οὗτοι	plural	near
ἐκεῖνος	singular	far
ἐκεῖναι	plural	far

---

50 Ray Summers, *Essentials of New Testament Greek* (Nashville: Broadman Press, 1950), p. 47.

The purpose of demonstrative pronouns in both English and Greek grammar is to help identify where the speaker identifies him or her self in relation to the object. Fundamental to preterist eschatology is a first-century fulfillment of the Olivet Discourse. The preterist interpretation of the Olivet Discourse requires Jesus to place Himself in a relatively near relation to the events of Matthew 24—25. If this is the scenario, as the preterists contend, then Jesus would use οὗτος and οὗτοι in order to indicate relatively near events.

In four verses, Jesus used the relatively distant demonstrative pronouns: ἐκείναις ταῖς ἡμέραις (24:19); αἱ ἡμέραι ἐκεῖναι (24:22); τῶν ἡμερῶν ἐκείνων (24:29); and, τῆς ἡμέρας ἐκείνης (24:36).[51] When speaking with regard to His second coming, Jesus used the relatively distant demonstrative pronouns. When Jesus spoke concerning the events that will occur prior to His coming, He used the relatively near demonstrative pronouns since this would correspond to His perspective at the time of His coming: ταῦτα (24:8, "these") and οὕτως (24:33, "these"). In other words, Jesus was speaking of His future coming, and then used the near demonstratives to describe the eschatological events that will precede that return.

When Jesus said, "Truly I say to you, this [αὕτη] generation will not pass away until all these [ταῦτα] things take place" (24:34), He was referring to the same generation that belong in the distance (eschatologically). By identifying the demonstrative pronouns, it becomes clear that Jesus was referring to the generation that witnesses the events of the Olivet Discourse with His coming in a future time. If Jesus intended to speak of a first-century fulfillment then He would have used the relatively future demonstrative, ἐκεῖναι, for the events that would occur among the generation that would witness His coming. In other

---

51 Perhaps a fifth reference could be added in 24:38 (ταῖς ἡμέραις [ἐκείναις]) due to the likelihood that the pronoun was omitted accidentally. Both the United Bible Societies and Nestle-Aland Greek texts of the New Testament include ἐκείναις in brackets. Metzger rated its inclusion with a "C" grade. See Bruce M. Metzger, *A Textual Commentary on the Greek New Testament*, 2nd ed. (Stuttgart: United Bible Societies, 1994), p. 52.

words, Jesus was not using relatively far demonstratives to describe what He prophesied of Himself in relatively near demonstratives because He referenced the future from His present earthly location. Only the generation witnessing all the events prophesied in the Olivet Discourse will be the generation to witness His return.

Commenting on the parallel passage to Matthew 24 in Luke 21, Lukan scholar Darrell Bock assented:

> What Jesus is saying is that the generation that sees the beginning of the end, also sees its end. When the signs come, they will proceed quickly; they will not drag on for many generations.
>
> Nonetheless, in the discourse's prophetic context, the remark comes after making comments about the nearness of the end to certain signs. As such it is the issue of the signs that controls the passage's force, making this view likely. If this view is correct, Jesus says that when the signs of the beginning of the end come, then the end will come relatively quickly, within a generation.[52]

Understanding Matthew 24:34

Although Matthew 24:34 is the preterist mantra, the reference therein to "this generation" is a difficult passage to correlate with the preterist system. Preterists seek to demonstrate that whenever "this generation" was used in the gospels, it refers to the first-century generation. In Matthew 23:36, "this generation" does refers to those who would witness the destruction of the Temple in A.D. 70. While the latter statement is correct, the former assertion is wrong. For instance, it is not true that the prophecies of Matthew 24:4-33 were all fulfilled in A.D. 70. The only manner in which such a view could be affirmed is by ignoring the other more obvious verses which demand an eschatological

---

52 Darrell L. Bock, *Luke 9:51—24:53* (Grand Rapids: Baker, 1996), pp. 1,691-92.

fulfillment (e.g., the meaning of παρουσία and the interpretation of Matt. 23:39; 24:22; and 24:27, 30).

The correct interpretation is to understand "this generation" in reference to those who witness "all these things" of Matthew 24 (Luke 21:32 reads, "all things"), which includes the literal and physical return of Jesus Christ. The issue concerning the near and far demonstratives has already been discussed; therefore, analysis here will focus upon the verb γένηται ("take place"). The better way to understand γένηται is as an ingressive aorist, which means an event has occurred but the emphasis is upon initiation. The destruction of the Temple should be understood from its initiation, which would bear the meaning "begin to take place." The prophetic chronology for "all these things" of Matthew 24:34 would begin with the first-century generation, but not find final fulfillment until the second coming.

One should note that the texts of prophecies were the first to which commentaries at Qumran were organized. The *pesharim* was not intended to explain the prophetic texts, but to reveal the mysteries concerning prophetic fulfillment. Such mysteries would be hidden from the prophet himself, but revealed to the Teacher of Righteousness (*Pesher on Habakkuk*, or *Habakkuk Commentary*, 7:1-5). In other words, the Qumran literature indicated more than historical prophecies for past generations, but also used the term "last generation" to indicate several generations. The Qumran usage of "last generation" is similar to the New Testament usage in 1 John 2:18 for the ἐσχάτη ὥρα ("last hour"), which means the last period in history for the current age.

THE THEOLOGICAL SYSTEMS OF PRETERISM

Amillennialism

The prefix *a* means *no*, which can give the appearance that amillennialists do not believe in a future reign of Christ even when the Old Testament clearly prophesies of a future kingdom in fulfillment of the promises of God. In fairness, amillennialists do not reject a literal return of Jesus Christ (only full preterists affirm that notion), but they do reject the belief in a literal millennial reign of Christ on earth. Therefore, the current age is the kingdom of God. Amillennialists recognize this confusion, which is why some favor the term "realized millennialism."[53] At the perfection of the current age, amillennialists believe the eternal state will be established without the need for a literal 1,000-year reign.

The kingdom of God is both a present reality in the current age and a future hope in the eternal state. Amillennialists believe the kingdom began at the birth of Christ and it will be perfected at the time of His second coming. The kingdom exists at the present since Christ is presently ruling from heaven; it is the time from the first coming to the second coming. Christ will not reign for a literal 1,000 years since the current age is "the millennium now." Hoekema explained the two views concerning the millennium.

> The amillennial position on the thousand years of Revelation 20 implies that Christians who are now living are enjoying the benefits of this millennium since Satan has been bound for the duration of this period [i.e. the millennium is the church on earth]. . . . Amillennials also teach that during this same thousand-year period the souls of believers who have died are now living and reigning with Christ in heaven while they await the

---

53 Jay E. Adams, *The Time Is at Hand* (Philadelphia: Presbyterian and Reformed Publishing, 1970).

resurrection of the body [i.e. the millennium is the church in heaven].[54]

The preceding explanation should make it apparent why amillennialists refer to an already form of the kingdom and yet a future eschatology. The current age is thought to be the fulfillment of Revelation 20 since believers are in the millennium. The departed saints, now in heaven, are living and reigning with Christ in heaven. There will be a general resurrection of believers and unbelievers at the second coming of Christ. In terms of the future, amillennialists regard the second coming of Christ as a single event, which is in contrast to premillennialists who understand the second coming of Christ to occur in two phases. Concerning the tribulation period, amillennialists reject the idea of a specific seven-year period. Believers who are alive at the return of Christ will be transformed and glorified as they meet Christ in the air and return with Christ to earth. After the second coming, those who have rejected Christ will be sent into everlasting punishment at the final judgment. Conversely, believers will enter the everlasting glory of the eternal state. At this time, both heaven and earth will be created new.

Just as there are different forms of preterism, so are there different forms of amillennialism. Some amillennialists determine their view of Scripture based upon a preterist perspective, and these amillennialists refer to the A.D. 70 destruction of the Jewish Temple. Other amillennialists understand the fulfillment of Biblical eschatology continuing to A.D. 300 approximately and the reign of Constantine. Some amillennialists classify themselves as historicists, which means Biblical eschatology describes events of the last 2,000 years of the church age. Other amillennialists regard Biblical eschatology as the cosmic battle between good and evil.

54 Anthony A. Hoekema, "Amillennialism," in *The Meaning of the Millennium: Four Views*, ed. Robert G. Clouse (Downers Grove, IL: InterVarsity Press, 1977), p. 181.

Postmillennialism

Postmillennialism is the view that the kingdom of God is the current age of the church. Presently, in the church age, the kingdom is being extended in the world through the preaching of the gospel. Through the preaching of the gospel (and saving work of the Holy Spirit), the church will introduce a golden age wherein Christians are no longer expanding the kingdom, but are actually reigning in the kingdom. At this time, the majority of people in the world (not necessarily all) will become "Christian."

Postmillennialists believe the present church age is expanding morally and spiritually until it introduces the golden age. The millennium is not a literal 1,000 years; it is simply a long period of time. After the millennium, which is "a long period of righteousness and peace,"[55] Christ will return. Postmillennialism, therefore, affirms three essentials: (1) the world will become Christianized through the preaching of the gospel; (2) the preaching of the gospel will usher in a long period of peace and righteousness; and, (3) the return of Christ will be subsequent to the golden age, commonly called the millennium.

There is disagreement among postmillennialists as to whether the term "millennium" refers to the entire church age or is limited to the golden age. For instance, Kik applied the term to the expanding of the "gospel dispensation" and "the victorious reign of the saints upon earth regardless of martyrdom and suffering."[56] Conversely, Loraine Boettner limited the millennium to "a golden age of spiritual prosperity during this present dispensation, that is, during the Church age, and is to be brought about through forces now active in the world."[57] A major feature of postmillennialism is its staunch optimism that the world is getting better. Boettner wrote:

---

55 Loraine Boettner, *The Millennium*, rev. ed. (Phillipsburg: Presbyterian and Reformed, 1984), p. 4.

56 J. Marcellus Kik, *An Eschatology of Victory* (Nutley, NJ: Presbyterian and Reformed, 1974), p. 49.

57 Boettner, *Millennium*, p. 14.

That a great spiritual advance has been made should be clear to all. Consider, for instance, the awful moral and spiritual conditions that existed on earth before the coming of Christ—the world at large groping helplessly in pagan darkness with slavery, polygamy, oppressed conditions of women and children, the almost complete lack of political freedom, the ignorance, poverty, and primitive medical care that was the lot of nearly all except those who belonged to the ruling classes. . . . Today the world at large is on a far higher plane.[58]

There may be disagreement among evangelicals regarding the nature of the millennium, but all non-postmillennialists challenge the notion that the world is getter better. Covenant premillennialist George Ladd wrote, "The argument that the world is getting better is a two-edged sword. One can equally well argue from empirical evidence that the world is getting worse."[59] Likewise, dispensational premillennialist Herman Hoyt responded:

There is a sense in which the world is getting better, as Boettner affirms. But there is a sense in which the age is growing worse. . . . All progress, including moral and spiritual progress, should be reason for hope in a coming millennium here on earth ushered in by the Lord Jesus Christ. But the spiritual decline is reason for warning of an approaching end of the age with judgment from Christ. This decline is coming in spite of the spiritual influence of the church and suggests that real hope must be vested in the personal appearance of the Lord Jesus Christ. This is not to ignore international good will, the translation and dissemination of Scriptures, the worldwide missionary movements, the increasing Christian population and the many other factors contributing to a better society. But in assessing these values, one dare not shut his eyes to the trends that point to the disintegration and demoralization of society in preparation for the end of the age.[60]

---

58 Loraine Boettner, "Postmillennialism," in *Meaning of Millennium*, pp. 125-26.

59 George Eldon Ladd, "An Historic Premillennial Response," in *Meaning of the Millennium*, p. 143.

60 Herman A. Hoyt, "A Dispensational Premillennial Response," in *Meaning of the Millennium*, pp. 146-47.

Amillennialist Anthony Hoekema also challenged the postmillennial belief that the world is getting better.

> Boettner's second argument is that the world is growing better (pp. 125-33). Many readers will be inclined to take issue with the author on this point. To begin with, his sketch of world conditions is seriously out of date. Little or nothing is said, for example, about the war in Vietnam, the tension in the Middle East, the ecological crisis, the world food shortage or the energy crisis. . . . Besides, the author seems to pick out only the favorable aspects of world conditions while ignoring unfavorable aspects. He mentions, for example, how much progress has been made in the areas of transportation and communication. But certainly modern inventions are used for purposes which are evil as well as good![61]

Postmillennialism did arise during an age of scientific and educational advances, but it virtually diminished in light of the two world wars in the 20th century. A major fault of postmillennialism is its failure to interact with the historical facts. If taken consistently, postmillennialism could embrace any organization that is making society better as advancing the kingdom even though the same organization could be contributing to evil in the society. For instance, there were some who supported the Nazi party since they believed that Kaiser Wilhelm's policies were making society better. *At times*, postmillennialism will blur the distinctions between good and evil. Postmillennial teaching regards the expansion of the kingdom as eventually affecting every sphere of life (culturally, economically, politically and socially). When the church emerges triumphant, through the preaching of the gospel, postmillennialists teach that wickedness "will be reduced to negligible proportions, that Christian principles will be the rule, not the exception, and that Christ will return to a truly Christianized world."[62]

There is a strong relationship between preterism and postmillennialism.

---

61 Anthony A. Hoekema, "An Amillennial Response," in *Meaning of the Millennium*, p. 151.
62 Ibid.

Advocates of such positions have deceived the church into thinking that God has rejected Israel. Consequently, they believe it is necessary for the church to build the kingdom of God throughout the world. John Walvoord's comments on postmillennialism are equally applicable regarding preterism: "In order to find fulfillment of millennial promises in the present age, it is necessary for them to follow an allegorical or figurative system of interpretation in great areas of Biblical prophecy."[63] The unrelenting attempt to find the fulfillment of Biblical eschatology in the rejection of Israel, as demonstrated in the destruction of Jerusalem, is the motivating dynamic behind preterism. The church is now the means through which millennial blessings will flow, and it is for this reason that a relationship can be made between the foundation of preterism and the postmillennial system.

Unfortunately, postmillennialism today is experiencing resurgence in the Christian reconstruction movement. Christian reconstruction, or dominion theology, argues that Christians are to exercise dominion in all spheres of life. Dominion will occur as the church preaches the gospel and institutes the law of God in the church and the world. Prominent postmillennialists who are also preterists include: David Chilton, Gary DeMar, Kenneth L. Gentry Jr., Gary North and Douglas Wilson.

As a postmillennial view, reconstructionism teaches that when God created man He gave to humanity a mandate to subdue the earth on His behalf. The result of this mandate would be that Christians would establish the kingdom of God on earth (Gen. 1:28). Both Jews and Gentiles failed to fulfill this mandate, therefore it was in Jesus' first coming that He established and restored the Old Testament Law to complete fruition (Matt. 5:17-19). The Old Testament Law is now to be the Christian's rule of life, in addition to society. Through the provisions of Christ's death, resurrection and ascension, reconstructionists teach that Satan was defeated and also

---

63 John F. Walvoord, *The Millennial Kingdom* (Findlay, OH: Dunham, 1959; reprint, Grand Rapids: Zondervan, 1995), p. 24.

bound. Furthermore, Satan and his minions' stronghold upon the world have been eradicated. Although satanic activity still occurs in the world, this activity is greatly restrained.

Reconstructionism affirms that at the end of history every sphere of society, including all the nations, will eventually be subjugated to Christ's rule; at this point, the kingdom of God will be completely established on Earth, and only then will Christ return to this Earth in order that He will receive His kingdom. In light of the mandate given in Genesis, reconstructionism teaches the idea that the fulfillment of the mandate will be in the present age and without Christ's bodily presence. In other words, it is not in the millennium that Christ will lead His people in the progress of fulfilling the mandate; rather the church will accomplish this task in the present age.

Millennial Differences and Similarities

Postmillennialism differs from amillennialism and premillennialism in the sense that they adopt an optimistic view that a golden age of victory will be realized without a cataclysmic return of Christ. The postmillennial viewpoint would be similar in one sense to premillennialism since both views anticipate a future millennium when the Old Testament prophecies will be fulfilled. However, it is decisively antagonistic toward dispensational premillennialism because of the strong emphasis upon the fulfillment of Old Testament prophecies by Israel in the Davidic (millennial) kingdom rather than the fulfillment by the church in a golden age instituted through gospel preaching. Postmillennialism would be similar to amillennialism since there is a single coming of Christ, a general judgment and resurrection, which will be followed by the eternal state. Consequently, it is possible to be an amillennial preterist or postmillennial preterist.

Preterists believe the tribulation period has already occurred and that Christ has already returned (spiritually) in association with the A.D. 70 destruction of Jerusalem; therefore, it is not possible to be a premillennial preterist. Amillennial preterists teach that the church is already in the millennium, and many postmillennial preterists are now teaching the same, which would also make premillennial preterism impossible. Millard J. Erickson identified some of the differences between the postmillennial and premillennial views.

> Further, this earthly millennium will not come into reality through a gradual process or progressive growth or development. Rather, it will be dramatically or cataclysmically inaugurated by the second coming. While the millennium expected by postmillennialists may begin so gradually that its beginning will be virtually imperceptible, there will be no doubt about the beginning of the millennium as premillennialists envision it. The return of Christ will be similar to His departure—dramatic and external, readily observable by anyone, and consequently unmistakable.[64]

Interestingly, some postmillennialists have identified commonality with progressive dispensationalists. Chris Strevel, pastor of Covenant Presbyterian Church, applauded the progressives on five points: (1) "soteriological clarification," (2) "covenantal unity," (3) "ethical renewal," (4) "present realization," and (5) "future fulfillment."[65] Nevertheless, Strevel noted three main differences that still exist between postmillennialism and progressive dispensationalism. *First*, differences exist as to the nature of the present kingdom. Postmillennialism is pleased that there is an emphasis upon the earthly aspects of the kingdom impacting present life, but finds disharmony with the fact that the majority of the fulfillment will occur in the millennium. The reason for the difference is that postmillennialism anticipates a glorious age of the church as a fulfillment of Old Testament

---

64 Millard J. Erickson, *Contemporary Options in Eschatology: A Study of the Millennium* (Grand Rapids: Baker, 1977), pp. 91-92.

65 Chris Strevel, "Dispensational Theology: A Flawed Hermeneutic Produces Flawed Eschatology," SCCCS Conference on Left Behind or Moving Forward (Summer 2001).

prophecies, and this age will be realized through the preaching of the gospel. All nations will become Christian and will live in peace. The prophecies will be fulfilled in history and time. Once the church is victorious by the institution of the glorious age, then there will be the second coming of Christ (bodily). Therefore, the emphasis is that the kingdom is present reality wherein the church is rejoicing and the kingdom is growing through the preaching of the gospel, and will climax in a "golden age of righteousness, peace, and prosperity that will mean the salvation of the world under the reign of Messiah the Prince."[66]

Second, there is also disagreement with the "substance of Christian obedience." Postmillennialists are displeased that greater emphasis is not given to the law of God in terms of daily Christian living. *Thirdly*, there is the disagreement of the "place of national Israel." Progressive dispensationalism teaches that the church is receiving benefit of a "partial and glorious experience" of some aspects of the Davidic kingdom, which (according to postmillennialism) is commendable since this teaching emphasizes covenantal unity, as some Old Testament prophecies find fulfillment in the church. According to progressive dispensationalists, "The present dispensation is not the full and complete revelation of the eschatological kingdom. It is a progressive stage in the revelation of that kingdom."[67] Postmillennialism views progressive dispensationalism as still in need of improvement for the following reasons: (1) it does not teach Israel's excommunication, as does preterism; (2) it does not interact with phrases such as "it has been fulfilled" (e.g., passages like Acts 2:16); and, (3) it does not realize the complete lifeline implications of the present kingdom in every sphere of life.[68]

---

66 Chris Strevel, "The Certainty of the World's Conversion" [article online] (Covenant Presbyterian Church, 5 July 2001); http://covenant-presbyterian.church/articles/from-the-pastors-desk/the-certainty-of-the-worlds-conversion; Internet; accessed 12 May 2017.

67 Craig A. Blaising and Darrell L. Bock, *Progressive Dispensationalism* (Wheaton: BridgePoint, 1993), p. 260.

68 Strevel, "Dispensational Theology."

A consistent hermeneutic demands an unambiguous distinction between Israel and the church, yet progressive dispensationalism has blurred those distinctions to such an extent that postmillennialism can actually commend some of the changes (which is disconcerting when one considers the manner in which postmillennialism views the future of Israel. For instance, postmillennialists may cite John 12:28-32, Eph. 1:19-23, and Rev. 1:9 to teach that the kingdom is not imminent; rather, it has arrived at Christ's first coming. According to postmillennialism, the kingdom is presently comprised of every blessing and promise (cf. Luke 1:46-54; 2 Cor. 1:20), which are believed to have fulfillment in Jesus Christ because of His obedience. As the church is changed by the power of the gospel, follows Christ's example and lives under His lordship, the result will be changed institutions in every sphere of life. The kingdom presently encompasses all the enemies of Christ being conquered so that the church is somewhere between the "session" and "final victory."

Furthermore, it is believed that Israel has been excommunicated; therefore, preterists of both amillennial and postmillennial persuasion believe that their view is superior. In other words, the kingdom that the Jews were expecting was not the kingdom that Jesus offered at His "triumphal entry." Israel will be restored to the olive tree of faith (cf. Rom. 11), but she will not be the mediator of all salvation blessings to the world. The inheritance that the Jews will possess will be as heirs of God's promises in the same manner as the church today.

CONCLUSION

Both preterist amillennialism and preterist postmillennialism replace God's program for Israel with the church despite the fact that Scripture never claims that God has permanently rejected Israel (cf. Deut. 28—30). Indeed, the Old Testament clearly teaches a restoration of a future national

Israel (Joel 3:1; Amos 9:11-15; Zeph. 3:20; Zech. 12:10); thus, it is Biblical to affirm that great blessings are yet to come for the nation of Israel in the future. Although she has been temporarily set aside as a nation in the fulfilling of the covenants, God will ultimately bring the nation to a place of prominence where she will be a blessing to all nations of the world. God's covenant people, Israel, are not rejected (which is evident in the fact that there has always been a believing remnant within the nation of Israel, even when the majority lived in unbelief); rather, "judicial blindness" was brought upon the people.[69] The stumbling block to the Gentiles (and preterist amillennialists and preterist postmillennialists) was not that Israel should fall and be rejected permanently; rather, the temporary "casting away" was to allow salvation to come to the Gentiles in order that Israel would be provoked to jealousy (Rom. 11:7-11).

God has principally focused upon Gentiles in this present dispensation because of Israel's hardness of heart; however, a future blessing for the nation of Israel is to be eagerly expected. Paul wrote, "For if their rejection is the reconciliation of the world, what will *their* acceptance be but life from the dead?" (v. 15).[70] Abraham is the root of promise and Israel is the stock of promise, thus Gentiles cannot boast with regard to being grafted into the rich root of the olive tree (vv. 16-18). Gentiles should remember they are not the natural branches, and they are indebted to a Jewish root for their blessings (vv. 17-32).

When God resumes His covenant program with Israel as a nation, her spiritual condition will be an entire contrast with her present state. Israel is currently hardened to a degree. The natural branches of the olive tree have been "broken off" because of her unbelief, but the hardening is not complete because God still has a remnant of faith. When "the fullness of the Gentiles has come in," God will again turn to Israel and "all Israel

---

69   John Nelson Darby, *The Collected Writings of J. N. Darby*, 34 vols., ed. William Kelly (Sunbury, PA: Believer's Bookshelf, 1971) 26:109.

70   John F. Walvoord, *Israel in Prophecy* (Grand Rapids: Zondervan, 1962), p. 56.

will be saved" (vv. 25-26). The "all Israel" refers to a turn to God by Israel on a national scale. A mass turning to God by the Jews does seem impossible today. However, Romans 11:28-32 emphasize the certainty that the event will occur because "the gifts and the calling of God are irrevocable" (v. 29). God never retracts on His acts of grace (v. 29). "God has shut up all in disobedience" for the precise purpose that He can show mercy upon the Jewish nation (v. 32). God's ways are unsearchable beyond all understanding, and the church does well when she finds herself not teaching doctrines contrary to the Lord's eternal plans (vv. 33-36).

CHAPTER 3

PROPHETIC TIMING AND THE MILLENNIUM: HISTORICISM

Historicism is the view that the timing of Bible prophecy occurs during the entirety of the church age. Whereas preterism, historicism and futurism all interpret general eschatology as unfolding certain historical events, historicists differ from the other two views by believing that prophetic books and texts of the Bible are entirely symbolic in form. Therefore, major Bible prophecies are interpreted in a non-literal manner according to the belief in fulfillment during the entire course of church history. Historicists will agree with both preterists and futurists that Christ did bring judgment upon Israel in A.D. 70. Historicists and futurists will differ with preterists in believing that the coming of Christ subsequent to the tribulation is future. Historicists will differ from futurists in believing that major Bible prophecies have been and are being fulfilled throughout current church age. Historicism results in "the progressive and continuous fulfillment of prophecy, in unbroken sequence, from Daniel's day and the time of John, on down to the second advent and the end of the age."[71]

The historicist interpretation of Biblical prophecies certainly has found representation throughout the entirety of church history. Adventist scholar LeRoy Edwin Froom traced the view through such prominent church figures as Hippolytus (ca. 170-236) in early church history, Joachim of Fiore (ca. 1135-1202) and John Wycliffe (ca. 1329-84) in the Middle Ages, Martin Luther (1483-1546) and John Knox (ca. 1817-1892) during the Reformation, and Isaac Newton (1642-1727) and John Wesley (1703-91) of prior centuries, and into contemporary Christianity.[72] From the time of the Reformation to the 20th century (approximately), virtually all Protestants held the historicist view. The majority of the 19th-century cults, such as Jehovah's Witnesses (1884) and Mormonism (1829), and the *pseudo*-cult of Seventh-day Adventism[73] (1860), adopted the historicist interpretation.

THE THEOLOGICAL SYSTEM OF HISTORICISM

Historicism equates the current church age with the period of the tribulation. Some historicists teach the tribulation began in A.D. 300 with the rise of the papacy as the Antichrist. The Protestant Reformers

---

71   Leroy Edwin Froom, *The Prophetic Faith of Our Fathers*, 4 vols. (Washington, DC: Review and Herald Publishing Association, 1950), 1:22-23.

72   Ibid., 1:2.

73   The Adventist doctrine of the "investigative judgment" is antithetical to the Biblical gospel. Christians have debated whether every Adventist denomination should be properly classified as a cult. Adventist denominations that affirm the "investigative judgment" are rightly classified as teaching cultic doctrine, but for the purpose of this chapter, the author is not engaging in the debate regarding the entire theological structure of Seventh-day Adventism.

supplemented Augustine's amillennialism with the view that the papacy (as a system) was the Antichrist. The seal, trumpet and bowl judgments are fulfilled throughout various historical events in Europe. The seal judgments could include the rise of Islam, whereas the trumpet judgments could include the march of Napoleon across Europe. Since the major of these judgments have already occurred in church history, it is not uncommon for historicists to anticipate the Battle of Armageddon. The Branch Davidian leader David Koresh was a premillennial historicist. He was anticipating the Battle of Armageddon since he regarded himself as the last of the seven angels of Revelation.[74]

The majority of historicists interpret the Olivet Discourse (Matt. 24—25, Mark 13; Luke 21:7-36) preteristically; however, the book of Revelation is interpreted historicistically. William Hendrickson and Seventh-day Adventists are exceptions to historicists that do not interpret the Olivet Discourse preteristically. The only *group* of historicists today is the Seventh-day Adventists. Charles Hodge and Jonathan Edwards were postmillennial historicists. Martin Luther was an amillennial historicist.[75] William Miller and John Gill were premillennial historicists. Whereas preterists generally are only postmillennial or amillennial, the historicist view of prophetic timing fulfillment can accommodate all millennial views (pre-, post- and a-). Every historicist predicts dates

---

74 James D. Faubion, *The Shadows and Lights of Waco: Millennialism Today* (Princeton, NJ: Princeton University Press, 2001), p. 59.

75 John Calvin interpreted the Olivet Discourse historicistically, but whether he was clearly amillennial or postmillennial is still a matter of research. The influence of the Reformer's eschatology is evident in the Westminster Standards—the official teaching of all Presbyterian Churches—which is entirely historicist. The Antichrist is said to be the beast of Revelation in contrast to the preterist notion of first-century Rome or futurist teaching of an eschatological individual. One should note that covenant theology is not found among the Protestant Reformers. Prior to the 1647 Westminster Confession of Faith, there were no references to covenant theology. The Westminster Confession is one of the first documents to mention a covenant of works and covenant of grace. Covenant theology was not fully systematized until Cocceius. Covenant theology was introduced in America through the Puritan influence of the writings of Francis Turretin and Herman Witsius; it was communicated extensively in America with the writings of John Cotton and others. Covenant theology, as a theological system today, is a combination of the theology of the Reformers, the writings of Cocceius, and the Westminster Confession (i.e., certainly not an exegesis of Scripture in all areas of doctrine and theology, especially ecclesiology and eschatology).

for the fulfillment of Bible prophecy since they believe current events fulfill the Olivet Discourse and prophetic books (such as Daniel and Revelation). John Gill, for example, believed that the Olivet Discourse was fulfilled preteristically but separated it from prophetic teaching in the Epistles and Revelation.

Historicism was dominant in the United States until the Civil War. Dispensational premillennialism became dominant after the American Civil War. One reason for the decline of historicism was the "Great Disappointment" of William Miller, who brought the doctrine into disrepute for centuries. The popularity of dispensationalism was due to the fact that its teachers were communicating accurately that the rapture was a timeless event and the tribulation was eschatological (i.e. any "date setting" was unbiblical). Dispensationalism was entirely anti-date setting. Unfortunately, many dispensationalists today resort to historicist interpretations when they quote Matthew 24:4-8 (for example) as being fulfilled in the present time. The lack of interpretative consistency is unfortunate since historicist interpretation militates against a pretribulational rapture. Although the intricacies of their system allow them to embrace any of the three millennial views, historicists cannot believe in pretribulationism because they believe the tribulation has already commenced. Therefore, "dispensationalist" teachers who quote events of the tribulation as being fulfilled today are practicing historicist principles that undermine the teaching of a pretribulation rapture.[76]

Historicists generally attribute the rise of futurism and preterism, from an almost unanimous view among Protestants,[77] to the rise of Roman Catholic leaders during the Counter Reformation (beginning in 1534). For instance, historicists understand the prophecies in Revelation of the "beast"

---

76 Ron J. Bigalke Jr., "The Olivet Discourse: A Resolution of Time," *Chafer Theological Seminary Journal* 9 (Spring 2003): 106-40.

77 George E. Ladd commented, "This 'historical' type of interpretation with its application of the Antichrist to papal Rome so dominated Protestant study of prophetic truth for three centuries that it has frequently been called the 'Protestant' interpretation" (*The Blessed Hope* [Grand Rapids: Eerdmans, 1956], p. 32).

in chapter 13 as an ecclesiastical system best represented by the Roman Catholic Church. Since the Reformers identified the Roman Catholic Church as the beast of Revelation, historicists claim that it was critical for the Roman Catholic Counter Reformation to promulgate an eschatological system to alleviate the papacy of that ignominy. Regarding the Protestant interpretation of the Antichrist, *The Catholic Encyclopedia* reads:

> To the "reformers" particularly the Apocalypse was an inex-haustible quarry where to dig for invectives that they might hurl then against the Roman hierarchy. The seven hills of Rome, the scarlet robes of the cardinals, and the unfortunate abuses of the papal court made the application easy and tempting. Owing to the patient and strenuous research of scholars, the interpretation of the Apocalypse has been transferred to a field free from the *odium theologicum* ["theological hatred" due to differences in religious belief]. But then the meaning of the Seer is determined by the rules of common exegesis. Apart from the resurrection, the millennium, and the plagues preceding the final consum-mation, they see in his visions references to the leading events of his time. Their method of interpretation may be called his-toric as compared with the theological and political application of former ages. The key to the mysteries of the book they find in 17:8-14. For thus says the Seer: "Let here the mind that hath understanding give heed".[78]

The alleged action of the Roman Catholic Church was a Jesuit effort to circulate an eschatological system of belief that would remove the stigma upon the Catholic Church. Francisco Ribera (1537-91) and Luis de Alcazar (1554-1613), 16th-century Spanish Jesuits, would challenge the histori-cist view in an effort to confuse the Protestant prophetic interpretation.[79]

78 C. van den Biesen, "Apocalypse," in *The Catholic Encyclopedia* [online] (1 March 1907, New Ad-vent), <http://www.newadvent.org/cathen/01594b.htm>; Internet; accessed 24 May 2017.

79 Francis D. Nichol, ed., "History of the Interpretation of Daniel," in *The Seventh-day Adventist Bible Commentary*, 7 vols. (Washington, DC: Review and Herald Publishing Association, 1953-80), 4:42; James Durham, *A Commentarie Upon the Book of the Revelation* (Edinburgh: Christopher

Sometimes Roman Jesuit, Robert Bellarmine (1542-1621), is added along-side Ribera as also contributing to the futurist view.[80]

Francisco Ribera of Salmanca, Spain, is generally credited with the origin of the futurist view as a Catholic response to the historicism of the Reformers. Approximately 1590, he published a 500-page exposition of the book of Revelation. The official eschatological position of the Roman Catholic Church followed Ribera's exposition. The historicists objected strongly to futurism since it does not address the history of the church in prophetic analysis, which historicists believe produces a historical and prophetical vacuum. Historicists remain critical that major Bible prophecy will not find fulfillment until the final seven years of Daniel's 70th week occurs. The futurism of Ribera placed the Antichrist in a distant future from the time of the Protestant Reformation. According to Ribera, the reign of Antichrist would not be until the last three and one-half years of Daniel's 70th week.

Jesuit Interpretation and the Protestant Reformers

The Protestant Reformers never abandoned the amillennialism of the Catholic Church. For instance, it was through his use of the Scriptures, which the Reformers rightly claimed as their sole authority (*sola Scriptura*), that Ribera was able to use in order to demonstrate the truth of the futurist position. One accusation against futurism is that it was a Catholic effort. However, Martin Luther was also a Catholic when the Holy Spirit illumined his mind to embrace the Biblical teaching of justification by faith alone (in contrast to Romanism). In like manner, Ribera may have been another individual whose mind the Holy Spirit illumined within great spiritual darkness so that he could understand the Word of God literally.

Higgins, 1658), p. 667.
80 Froom, *Prophetic Faith*, 2:486.

What needs to be brought to mind is the fact that Ribera contradicted official Catholic dogma. He did not present his interpretation in a pamphlet against the Reformers; rather, he composed a major commentary on the book of Revelation. Indeed, it would be odd for Ribera to formulate a doctrine opposed to official Catholic doctrine. If it is said that Ribera wrote his commentary to convince the Reformers of the futurist system, it is not possible to imagine any Protestant taking seriously the interpretation of a Jesuit bishop. If it is said that he wrote to convince Catholics that the Pope was not the Antichrist, his literal interpretative method would have been completely opposed by the Catholic Church (which would be an argument in favor of the Reformers). The more natural approach is to conclude that Ribera's futurism was the result of a literal interpretation of the Word of God, which, in turn, would lead to the conclusion that the Antichrist was an individual who would appear during a seven-year period just prior to the return of Christ.

Furthermore, any who opposed the dogma of the Roman Catholic Church (especially in Spain) would be branded as the worst type of heretic and would be murdered if the Spanish Inquisition captured them.[81] The Spanish Inquisition began in 1478 and continued well into the 18th century, which is during the time Ribera wrote his commentary. Ribera would have demonstrated great courage to publish his teachings, especially in Spain. Perhaps Ribera not only learned that the Reformers were wrong in proclaiming the Catholic Church as the Antichrist, but also the Roman Church was wrong in spiritualizing Bible prophecy. Either way, Ribera came to his conclusions through a literal interpretation of Scripture. The accusation that Ribera originated the futurist view does not accurately consider the development of eschatological systems. Larry V. Crutchfield demonstrated meticulously the belief of the early church

---

81 Philip Schaff, *History of the Christian Church*, 8 vols. (New York: Charles Scribner's Sons, 1858; reprint, Peabody, MA: Hendrickson, 1996), 6:533.

WHEN? *The Biblical Timing for Prophetic Fulfillment*

fathers in the return of the Lord and the establishment of His kingdom on earth.[82]

> The position of the early fathers on the tribulation and its relation to the saints and Christ's return, is impossible to completely decipher. Many of them, especially in the first century, did indeed make explicit statements which indicated a belief in the imminent return of Christ. The doctrine of imminency is especially prominent in the writings of the apostolic fathers. It is on the basis of Christ's impending return (e.g., Didache) and on the strength of the literal fulfillment of past prophecy (e.g., Barnabas), that they exhorted the Christian to live a life of purity and faithfulness.
>
> In addition to direct statements on imminency, in some fathers language decidedly associated with the rapture is also found. And still others maintained that the saints will escape the time of persecution under Antichrist in a manner reflective of Revelation 3:10. But due to the circumstances of that period of church history, there was no exact correlation between tribulationism as held by the early fathers and views commonly held today.[83]

Crutchfield mentioned first-century fathers, such as Clement of Rome, Ignatius, Hermas and Barnabas, and second-century fathers, such as Tertullian and Cyprian, as a few examples of those early church fathers affirming an imminent return of the Lord. Therefore, the early church held to a futurist, premillennial interpretation of prophecy in a primitive and non-systematized

---

82 Larry V. Crutchfield, "The Early Church Fathers and the Foundations of Dispensationalism: Part I," *The Conservative Theological Journal* 2 (March 1998): 19-31; idem, "The Early Church Fathers and the Foundations of Dispensationalism: Part II," *The Conservative Theological Journal* 2 (June 1998): 123-40; idem, "The Early Church Fathers and the Foundations of Dispensationalism: Part III," *The Conservative Theological Journal* 2 (September 1998): 247-69; idem, "The Early Church Fathers and the Foundations of Dispensationalism: Part IV," *The Conservative Theological Journal* 2 (December 1998): 375-403; idem, "The Early Church Fathers and the Foundations of Dispensationalism: Part V," *The Conservative Theological Journal* 3 (April 1999): 26-52; idem, "The Early Church Fathers and the Foundations of Dispensationalism: Part VI," *The Conservative Theological Journal* 3 (August 1999): 182-97.

83 Crutchfield, "Foundations of Dispensationalism: Part VI," 194.

form. Ladd was incorrect when he stated the "futurist, premillennial interpretation" was "not of the pretribulation type."[84] Erickson attempted to be
more truthful: "To be sure, the premillennialism of the church's first centuries
may have included belief in a pretribulational rapture of the church . . . while
there are in the writings of the early fathers seeds from which the doctrine
of the pretribulational rapture could be developed. . . ."[85]

If the church of the Middle Ages had not abandoned the futurist,
premillennialism of the early church, one may only speculate what doctrinal
developments may have "grown" from those "seeds"—rather than allegori-
cism inhibiting germination. Posttribulationists will often refer to their view
as "historic premillennialism." The term is not accurate though since the
eschatological system of the early church is difficult to classify. The difficulty
is the consequence of frequent contradictory perspectives of the early church
without any conscientious regard for consistency. The early church was largely
premillennial.[86] Walvoord referred to the belief of the early church fathers
being "that the coming of the Lord could occur any hour."[87]

The term "imminent intratribulationism" is more accurate to describe
the beliefs of the early church, rather than asserting that they embraced a
contemporary form of posttribulationism. (With the exception of Caius, there
is no church father who opposed premillennialism until the advent of Origen's
allegorical method of interpretation, which then dominated eschatological
thought through the spiritualized [Gnostic] interpretation of Revelation 20
by Augustine, and as a consequence of the legalization of Christianity by
Constantine.) In the midst of continual persecution, the early church believed
the tribulation was presently upon them and anticipated the imminent return

---

84 Ladd, *Blessed Hope*, p. 35.

85 Millard J. Erickson, *Contemporary Options in Eschatology: A Study of the Millennium* (Grand Rap-
    ids: Baker, 1977), pp. 112, 131.

86 Larry V. Crutchfield, "The Blessed Hope and the Tribulation in the Apostolic Fathers," in *When the
    Trumpet Sounds*, gen. eds. Thomas Ice and Timothy Demy (Eugene, OR: Harvest House, 1995),
    pp. 91-94, 101.

87 John F. Walvoord, *The Return of the Lord* (Grand Rapids: Dunham Publishing, 1955), p. 80.

of Jesus Christ within this context. Although indeterminate, the climax of the tribulation would be the rapture of the church; the rapture was therefore an imminent event. The belief in the imminent return of Jesus Christ by the early church fathers is a primary aspect of pretribulational thought.

The absence of any systematic eschatology by the early church fathers is the consequence of the lack of consistency by them regarding the exact chronology of the premillennial return of Jesus Christ. Since the early church did believe in an imminent return of the Lord, it would seem that any references to them by posttribulationists must explain how they could believe in a doctrine of imminence, yet also thought they were experiencing the tribulation. The reason why the early did not give systematic thought to eschatological doctrines is understandable. "The church soon became involved in problems other than the study of prophecy, however, and church councils in the fourth century and in following centuries were concerned primarily with the doctrine of the Trinity, the doctrine of sin, and various controversies. Paganism and ritualism engulfed the church after the fourth century, and it was not until the Protestant Reformation in the sixteenth century that Biblical doctrines began to be restored."[88]

The systematic teaching of premillennial pretribulationism is a consequence of the Protestant Reformation. Amillennial and postmillennial theologies essentially deny the principle of *sola Scriptura* by not applying the Reformation hermeneutic consistently. (Due to their own historical context, the Protestant Reformers themselves cannot be *directly* accused of this deficiency.) However, it is not clear why the majority of modern posttribulationists deny imminency. Although posttribulationists make frequent appeals to the church fathers for defense of their view, it is unmistakable that there is a lack of continuity between the early church and posttribulationists today. Nevertheless, the early church simply did not articulate a systematized form of eschatological doctrine.

---

88 Ibid., p. 81

A major change to prophetic interpretation occurred in the second and third centuries with Origen (ca. 185-254). He absolutely ignored the literal, normal meaning of Scripture, and it was his method of spiritualizing and allegorizing that became unusually excessive throughout the church. Augustine of Hippo is best known as the father of amillennialism. Augustine dated the beginning of the millennium to the first coming of Christ and taught the kingdom of God was present on earth. He modified Origen's allegorical method by confining it solely to Bible prophecy. Following the teachings of Augustine, the church developed a sense of triumphalism that remained the dominant view of prophecy until Joachim of Fiore (ca. 1135-1202). Joachim developed the day-year theory, which understands the 1,260 days of Revelation as 1,260 years. He taught that Babylon was Rome, the Pope was the Antichrist, and the Age of the Spirit would begin in A.D. 1260. Joachim's historicism thrived during the Middle Ages (among those who did not merely allegorize prophetic truths) and into the period of the Reformation.[89]

Ribera's futurism and Alcazar's preterism were products of the counter-Reformation since the majority of the Reformers still followed the historicist views of Joachim. Of course, Ribera and Alcazer interpreted differently, but they were united in their efforts to remove the stigma of Babylon upon Rome, and thus opposed any teaching from contemporary history that the Antichrist was Pope. In removing such stigmas, they would free Rome from the accusations raised by the historicism of the Protestant Reformers; it is wrong though to attribute futurism and preterism to a counter-Reformation movement since both views were in existence, in some form, prior to the writings of Ribera and Alcazer. The Jesuit theologian and shrewd controversialist, Cardinal Robert Bellarmine (1542-1621) of Italy, is said to have refined the futurism of Ribera. In the third book of his *Disputationes de Controversiis Christianae Fidei Adversus Huius Temporis Haereticos* (1586–93; "Lectures

---

89   David Larsen, "Joachim of Fiore: The Rebirth of Futurism," *Covenant Quarterly* 60 (2002): 1-15.

Concerning the Controversies of the Christian Faith against the Heretics of This Time"), Bellarmine argued that the prophecies of the Antichrist in Daniel, Revelation and throughout the Pauline epistles bore no identification to the papacy. Bellarmine sought to demonstrate that the Antichrist was not the papacy; rather, it was a single man who would be revealed at the end times.[90]

Luis de Alcazar (1554-1613) advanced the preterist view of the book of Revelation. He taught that Nero was the Antichrist and had already fulfilled the prophecies of Revelation 1—11 in the A.D. 70 destruction of Jerusalem. He taught that Revelation 12—19 was fulfilled by the fall of pagan Rome in A.D. 410. Revelation 20 was interpreted as the final judgment of the Antichrist and the day of judgment. Revelation 21 was the current age wherein the New Jerusalem is the Roman Catholic Church.[91] Both Ribera and Alcazar placed the Antichrist outside the Middle Ages and Protestant Reformation, which is the time that Protestant historicists identify the 1,260-year reign of Antichrist.

With the exception of the kingdom of the cults, historicism has few advocates in contemporary times. Protestant historicists believe the reason for this is the outcome of Ribera's futurism and Alcazar's preterism. The result has been an easing of the pressure once felt by the papacy during the Reformation. However, the historicist claim that the idea of the Antichrist as an individual is a recent development by Catholic scholars during the Reformation is not true. McGinn demonstrated that the only view of the Antichrist in the early church was that of an individual.[92]

---

90 Roberti Bellarmini, *Disputationes de Controversiis Christianae Fidei Adversus Huius Temporis Hae-reticos*, 3 vols. (Ingolstadt: David Sartorius, 1593-93). See also, James Broderick, *Robert Bellarmine, Saint and Scholar* (Westminster, MD: Newman Press, 1961); Giorgio de Santillana, *The Crime of Galileo* (Chicago: University of Chicago Press, 1955), pp. 74-109; and, William Whitaker, *A Disputation on Holy Scripture, Against the Papists, Especially Bellarmine and Stapleton*, trans. and ed. William Fitzgerald (1588; reprint, Cambridge: University Press, 1849).

91 Froom, *Prophetic Faith*, 2:507.

92 Bernard McGinn, *Visions of the End: Apocalyptic Traditions in the Middle Ages* (New York: Columbia University Press, 1979), pp. 16-17.

Protestant historicists believe that Daniel's 70th week and the 2,300 year-day prophecy have a common starting point. The rebuilding of the walls of Jerusalem (Neh. 5:15) in 454 B.C. is the starting point for the 2,300 years and 490 years. Therefore, there are 1,810 year-days remaining subsequent to the end of the 70th week. The entire prophecy of Daniel 9:24-27 is reinterpreted to fit the historicist scheme. Historicists radically reinterpret Daniel 9:24. According to Hebrews 9:26, the prophecy of Daniel 9:24, "to make an end of sin," is fulfilled. The forgiveness of the sins of the church is the fulfillment of "make atonement for iniquity." The prophecy "to bring in everlasting righteousness" means to accomplish everlasting justification. "To seal up vision and prophecy" is the vision of the 2,300 year-days and the seal placed upon Daniel the prophet (i.e., 490 years are cut-off from the vision of the 2,300 years which means 1,810 years remain). The prophecy "to anoint the most holy" was fulfilled on Pentecost with the outpouring of the Spirit on the church. Historicists offer the same radical reinterpretation to Daniel 9:27. The confirming of the covenant "with the many for one week" was the seven years from A.D. 29 to 36. The covenant with Israel would be confirmed for the last of the week. During this time, no Gentiles could be accepted. The "middle of the week" was A.D. 33 when Jesus Christ "put a stop to sacrifice." His sacrifice would end on the cross in the "middle of the week." The historicist view has to spiritualize these prophecies in order to find fulfillment with historical events.

Froom blamed the futurist Protestants (inspired by Jesuits, in his view) for abandonment of the historicist school.

> The inroad of the Futurist theory also served to divert attention and understanding from the relationship of the seventy weeks to the terminus of the 2300 years. If the seventieth week is separated from the sixty-nine weeks, then the inseparable relationship of the remaining 1810 years of the 2300 is hidden, and the divine har-

mony and understanding of the whole is ruptured. By fixing the eyes upon a transcendent future, one obscures the epochal events of the present. And when the 2300 days are conceived of as but literal time, any consideration of a nineteenth-century terminus is obviously puerile. Confusion of the Historical School of interpretation, and its final breakdown, is now definitely under way.[93]

Tanner wrote similar to Froom.

Accordingly, towards the close of the century of the Reformation, two of her most learned doctors set themselves to the task, each endeavouring by different means to accomplish the same end, namely, that of diverting men's minds from perceiving the fulfilment of the prophecies of the Antichrist in the Papal system. The Jesuit Alcasar devoted himself to bring into prominence the *Preterist* method of interpretation . . . and thus endeavoured to show that the prophecies of Antichrist were fulfilled before the Popes ever ruled at Rome, and therefore could not apply to the Papacy. On the other hand the Jesuit Ribera tried to set aside the application of these prophecies to the Papal Power by bringing out the *Futurist* system, which asserts that these prophecies refer properly not to the career of the Papacy, but to that of some future supernatural individual, who is yet to appear, and to continue in power for three and a half years. Thus, as Alford says, the Jesuit Ribera, about A.D. 1580, may be regarded as the Founder of the Futurist system in modern times.[94]

Froom perceived the development of the futurist view as a counter Protestant position in the 16th century that is the majority belief among Protestants in the modern church. He credited Samuel R. Maitland (1792–1866) as the first Protestant to accept Ribera's futurist interpretation of the Antichrist.[95] Maitland, curate of Christ's Church in Gloucester, first

---

93   Froom, *Prophetic Faith*, 3:658.

94   Joseph Tanner, *Daniel and the Revelation* (London: Hodder and Stoughton, 1898), pp. 16-17.

95   Froom, *Prophetic Faith*, 3:541.

published *An Enquiry into the Grounds on which the Prophetic Period of Daniel and St. John, Has Been Supposed to Consist of 1260 Years* (1826), which was widely read and opposed the day-year theory. James Todd, professor of Hebrew at the University of Dublin, began teaching futurism and published several pamphlets and books. John Newman, a leading figure of the Oxford Tractarian Movement, published a pamphlet that endorsed futurism, and eventually converted to Roman Catholicism.[96]

Froom's conspiracy theory falls to understand that Ribera did not originate the futurist view. Ribera revived a view that was widely held by many of the early church fathers. Since premillennial dispensationalism is based upon a futurist interpretation of Daniel and Revelation, Ribera's futurism revived premillennial teaching. However, it needs to be noted that the view was not completely systematized in his time. Nevertheless, Froom connected the development of futurism to another Jesuit priest, the Spaniard, Manuel de Lacunza (1731-1801).

Lacunza wrote *La Venida del Mesías en Gloria y Magestad* ("The Coming of the Messiah in Glory and Majesty") pseudonymously as Juan Josafa [Rabbi] Ben-Ezra about 1791. The work was entirely premillennial and opposed to Roman Catholicism. Although Lacunza argued for a literal and premillennial second coming, he was not a pretribulationist. He held a peculiar view of a 45-day partial rapture. His book was discussed at the Albury Conference (with Edward Irving in attendance) at the home of Henry Drummond.[97]

Contrary to belief among some dispensationalists, John Nelson Darby was not present at the Albury Conference. During the 19th century, the French Revolution and the actions of Napoleon anguished Christians, which caused some to fear that the Emperor may be the Antichrist, and thus developed a renewed interest in Biblical prophecy. Lady (Theodosia)

---

96 Ibid., 3:655-58.

97 Harold H. Rowdon, *The Origins of the Brethren, 1825-1850* (London: Pickering & Inglis, 1967), p. 87.

Powerscourt held one of many similar meetings that arose to address prophetic concerns. Darby was invited to the Powerscourt Conferences of 1831 to 1833, which had a lasting influence upon him. The transition from the present church age to the millennial kingdom in which Israel had prominence under Christ's rule was understood by interpreting the 70th week of Daniel 9 as future. Based upon his resolute belief in a literal interpretation of Scripture, he developed a precise design for eschatological events. Darby believed in a distinction between Israel and the church that extends into eternity. He also taught dispensations are economies of God, and that the church age is a parenthesis. Darby first began to articulate his views of a pretribulational rapture and to develop his dispensational thinking during convalescence (from December of 1826 to January of 1827). By 1833, he developed a complete systematization of premillennial dispensationalism.

The problem with Froom's conspiracy theory is that he believes premillennial dispensationalism is unbiblical if it bears any connections or similarities to the writings of two Jesuit priests. No problems exist in crediting Ribera with reviving futurism during the Protestant Reformation. God can use both believers and nonbelievers to accomplish his purposes. Furthermore, the actual issue is not who developed the futurist view, but whether it is Biblical.

CONCLUSION

Often historicism has thrived during momentous eras of the church (e.g., during persecution or revival). What is evident regarding classic historicism is the vigorous promotion of the teaching that the Antichrist is an ecclesiastical system (viz. the Roman Catholic Church), and the vehement denial of the Biblical teaching that the Antichrist will be an individual. The Reformers endured such incredible persecution under the Catholic Church that it was only natural to spiritualize Scripture and understand the pope to be the Antichrist (it is, therefore, understandable why the Reformers developed their conclusions!). The Reformers abandoned the allegorical method of interpretation (characteristic of Roman Catholicism) in all areas but eschatology. Amillennialism is the prophetic viewpoint of the Catholic Church, and a non-literal millennium was also the prophetic viewpoint of the Protestant Reformers. The reason that many of the Reformers retained the amillennialism of Catholicism was due to the time in which they lived. They did embrace a grammatical-historical interpretation of the Scripture in regards to soteriology and ecclesiology. Since eschatology was not a major issue during the Reformation, the Reformers did not have the opportunity to apply their hermeneutic consistently. Although human personalities do not endure, thankfully, the Word of God does abide forever.

CHAPTER 4

PROPHETIC TIMING AND THE MILLENNIUM: IDEALISM

The idealist approach to Biblical eschatology is often termed the spiritualist or historical-spiritualist view.[98] Whereas preterism, historicism and futurism affirm a chronology for prophetic fulfillment, idealists do not. The focus of preterism is upon past fulfillment of major prophecies. Since historicists understand major prophecies as fulfilled and being fulfilled during the present age, it is impossible for them not to attempt predictions of prophetic fulfillment (i.e. "date setting"). Since the majority of unfulfilled prophecy relates to the tribulation, second coming and the millennium, futurists should never attempt to predict dates for prophetic fulfillment.

Idealists assume the book of Revelation, and parallel passages such as the Olivet Discourse, are not referring to real time chronology. As a

---

98 Prophetic idealism should not be confused with philosophical idealism. The latter is concerned with the nature of reality primarily as mind or spirit in contrast to matter or material.

variation of historicism, it reduces Revelation and the Olivet Discourse to an unclear and mystical allegory simply representing an ageless battle between good and evil. Bible prophecy is then mere myth,[99] in contrast to an unveiling of future and real-time events. For example, in contrast to eschatological individuals, the first and second beasts of Revelation are symbolic references to imperial and provincial Rome. Idealism, as an approach to Biblical eschatology, was rarely followed outside liberal scholarship and was not a significant factor in the mainstream of current evangelical debate regarding when prophecy will be fulfilled. Historically, idealism was primarily the view of liberals. Today, however, idealism is experiencing resurgence among evangelicals.

THE THEOLOGICAL SYSTEM OF IDEALISM

Idealists believe Biblical eschatology is not associated with chronology. For this reason, it is considered atemporal. Idealists believe the primary reason for Biblical eschatology is a spiritual, or inspirational, meaning. Therefore, they emphasize the symbolic and teach it is impossible to develop a chronology of prophetic events. The message of Biblical eschatology is deconstructed to mean the church will be victorious. Idealists believe the primary purpose of Biblical eschatology is to edify, exhort and encourage believers that God is victorious over the evil in the world.

The idealist view does not give complete attention to the original languages and is less systematic exegetically. Most idealists do not engage the scholarly literature (emphasizing instead the abuses and misinterpretations

---

99 One should make note that many who do not interpret Biblical eschatology literally also do not interpret Genesis 1—11 literally. Consequently, the same descriptive language of the Biblical accounts of creation and climax forms a relationship between belief in a literal six-day creation and cataclysmic eschatological events prior to the establishment of the millennial kingdom, and the consummation of human history.

of Biblical prophecy), as do the other views of Biblical eschatology. In his representation of the idealist view of Revelation, Sam Hamstra Jr. wrote, "The heart and soul of the idealist approach is that Revelation is an apocalyptic book that presents spiritual precepts through symbols, rather than a book of predictive prophecy fulfilled in specific events or persons in human history."[100] The prophetic is perceived in contrast to the apocalyptic.[101] Of course, there are those who classify Revelation as apocalyptic and prophetic.[102] Robert Thomas demonstrated that the best approach to Biblical eschatology is the literal method. He wrote, "A dispensational view holds that the book is primarily prophetic rather than apocalyptic and that biblical prophecy deserves literal interpretation, just as do other literary genres of Scripture."[103]

> Revelation is best understood as a prophecy, which is a classification that considers the book's numerous assertions to be prophecy (1:3; 22:7, 10, 18, 19), and thus it exhorts God's people with moral imperatives, in addition to predicting "things which will take place after these things" (i.e., "the things which you have seen," ch. 1; and, "the things which are," chs. 2-3). Understanding the book of Revelation as prophecy would require interpreting it according to the grammatical, historical method that is customarily used for all Scripture.[104]

Martin Luther (and the other Protestant Reformers of the 16th century) caused immeasurable transformation to the church by demanding

---

100 Sam Hamstra Jr., "An Idealist View of Revelation," in *Four Views on the Book of Revelation*, gen. ed. C. Marvin Pate (Grand Rapids: Zondervan, 1998), p. 129.

101 Although Hamstra understood the majority of Revelation to be "apocalyptic," he concluded that Revelation 20—21 is prophetic (Ibid., pp. 127-28).

102 George Eldon Ladd, "Why Not Prophetic Apocalyptic?" *Journal of Biblical Literature* 76 (1957): 192-200.

103 Robert Thomas, "A Classical Dispensational View of Revelation," in *Four Views on Revelation*, p. 224.

104 Ron J. Bigalke, "Apocalypticism," in *Encyclopedia of Christianity in the United States*, 5 vols., eds. George Thomas Kurian and Mark A. Lamport (Lanham, MD: Rowman & Littlefield, 2016), 1:109.

reform. They declared the theology of the church in Western Europe was a deviation of Biblical, apostolic teaching. The rallying call of the Reformers was *sola Scriptura*, which meant the Bible alone was their authority, in contrast to the pope, church councils, or tradition. In calling the church to live with the Bible alone as her authority, the Reformers did not attempt to transform their eschatology. The neglect to apply the principle of *sola Scriptura* to all Scripture has resulted in many Christians denying a literal, plenary interpretation of the Bible. For instance, the historical portions of the Bible are considered allegorical, and the prophetic sections of Scripture suffer an even worse fate.

From the time of the Reformation until the 1820s, historicism was the dominant view among Protestants within premillennial circles. Apart from the Seventh-day Adventists (or the cults), there is little inducement to historicism as a system of prophetic interpretation today. In the 1820s, John Nelson Darby revived and defended dispensational futurism.[105] From the time of Darby, futurism became the dominant view of conservatives and surmounted historicism. Darby was the cascading source of the revived study of the literal interpretation of the prophetic Scriptures. At the beginning of the 21st century, preterism is escalating in an effort to surmount futurism.

By 1614 (just shy of the centennial birth of the Reformation), the preterist view of Biblical prophecy was roused. The preterist view denied the clear meaning of Biblical prophecy by relegating the majority of prophetic statements to a first-century fulfillment. Since most of Biblical eschatology was already fulfilled, this meant God had completed any plans for national Israel and now the church inherited all the promises to Israel. The view relegates most of Biblical eschatology to allegorical interpretation, which actually weakens the very foundation of the New

---

105 Darby said he first understood the pretribulational rapture during convalescence, due to an accident with his horse, from December 1826 until January 1827 [John Nelson Darby, *Letters of J. N. Darby*, 3 vols. (London: Stow Hill Bible and Tract Depot, n.d.; reprint, Sunbury, PA: Believers Bookshelf, 1971), 3:298-99].

Testament. The postmillennial form of preterism is mostly responsible for keeping preterism alive in the present time.

In his book *Every Prophecy of the Bible* (formerly titled, *The Prophecy Knowledge Handbook*),[106] Walvoord completed the enormous task of compiling a list of every significant Bible prophecy and included an exposition of each. He expounded more than 1,000 individual verses and demonstrated the literal fulfillment of half of those prophecies already. His work is unavoidable evidence that prophecy should be understood literally, since God always fulfills his Word exactly as He said. When the history of humanity is completed, every prophecy will be literally fulfilled. Since half of the Biblical prophecies have been fulfilled literally, it would make sense to expect that God will fulfill those remaining prophecies in the same accurate and historical manner.

In contrast to Walvoord's work, the majority of non-literal approaches to Biblical eschatology teach that prophetic texts are not actually relevant to specific events or historical fulfillment; rather, they merely provide comfort that the church will be victorious in Christ. As opposed to stimulating the church to confidence in God's sovereignty over world affairs, the non-literal approach to Biblical prophecy mollifies the church into a narcissistic view of a world in troubled times. Whereas preterism and historicism do find historical meaning in prophetic texts, as does the futurist, who anticipates a historical fulfillment in the final events of God's Divine plans for history, idealism offers little hope that the kingdom of God will be truly consummated when Christ returns to Earth in power and glory, and will then be extended into the new heaven and new Earth, or eternity itself.

Much of the church today is opting for non-literal interpretations of the Genesis record believing God used the process of evolution to bring creation into existence. The church is not only applying the approach that

---

106   John F. Walvoord, *Every Prophecy of the Bible* (Colorado Springs: Chariot Victor Publishing, 1999).

the Bible does not mean what it says to the creation account, but also to Biblical eschatology. The mentality is that prophecy cannot be understood or mean what it says, but such thinking is contrary to the Old Testament (or even the book of Revelation), which explains the symbolism of the prophetic books. The issues in Biblical eschatology are relevant today because they deal with the whole counsel of God's Word and the hope of the Christian. Furthermore, it is also vital to understand the prophetic Word so the believer can comprehend the final human drama for the world, the nation of Israel and the church. The knowledge of Biblical eschatology allows the believer to take comfort in the sovereignty of God and causes the believer to live humbly in light of God's eternal decrees (i.e., by not reducing them to mere human intellect).

D. H. Kromminga noted accurately: "The preterist and the futurist methods, or approaches, stand at opposite extremes."[107] The "opposite extremes" may help explain the later ascendancy of historicism and idealism, while the futurist and preterist views are in the forefront. From the 1820s until fairly recently, futurism generally remained unchallenged. Preterism has emerged, as the opposite extreme of futurism, to challenge the ascendancy of futurism within evangelicalism. Another method, known as idealism, is also gaining ascendancy as an eclectic, spiritualizing, system of prophetic interpretation.

Idealists interpret Biblical eschatology as symbols and metaphors of the emblematic panorama of the battle between good and evil, as opposed to it being a real account of events that will occur in history. Biblical eschatology does not predict future events, but insinuates a grand moral theme that is in the background of world events. The battle between good and evil is symbolized in the prophetic Word, and the moral theme is that good will ultimately triumph. There is no relation to real time in history, just allegorical representation.

---

107   D. H. Kromminga, *The Millennium and the Church: Studies in the History of Christian Chiliasm* (Grand Rapids: Eerdmans, 1945), p. 295.

Eclecticism, or realized eschatology, has modified the spiritualizing method of idealism. Interpreters who are eclectic in their approach recognize a consummated new heaven and new Earth preceded by the coming of Christ to deliver His people and judge the wicked. Biblical passages which prophesy of the tribulation are not literal, hence there is no rapture or 1,000-year reign of Christ on Earth. Idealism cannot be represented premillennially, but only postmillennially or amillennially.

Amillennialism views the millennium as a representative period between the death and resurrection, and the second coming of Christ. The "latter days" are the current church age. The perspective of the idealist is to view Biblical eschatology "as representing the ongoing conflict of good and evil, with no immediate historical connection to any social or political events."[108] The combined view (eclecticism) stresses courageous living, perseverance, assurance in the defeat of evil, viewing Christ in a new and wonderful manner, and viewing history in the mind of God and hands of Christ who will review the moral destinies of mankind. The only predictive element is in the sense that good will overthrow evil when Christ returns.[109]

Of course, preterist amillennialism and postmillennialism favors an historical interpretation of the identification of Antichrist and the establishment of the kingdom of God. By contrast, idealist postmillennialism and amillennialism either wholly (or above and beyond historicism of some variety) comprehend the establishment of the kingdom of God repeatedly, which means many antichrists arise in conflict with the kingdom of God for the duration of history and this process will merely end in destruction. Since it is believed that the kingdom of God was established at the resurrection of Christ, during which He secured victory over Satan and the curse, the view can also be known as inaugurated millennialism. Christ is currently

---

108   C. Marvin Pate, "Introduction to Revelation," in *Four Views of Revelation*, p. 23.

109   Raymond Calkins, *The Social Message of Revelation* (New York: Woman's Press, 1920); Elisabeth Schüssler Fiorenza, *Revelation: Vision of a Just World* (Minneapolis: Fortress, 1991; Paul Minear, *I Saw a New Earth: An Introduction to the Visions of the Apocalypse* (Cleveland: Corpus, 1968).

reigning over the church in heaven at the right hand of the Father. The end of the current age will witness the return of Jesus Christ to judge the wicked, after which the church will enter the eternal state.

Fulfillment of Bible Prophecy

The fulfillment of Bible prophecy is one of the most persuasive arguments in defense of the supernatural nature of the Old and New Testaments. Liberal theologians, who do not accept the supernatural nature of the Bible, endeavor to propose naturalistic explanations for the fulfillment of prophecy.[110] These theologians will claim that Biblical prophecies are general enough so that a number of different interpretations are possible. While it is true that some prophecies are general in nature, many are so specific that only one interpretation is possible (cf. Isa. 9:6; Mic. 5:2).

Another explanation by liberal theologians for the fulfillment of Bible prophecy is the assumption of artificial fulfillment. According to this view, an *au fait* ("to the fact") person with a particular Biblical prophecy in mind could also devise a plan to fulfill the prophecy. The fulfillment of prophecy was void of any supernatural nature, as it was understood to be the result of an *au fait* individual working the text of their own innate cunning, which meant Biblical eschatology was devoid of Divine intervention in the outcome of world affairs.

Examples of such careless understanding of Biblical eschatology are found throughout the history of the church, yet the supernatural nature of the prophecy is misrepresented. Furthermore, as already stated, there are some prophecies that are so specific that it is impossible to accept the view that someone conspired to make themselves the fulfillment. Some prophecies involve entire cities and nations, making it impossible to

---

110   Aage Bentzen, *Introduction to the Old Testament*, 2 vols. (Copenhagen: G. E. C. Gad, 1952); Martin North, *The History of Israel* (London: Adam and Charles Black, 1958); Robert H. Pfeiffer, *Introduction to the Old Testament* (New York: Harper and Row, 1948); Gerhard Von Rad, *Old Testament Theology*, 2 vols. (New York: Harper and Row, 1962).

accept the presumption of artificial fulfillment (e.g., Isa. 13:19-22; Ezek. 26:3-5; Obad. 2; Mic. 1:6).

Hugh Schonfield used such naturalistic explanations regarding the fulfillment of Messianic prophecy by Jesus.[111] Of course, if one discounts the deity of Jesus Christ (so common to liberal theologians) then passages stating Jesus consciously fulfilled messianic prophecies can be rationalized (e.g., Matt. 20:17-19; Mark 14:2; Luke 18:31-34; John 19:28). Therefore, in this instance, the rejection of literal interpretation reveals the total depravity of the unregenerate. The words of the Lord to the prophet Jeremiah are appropriate in this context: "You have seen well, for I am watching over My word to perform it" (1:12). As God incarnate, Jesus Christ is well qualified to fulfill prophecies in accordance with this statement of the Lord.

If liberal theologians cannot explain their concept of artificial fulfillment in the life of Christ and prophecies involving entire cities and nations, they will further reinterpret the supernatural nature of Scripture by redating the prophetical books. According to this view, prophecy does not predict historical events; rather, it merely records it. Since some prophetic Scriptures are so detailed, liberals must reject any notion that history can be prewritten by God, so the only alternative for them is to redate Biblical prophecy in an obstinate fashion.

Responding to Idealism

The book of Revelation is an example of predictive literature. Another example of this type of literature in Scripture is the book of Daniel. Similar to Daniel, the book of Revelation was addressed to God's people who were undergoing persecution (yet this was not the only purpose for writing).[112] Daniel was written during the Babylonian Captivity (1:1, 21),

---

111 Hugh J. Schonfield, *The Passover Plot* (New York: Random House, 1966).

112 The book of Revelation reveals Jesus Christ as the one who will come to judge the world and establish a righteous kingdom on earth. Revelation was also written not only to complete the prophetic truths revealed primarily in the Old Testament (particularly in regard to Israel's destiny)

and Revelation was written when the early church was enduring intense persecution by imperial Rome.

The church was warned of imprisonment (Rev. 2:10). Antipas, a leader among the church in ancient Pergamum, was martyred (2:12-13). The Roman and Jewish persecution left many church communities impoverished (2:9; 3:9); rather than hopelessness filling their hearts, the church was exhorted to hope in God who can deliver His people. The prophetic Word encourages the reader to withstand persecution, principally by predicting the rapidly approaching end of the world, when God will rescue His own by destroying the powers of evil. Certainly, this prediction is presented in symbolic language. To the original readers of the book, the meaning of these symbols was understandable. To modern readers the symbols seem obscure, and diligent study is required to understand the original meaning of the book.

Furthermore, any understanding of the Olivet Discourse, which complements the book of Revelation, cannot ignore the canonical writings that supplement its study (e.g., Dan.; Ezek.; Zech.; 1 Thess. 4:13—5:10; 2 Thess. 1—2; 1 John 2:18-23; 4:1-6). Certainly, there are non-canonical writings (e.g., the apocryphal 2 Esdras and pseudepigraphal 1 Enoch) that employed extensive symbolism as a means of communicating the hope and encouragement that God will reign victoriously over the kingdoms of the world. However, there is no reason for concluding that Biblical eschatology is apocalyptic literature in the sense that it is of the same "genre" of non-canonical, extra-biblical writings. There is no other book in the New Testament that is comparable to Revelation; however, it does have an accompaniment in the Old Testament, the book of Daniel.

Idealists are correct that one of the reasons for Revelation is to provide hope and encouragement to those Christians throughout church history

---

but also in the New Testament (involving both the church and Israel). Revelation provides harmony to God's plan and purposes for the ages. Since anti-Semitism is increasing in the church and the world, it is understandable why this purpose would not be recognized, and Revelation would be regarded as unimportant and/or ignored.

who have endured persecution in the name of Christ. Idealism is wrong in making a defining characteristic of Revelation, namely the assurance of God's victory in the world over evil, as the *only* purpose. The kingdom of God will rule over all kingdoms of the world; it will be characterized by peace and righteousness. The books of Genesis and Revelation are fitting bookends to the drama of redemption. Genesis 2—3 records the fall of mankind and all that was lost because of sin. Conversely, Revelation 20—22 records the restoration of mankind.

IDEALISM EXPLAINED

Interpretative Method

The dominant interpretative method of idealism is the redemptive-historical. The redemptive-historical[113] hermeneutic is based upon the following principles (some propositions being true and others false): (1) Scripture is progressive revelation; (2) Scripture can only be understood Christologically from Genesis through Revelation; (3) the people of God in both the Old and New Testaments were redeemed through faith in Christ; and, (4) the people of God in the Old Testament were under the same organic, covenant body as the people of God in the New Testament. Greidanus (Dutch Reformed covenant theologian)[114] believes that the redemptive-historical hermeneutic allows one to communicate Christ from all of Scripture. He wrote, a "Christian preacher cannot preach an Old

---

113 *The term redemptive-historical* is derived from the German word for "sacred history" (*heilsge-schichte*). Redemptive historians understand the past as God's self-revelation to humanity in the person of Jesus Christ. The life, death and resurrection of Christ are the means of God's redemptive purposes. Redemptive history attempts to unify the historical events by which God advances His saving kingdom.

114 Popular redemptive historians are: Geerhardus Vos (1862-1949); Klaas Schilder (1890-1952); Herman N. Ridderbos (1900-2007); Oscar Cullmann (1902-99); and, Charles G. Dennison (1945-99).

Testament text in isolation, but must always understand the text in the context of the whole Bible and redemptive history. . . ."[115]

The focus of the redemptive-historical hermeneutic is the progressive self-revelation of God to His covenant people through the medium of history. As "the Alpha and the Omega, the first and the last," God is "the beginning and the end" of all things in the Earth below and heaven above (Rev. 22:13). All history moves in the direction of the consummation of God's good purposes. The incarnation of Jesus Christ is the culmination of the two ages: "this present evil age" and "the one to come" (cf. Matt. 12:32; Gal. 1:4; Eph. 1:21). Since the powers of "the one to come" have already entered into history in the person and work of Jesus Christ, the two-age view of reality means "the *age* to come" (the kingdom of God) arrived sooner than expected (Mark 1:15; Luke 17:20-21). Those who are united by faith to Christ have been transferred from "this present evil age" into the power of "the one to come." In other words, they are now in the kingdom of God.

Although the church is already in the kingdom of God, there is still tension since the kingdom of God has not yet arrived in its completeness. "The age to come" is related to "this present evil age," which creates a transitory eschatological tension between the time of the first and second comings of Christ (cf. 2 Cor. 4:16). Redemptive-historical hermeneutics begin with this two-age knowledge of the Christian life. This hermeneutic attempts to bring the church into a greater awareness of her position in Christ by emphasizing the fact that the believer is already raised with Christ, but has not yet entered the complete eschatological fullness of the kingdom that will be realized at the second coming of Christ. The believer groans in "this present evil age" while longing for the return of the Lord.

The first coming of Christ in humiliation was to accomplish God's eternal redemption and the second coming will be in glory to consummate

---

115 Sidney Greidanus, *Preaching Christ from the Old Testament: A Contemporary Hermeneutical Method* (Grand Rapids: Eerdmans, 1999), p. 230.

the kingdom of God, and this completeness of time is the direction in which history is moving. Christ foreshadows and hints at the consolation of Israel throughout the Old Testament. Redemptive history means Christ has descended and now reigns as the fulfillment of the Old Testament types and shadows. Similar to the nation of Israel in the Old Testament, the church is the chosen nation—the sole investiture of God's grace—in the kingdom age and will be a blessing to all the nations of the world. The church is the heir and source of all the covenantal blessings. Presently, the church is situated at the end of the ages and has already realized eschatological fulfillment, in contrast to mere promise and typology. According to the new covenant, the church is the historical expression of the kingdom of God. The redemptive-historical approach is to understand Scripture as God's progressive revelation in the sense that all Scripture points to the person and work of Jesus Christ. All Scripture is interpreted in light of His historical life, death, resurrection and ascension.

Progressive revelation means the New Testament authors amplified the revelations of former ages. The New Testament amplifies the Old Testament themes and expounds upon them in light of Christ. The comprehensive knowledge of God's redemptive purposes for history is the result of a more comprehensive and personal knowledge of God. The more comprehensive knowledge of God is revealed in the events of redemptive history. According to the redemptive-historical hermeneutic, the Old Testament must be interpreted both Christologically and eschatologically in light of the person and work of Christ. History is the medium that God uses to reveal His redemptive purposes in a progressive manner. The redemptive-historical approach maintains that history is the means by which God progressively reveals His sovereign purpose of redemption. Eternal redemption in Jesus Christ and His eschatological kingdom is the central theme of Scripture.

Conversely, dispensationalism would disagree with the Christological interpretation of the Old Testament. The amount and content of Christocentric and salvific revelation that the redemptive-historical hermeneutic demands are far more than Scripture reveals. Even if there were agreement that a certain amount of Christocentric knowledge was available to certain individuals in the Old Testament (by means of covenants, visions, dreams or revelation), the number of individuals with such knowledge would be so minuscule so as to make salvation in the Old Testament virtually unfathomable. However, even though there was not a great amount of conscious Christocentric knowledge, there was salvation in the Old Testament by grace through faith (the content of that belief, not the nature of it, is what has changed between the testaments; certainly, there was a consciousness of sins and the need of God's grace, but there would be no need of Old Testament sacrifices if saints of that dispensation believed in Jesus Christ as the once-for-all sacrifice that the book of Hebrews declares).[116]

Israel and the Church

Idealism views the church as the eschatological fulfillment of the same Old Testament promises God made with Israel. The death and resurrection of Christ is the culminating event for believers of all ages; it unites them without distinction for the common purpose and entrance into the kingdom of God. The covenantal promises with Israel in the Old Testament found their fulfillment in the church at the death and resurrection of Christ. The church is now raised to its final mediation from glory. Idealism places extensive emphasis upon church covenant fulfillment.[117] In contrast to dispensationalism, idealism merely emphasizes the spiritual and salvation aspect of God's covenantal promises. Both systems would emphasize a doxological purpose to history, but the dispensationalist approach is much broader than the idealist. Dispensationalism emphasizes both spiritual and physical blessings within the doxological purpose of history.

---

116 Charles C. Ryrie, *Dispensationalism* (Chicago: Moody Press, 1995), pp. 118-21.
117 Hamstra, "Idealist View of Revelation," in *Four Views of Revelation*, p. 96.

The Kingdom of God

Idealism teaches the kingdom of God is a present, spiritual reality. The church is a partaker in the kingdom of God even though it is only presently seen by faith. The consummation of the kingdom of God occurs when all God's covenants are fulfilled in the "last days," or eschaton, with God's earthly creation. At this time, the kingdom of God will be apparent. The idealist position assumes, without Biblical exegesis, that God's covenants with Israel were conditional and because of the nation's disobedience, the promises have been reassigned to the church. The entirety of God's redemptive revelation is both promise and fulfillment, which nullifies a literal interpretation of the Biblical covenants in the Old Testament. Ryrie countered this belief quite well.

> Premillennialists point out that if the yet unfulfilled part of that covenant is to be fulfilled literally (the promise of the land of Palestine), this will have to occur in a future Millennium, since there has been no place in past or present history for a literal fulfillment. Amillennialists [idealists included] say that we need not expect a future fulfillment because (a) the promises were conditional and the conditions were never met; or (b) the land promise was fulfilled in the time of Joshua (Josh. 21:43-45); or (c) it was fulfilled under King Solomon (1 Kings 4:21); or (d) it is now being fulfilled by the church; or (e) it is fulfilled in the heavenly Jerusalem. I only observe that each of those five suggestions negates the validity of the other four. One receives the impression that the amillennialist does not really know how or when the Abrahamic Covenant should be fulfilled. He is only certain that it will not be in a future, earthly Millennium.[118]

Generally, idealists will teach the millennium was inaugurated at the resurrection of Christ. At His crucifixion and resurrection, Christ

---

118 Charles C. Ryrie, *Basic Theology: A Popular Systematic Guide to Understanding Biblical Truth* (Chicago: Moody Press, 1999), p. 447.

emerged victorious over Satan and ascended into heaven to begin His present reign over all creation in an "already and not yet" eschatological sense. The members of the church are now subjects of the kingdom since He was crowned King of Kings at his ascension.

Major prophecies, such as the Olivet Discourse and the book of Revelation, are interpreted as part of the redemptive-historical plan of God that began in the first-century Roman persecution of the church. Idealism must affirm a two-age[119] coming of the kingdom of God. Christ's first coming was the dawning of the first age, which John the Baptist proclaimed, "Repent, for the kingdom of heaven is at hand" (Matt. 3:2). At His death and resurrection, Christ emerged victorious over death and Satan. At His ascension, Christ began His eternal reign upon the throne of David (Luke 1:32-33; Acts 2:30-31). According to idealism, there is a present form of the kingdom that cannot be seen, but is understood by faith to be "already but not yet."

Idealism is wholly dependent on a two-age "Biblical" theology which focuses primary attention upon an "already not yet" eschatology. For example, emphasis is placed on the fact that God already "raised us up with Him, and seated us with Him in the heavenly *places* in Christ Jesus" (Eph. 2:6). However, the church still anticipates a bodily resurrection, for "we will not all sleep, but we will all be changed" (1 Cor. 15:51), and emphasizes the certainty of the glorification of the saints (Rom. 8:30). Glorification is the last stage of the believer's salvation and so the Christian still anticipates the complete fulfillment.[120]

---

119   Eric D. Pyle and James E. Doerfel, "Two-Age Eschatology" [online] (8 February 2001, Biblical Theology and Redemptive Historical Hermeneutics, <http://two-age.biblicaltheology.org/beliefs_index/eschatology.htm >; Internet; accessed 25 May 2017.

120   Gregory K. Beale, *The Book of Revelation: A Commentary on the Greek Text* (Grand Rapids: Eerdmans, 1999); William Hendrikson, *More Than Conquerors: An Interpretation of the Book of Revelation* (Grand Rapids: Baker, 1939); Anthony Hoekema, *The Bible and the Future* (Grand Rapids: Eerdmans, 1994); Herman Ridderbos, *The Coming of the Kingdom* (Philadelphia: Presbyterian and Reformed Publishing, 1962); Robert B. Strimple, "Amillennialism," in *Three Views of the Millennium and Beyond*, ed. Darrell L. Bock (Grand Rapids: Zondervan,1999); Geerhardus Vos, *Biblical Theology* (Grand Rapids: Eerdmans, 1953); Geerhardus Vos, *The Pauline Eschatology*

Idealism and the Olivet Discourse

Idealism interprets prophetic passages in context of the advent of Christ and His death, resurrection and ascension. For example, the Olivet Discourse in Mark 13 is understood as amplifying Jesus' teaching on discipleship.[121] The inclusive words of 13:5 ("And Jesus began to say to them") and 13:37 ("What I say to you I say to all") extend beyond the first disciples in the time of Jesus to contemporary readers. Brower explained this "text-centered, narrative-critical approach" as follows: "A controlled reading of the gospel, which takes the intention of the implied author seriously as a first-century document addressed to his implied readers, also in the first century allows modern readers to hear the same message and apply it to their own lives."[122]

Regarding the reader's understanding of Mark's Olivet Discourse, Brown wrote, "Detectable comprehensibility to a 1st-cent. audience is an important (even if not sufficient) guide to interpretation."[123] Other points made by the idealist are that the Olivet Discourse is related by means of the subsequent passion narrative in the course of an array of enduring themes. Mark 13 is the logical conclusion of the life of Jesus Christ, and closely related both to the central narrative and to the passion narrative and resurrection of Christ.[124] The last and most obvious conclusion to be drawn is the destruction of the temple.

Jesus did not proclaim the prophecy of the destruction of the temple easily. He is revealed as calling for a movement among the people to return

---

(Grand Rapids: Eerdmans, 1953).

121 Kent E. Brower, "'Let the Reader Understand': Temple and Eschatology in Mark," in *Eschatology in Bible and Theology*, eds. Kent E. Brower and Mark W. Elliott (Downers Grove, IL: InterVarsity, 1997), pp. 140-42.

122 Ibid., p. 120.

123 Raymond E. Brown, *The Death of the Messiah*, 2 vols. (New York: Doubleday, 1994), 2:1113.

124 R. H. Lightfoot, *The Gospel Message of St. Mark* (Oxford: Oxford University Press, 1950), pp. 48-59; T. J. Geddert, *Watchwords: Mark 13 in Markan Eschatology* (Sheffield: Sheffield Academic Press, 1989).

to God (1:38; 2:17; 8:34). Idealists, of course, reject any distinction between Israel and the church. Therefore, the return to God also entails becoming a part of "the true Israel"[125] (3:35; 6:7-13; 10:23-31). Preaching "the kingdom of God is at hand; repent and believe in the gospel" (1:15) is taken to mean a new and steadfast phase in God's plan of redemption will come to fulfillment (4:10-34). Brown wrote, "Before Jesus entered the Temple, he had looked for fruit from the fig tree but found none (11:12-14); after the reaction of the authorities the fig tree is found withered (11:20-21). Only when faced with obdurate irreformability does Jesus say (13:1-2) that not one stone will be left on another from the wonderfully built Temple."[126] Resistance to Jesus led to the passion narrative, which will eventually result in the destruction of the temple.

Brower argued for central placement of the destruction of the temple within the gospel of Mark. When this placement is observed, he believed Mark's "Little Apocalypse" becomes less complicated. The physical temple "is replaced by the crucified and risen Christ and His covenant community."[127] In the gospel of Mark, the destruction of the temple represents the expected political consequence of the rejection of Christ by the religious leaders and the subsequent Divine chastisement due to the rejection. Brower relied upon the Third Quest methodologies for his reducing Mark's Olivet to "apocalyptic imagery" void of literal interpretation.[128] The apocalyptic imagery "is the normal Jewish language used to draw out the significance of major socio-political events."[129]

As opposed to clarifying the Biblical text through literal interpretation, idealism adopts a liberal hermeneutic that obfuscates the Biblical text.

---

125   For example, see Greg K. Beale, "The Eschatological Conception of New Testament Theology," in *Eschatology in Bible and Theology*, p. 16.

126   Brown, *Death of the Messiah*, 1:456.

127   Brower, "Temple and Eschatology in Mark," p. 141.

128   For an analysis of these methodologies, see Ron J. Bigalke Jr., "The Historical Jesus Quests," *Journal of Dispensational Theology* 11 (March 2007): 19-31.

129   Brower, "Temple and Eschatology in Mark," p. 141.

The harm to the church is that liberal scholarship does not care for the apocalypticism of Jesus Christ; consequently, from one step to the next (i.e., obfuscate the meaning of eschatology, then soteriology), liberals attempt to erase the indictments that Jesus placed upon the whole of humanity.[130] From the example of the Olivet Discourse, it was demonstrated that idealism ignores the prophetic context in order to reinterpret the Biblical text to mean that God's ultimate goal for humanity will be realized (i.e., God is victorious; as if God could not say that clearly in one verse, which He has in other Biblical passages). Brower wrote, "Attention must be focused on the meaning of the events under discussion (in this case, the destruction of the temple), rather than the apocalyptic phenomena used to indicate significance."[131] Following this line of reasoning, he already concluded, "A whole plethora of modern 'Late, Great Planet Earth' notions are called into question."[132] Brower offered a negative response to finding signs in the Olivet Discourse concerning "the *timing* of the End." The Olivet Discourse "is confirmation that God's good purposes are now centered in Jesus and the new people of God . . . the End will be found in the climax of God's good purposes in Christ."[133]

CONCLUSION

The idealist interpretative process is becoming typical of those evangelicals who do not interpret Bible prophecy literally. Furthermore, such interpretative methodology eventually distorts other Biblical doctrines

---

130 For instance, He taught that humanity as a result of the fall is essentially evil (Matt. 12:34) and is capable of great wickedness (Mark 7:20-23). Jesus taught that humanity is totally depraved and spiritually destitute without Him (Luke 19:10). Humanity is in great need to repent before a holy and just God (Mark 1:15) and to be born from above (John 3:3, 5, 7). Jesus did not describe sin as ignorance, but as blindness (Matt. 23:16-26), sickness (9:12), enslavement (John 8:34) and darkness (8:12; 12:35-46).

131 Brower, "Temple and Eschatology in Mark," p. 141.

132 Ibid., p. 122.

133 Ibid., p. 142.

(i.e., a gradual erosion of Biblical truth when the text is distorted). The reasoning behind such interpretations is the belief that Biblical eschatology should be assigned to an apocalyptic literary genre that requires a non-literal interpretation. Idealists do not allow God to speak for Himself in prophetic passages, but use their own reasoning in redefining the nature of the prophetic Word in much of the same methodology of liberal scholarship. With such eclectic views, it seems the only agreement that idealists will achieve is that Biblical eschatology is never to be interpreted grammatically and historically (which is to say a literal interpretation), and with that approach it is only a matter of time before such thinking is applied to all Scripture.

CHAPTER 5

PROPHETIC TIMING AND THE MILLENNIUM: FUTURISM

Throughout the previous chapters, it has been demonstrated that understanding of the timing of prophetic fulfillment influences an understanding of the meaning of the millennium. All the views of prophetic timing have been proven as consistent with postmillennialism, but not with amillennialism and premillennialism. For instance, there can be preterist, historical, idealist and futurist postmillennialism; however, amillennialism can only be preterist, historicist or idealist (not futurist). Historicism is the only theological system that could be amillennial, postmillennial or premillennial. The theological system of futurism can accommodate both postmillennialism and premillennialism (not amillennialism). Knowledge of the various theological systems of prophetic timing fulfillment provides understanding of the logic and tenets of the various views regarding the meaning of the millennium. If the basic characteristics of preterism, historicism, idealism and futurism are understood, then it is not difficult to understand a particular interpretation regarding the millennium. Furthermore, the views of prophetic timing are more foundational as to what one believes Scripture to teach concerning the millennium.

THE THEOLOGICAL SYSTEM OF FUTURISM

In regards to the millennium, futurists believe the kingdom is not yet a reality. As the reign is heavenly, amillennialists understand the millennium as currently in existence between the first and second comings of Christ, and thus amillennialism cannot accommodate futurism. Consequently, this chapter will focus upon postmillennial and premillennial futurism.

Postmillennialism

Postmillennial futurists believe that prophetic fulfillment regarding the millennium is not yet. The postmillennial hope is anticipation of a glorious age of the church as a fulfillment of Old Testament prophecies. The kingdom age will be brought to realization through the preaching of the gospel message. All nations will become Christian and will live in peace. The prophecies will be fulfilled in history and time. Once Christianity is victorious by the institution of the glorious age, then there will be the second coming of Christ. The postmillennialist anticipates a time of fulfillment of Old Testament prophecies, but those prophecies will be fulfilled in the church, rather than fulfilled in Israel during the millennium. Whereas the millennial kingdom is fulfilled in time and history, the consummate kingdom will be the eternal state. Presently, the kingdom of God is conquering the nations through the preaching of the gospel. At the end of this period of peace and righteousness, Christ will return.

According to postmillennialism, the millennium is the period of the gospel dispensation and it began either with the ascension of Christ or the outpouring of the Spirit on Pentecost. Therefore, it is not a literal 1,000-year reign. The kingdom age will end with the second coming of Christ when that domain is given to the Father. The millennium will include the entire period of gospel preaching, which results in all nations becoming Christian, and peace among every nation. The millennium prophesied to Israel in the Old Testament is reinterpreted in application to the church (i.e., the relationship of Jews to the millennium will be in the church). The millennium ("a thousand years") mentioned in Revelation 20 is the period of the gospel dispensation, when the saints are reigning upon the earth, even though there is still martyrdom and suffering.

The basic tenets of postmillennialism are: (1) the preaching of the gospel will "Christianize the world"; (2) the "Christianization" of the world will result in a period of peace and righteousness; and, (3) the golden age will be followed by the return of Christ.

The millennium may refer to the entire gospel age or it may refer to the golden age only; (4) the millennium may include every person in the world being "Christianized" or it may contain some unbelievers; (5) the law of God will apply to all humanity as the manner in which one may be sanctified and in which the world is conquered; and, (6) the lordship of Christ for the believer and human government is true for both time and eternity.

Postmillennial interpretation requires the "thousand years" to be interpreted symbolically. The "thousand years" indicates an indefinitely long period of time. The Old Testament prophecies are interpreted figuratively, although to a lesser extent than non-futurist systems. The prophecies to Israel are understood to await fulfillment in the church. According to postmillennialism, Israel in the past was the chosen people. Although the Jews were chosen to receive the Scriptures, the Jews were "cast off" for disobedience. Therefore, the church is the people of God, which means the church and Israel in the Old Testament are the same, and the covenant of grace is foundational to emphasize only one people of God.

Regarding the Mosaic Law, Charles Hodge believed it was "a national covenant with the Hebrew people" and "a renewed proclamation of the original covenant of works."[134] Postmillennialists will generally refer to the Mosaic Law as "a national covenant," and teach that the covenant of works did not have any relation to the Law. The eschatology of postmillennialism must necessarily affirm covenant theology,[135] since understanding of the so-called "covenant of grace" determines interpretation.

The covenant of grace is the one promise that is seen to rule over all other covenants since the historical failure of the covenant of works (Gen. 3). According to covenant theology, God relates to humanity through two covenants: the covenant of works (*foedus operum*) and the covenant of grace (*foedus gratiae*). Sometimes the covenant of grace is understood under two aspects: (1) the Godward aspect, and (2) the manward aspect. The Godward aspect is called the covenant of redemption (*pactum salutis*), which is between God and Christ from all eternity and will result in the eternal redemption of all believers. The manward aspect is between God and the believer and will result in eternal redemption to the believer who has faith in Jesus Christ.

The excommunication from the garden of Eden and subsequent removal of the tree of life in Genesis 3:22-24 is thought to be evidence of the provisional nature of the covenant of works. The covenant of grace was made, from all eternity, to save humanity from the penalty of disobedience. The earliest reference to covenant theology is found in the Westminster Confession (1647); as a developed system, it originated with Johannes Cocceius (1603-69). Covenant theology teaches there is progressive revelation of the outworking of the covenant of grace throughout the Old Testament. The *protoevangelium* ("first gospel") of Genesis 3:15 announced the existence of the covenant of grace.

---

134   Charles Hodge, *Systematic Theology*, 3 vols. (reprint, Grand Rapids: Eerdmans, 1993), 2:375.

135   The earliest reference to covenant theology is found in the Westminster Confession (1647); as a developed system, it originated with Johannes Cocceius (1603-69).

The administration of the gospel is traced throughout Old Testament redemptive history according to belief in the progressive announcements of the covenant of grace. For instance, certain provisions of the covenant of grace were revealed to Noah. The first mention of the Noahic covenant (Gen. 6:17-19) was an administration of the covenant of grace. The second mention of the Noahic covenant (9:8-17) amplified the fact that there would be an all-inclusive non-salvation oriented covenant promising the constraint of judgment until the last day. The covenant of grace was afterward established with Abraham and his descendants. The Abrahamic covenant renewed the postlapsarian (the time subsequent to the fall of humanity) covenantal promise originally made in the covenant of works between God and Adam (3:15-17). At this moment, the covenant became national. In redemptive history, the covenant of grace is renewed in Abraham, as the father of all who believe (Rom. 4:11; cf. John 8:56).

God's promise of land to Abraham (Gen. 15:18; Exod. 6:4; Judg. 2:1) was typical of the blessings to be made manifest according to the new covenant (Gen. 2:4; Gal. 3:14; Heb. 8) and the final state (Heb. 11:10). As historically prior to the Mosaic covenant, the Abrahamic covenant was renewed under Christ but the Mosaic covenant was not. In terms of justification and soteriology, the Mosaic covenant was an administration of the covenant of grace. All believers who were justified under the Mosaic covenant were saved by grace though faith in Christ alone. In terms of the land promise though, the Mosaic covenant, with necessary changes, was a republication of the Adamic covenant of works. Israel received the land promise and maintained possession by grace. However, the nation fell into apostasy and was dispersed from the land for failing in obedience to a temporary, typical covenant of works (Gen. 12:7; Exod. 6:4; Deut. 29:19-29; 2 Kings 17:6-7; Ezek. 17).

According to 2 Corinthians 3:6, New Testament believers are "servants of a new covenant, not of the letter but of the Spirit; for the letter kills, but the Spirit gives life." The Mosaic covenant was predisposed to the ministry of the letter (the law) but the new covenant was inclined to the ministry of the Holy Spirit. Accordingly, the new covenant, as the certainty symbolized by the pre-incarnational types and shadows (2 Cor. 1:20; John 6:32; Heb. 7—9), is the fulfillment of the *protoevangelium* to Adam (Gen. 3:15) and the (Abrahamic) covenant of grace.

The exterior conditions of the covenant of grace are a faulty imposition that is placed upon Scripture and, as such, it distorts proper interpretation of both the Old and New Testament. Conversely, the grammatical-historical hermeneutic of consistent premillennialism is far more superior to interpret the testaments. The difference is that consistent premillennialists affirm the King will return to fulfill His covenantal promises to Israel, *and* to the church who are joint-heirs with the coming King.

The Jews in the present time, according to postmillennialism, have been rejected as the people of God, which means the church is now the people of God. The distinctions between the "church" in the Old Testament and the New Testament are fourfold: (1) church and state are no longer unified; (2) church is now independent of the state; (3) church will be universal; and, (4) the church is now different in terms of organizational structure. Therefore, the kingdom of God is a spiritual kingdom, and it is the church ("the truly regenerated") who bring that kingdom to the present age. Although not the kingdom specifically, a utopian and Christianized condition is visible in the actions of the church. Regarding the law of Moses, there are parts of it that are still in effect. There is, however, not a clear explanation as to what aspects are required and those components that are inoperative. Within postmillennialism, there is great confusion regarding which commandments apply to Israel and the church.

In regards to the current state of Israel, postmillennialists believe the restoration of the Jews to the land is not prophetic. Since the restoration of the Jews is a human work, the Jewish people do not have any right to their own land. Romans 9—11 is reinterpreted to mean that Israel has been rejected and has no future national destiny, and Israelites can be saved by faith and brought into the church. The prophecies of Israel's restoration are denied by postmillennialism based on the assumption that the promises to the church are symbolic.

Postmillennialism teaches that the church is the true Israel, and denies any distinction between Israel and the church. Believing Jews are simply amalgamated into the church. There will be a national conversion of Israel prior to the second coming of Christ, but this will occur subsequent to the millennium. The conversion of Jews occurs following a mass conversion of Gentiles to Christ. The national conversion of Israel is not a national restoration since regenerated Jews will be amalgamated into the church, and the conversion of Jews is part of the Christianization of the world.

The futurism of postmillennialism demands: (1) the second coming will occur subsequent to the millennium; (2) a symbolic interpretation of Scripture; (3) belief that the millennium will be a long period of peace and righteousness, although not a literal 1,000 years; (4) the preaching of the gospel, which includes a combination of believers and unbelievers, extends the kingdom of God; and, (5) the very end of the millennium will result in apostasy against the kingdom of God.

Postmillennialism fails to interpret adequately the covenants of God to Israel as a nation. Furthermore, it does not allow for two peoples of God (i.e., Israel and the church). Postmillennialism affirms that only the church is the elect people of God, and states that the law of God should be enforced today. The only commandments that are regarded as inoperative are the ceremonial laws. Postmillennialism does not explain the extent of Israel's rejection, nor clearly explain the role of Jewish believers as part of the church. Postmillennialism ignores Jewish history in its allegorization of Biblical prophecy.

Premillennialism

Premillennial futurists believe that prophetic fulfillment regarding the rapture, tribulation, second coming and millennium is in an eschatological period. Consistent futurism teaches that the tribulation, second coming and millennium are all future events pertaining to national Israel. The main difference between premillennialism and non-premillennial methods of interpretation is the testament priority (consistent premillennial systems affirm more discontinuity between the testaments and systematize prophetic doctrines from the priority of the Old Testament, as opposed to the New Testament changing the original meaning; non-premillennial systems formulate eschatology from the priority of the New Testament which allows change and reinterpretation of the Old Testament). A primary emphasis of consistent premillennialism is the relationship between the Old and New Testaments.[136]

The Relationship Between the Testaments

Jesus employed a consistently literal method as He interpreted the Old Testament. For instance, He accepted the narratives of Abel (Matt. 23:35), Noah (24:37-38), Abraham (3:9; 8:11; 22:32), Isaac and Jacob (8:11; 22:32), Moses (8:4; 19:8), David (12:3; 22:43, 45) and Jonah (12:40) as records of historical fact. Jesus never used an allegorical method of interpretation whenever He made application of the historical record. Never did Jesus divide Scripture into multiple meanings thereby distinguishing a surface level meaning based upon a literal reading of the Biblical text, and a deeper level meaning based on a numinous reading of the same text. Jesus rebuked the religious leaders because they developed sophistical methods for interpreting Scripture and replaced a literal understanding with

---

136   John S. Feinberg, "Systems of Discontinuity," in *Continuity and Discontinuity: Perspectives on the Relationship Between the Old and New Testaments*, gen. ed. John S. Feinberg (Wheaton: Crossway, 1988), p. 74.

their contrived traditions. On the contrary, no accusation of interpreting Scripture unnaturally (or non-literally) was ever attributed to Jesus by the religious leaders.[137]

Similar to Jesus, the apostles interpreted the Old Testament literally. Of course, non-premillennialists generally believe the New Testament writers changed the meaning of the Old Testament. In fairness, it is granted that certain New Testament citations appear to change the original meaning of the Old Testament or appear to interpret the Old Testament in a non-literal fashion, but the more one examines the grammatical-historical context in the New Testament, the more writers can be seen to interpret the Old Testament consistently according to a normal (plain) interpretation.

The principle for Biblical interpretation means there is one single meaning. After determining the single meaning, many legitimate applications can be gleaned from the text. Normal grammatical-historical interpretation avoids selectivity in the Biblical text, such as *sensus plenior* ("deeper meaning"), which actually changes meaning of the original. Consistently literal interpretation is essential to understand Biblical prophecy. Literal interpretation involves grammatical, historical and contextual interpretation. Among most evangelicals, a literal hermeneutic is employed; however, in the discipline of prophecy is when some begin to deviate and even disregard simple rules of interpretation. The goal of this section, then, is to demonstrate how Biblical prophecy is interpreted literally in the New Testament without ever changing the Old Testament meaning.

Literal Prophecy and Literal Interpretation

The first example of how the New Testament quotes the Old Testament is that of a literal Old Testament prophecy demanding a

---

137   Henry A. Virkler, *Hermeneutics: Principles and Processes of Biblical Interpretation* (Grand Rapids: Baker, 1981), p. 54.

literal New Testament interpretation. Micah 5:2, as it is quoted in Matthew 2:5-6, is a good illustration of this example.[138] Micah 4—5 provides two visions: (1) an ideal state wherein peace prevails; and, (2) an ideal ruler who will bring that restfulness to his people. The ideal state is described in chapter 4 and the ideal ruler, who is also a king, is described in chapter 5. According to Micah 5:2, the birthplace of the king will be Bethlehem. The prophecy was fulfilled literally in the birth of Jesus Christ, which was 700 years after its prediction (Matt. 2:5-6). The remaining prophecies, of course, will be fulfilled at the Lord's second coming. The example here of literal prophecy and literal interpretation is the most common principle to be followed in understanding Old Testament prophecies of the first and second coming of Christ to Earth (that do not involve "mystery" teachings).

Literal Prophecy and Application

The next example is to consider why and how Matthew quoted Jeremiah 31:15 in Matthew 2:18. The Jeremiah passage was a literal prophecy, but Matthew's reason for referring to the passage was for the purpose of application. The purpose of quoting Jeremiah 31:15 by Matthew was due to the author's intent to use fulfilled prophecy as evidence for the reader to believe the historicity of other events recorded. The quotation harkens to the time of weeping in response to the Babylonian captivity and the slaughtering of innocent children when Babylon conquered Judea. "Rachel" is representative of the mothers in Bethlehem who mourned the Herodian massacre of their innocent children. The parallel between the fulfilled prophecy of Jeremiah and the event in Bethlehem is remarkable. Both events are times of sorrow that were judgment upon Israel for her apostasy. Raymond Brown commented, "Further strengthening the parallel is the alternate tradition, probably current also in Matthew's day, that Rachel's tomb was on the outskirts of Bethlehem, five miles south of Jerusalem (cf. Gen. 35:19; 48:7; to this

---

138   Isaiah 7:14; 52:13-53:12; and, Zechariah 9:9 are other good examples (among many).

day, what is called Rachel's tomb is located there). Rachel might well weep for the infants of Bethlehem. . . ."[139]

In the prophecy of Jeremiah, there is a literal fulfillment in the contemporary event of the prophet's day and an application to those in Bethlehem. The one point of similarity is that Jewish mothers were weeping for children they would never see again. The fulfillment is the typology. Matthew's intent was to illustrate the fulfillment of prophecy as evidence for the reader to believe the historicity of the other events recorded. In this prophecy, there was a literal fulfillment in Jeremiah's day. In addition to the fulfillment, there was an application to those in Bethlehem.

Similarly, the quotation of Joel 2:28-32 in Acts 2:16-21 is an example of the use of a literal prophecy that demanded an application by those on Pentecost. Matthew's quotation is an example of history, whereas Peter's quotation is an example of prophecy. Both quotations have one point of similarity with the literal prophecy. For instance, in the Matthew passage, the Jewish mothers were weeping (as in Jeremiah's day). The passage in Joel refers to an outpouring of the Holy Spirit in the last days, yet within the Acts 2 passage (vv. 17-21), there is one point of similarity with the literal prophecy (viz. the outpouring of the Spirit in an unusual manifestation). Therefore, the New Testament does not change the Old Testament, as some would propose. The New Testament author quoted the Old Testament prophecy in the Matthew and Acts passages to illustrate the nature of a literal prophecy requiring a contemporary application.

Matthew's reason for quoting Jeremiah 31:15 in Matthew 2:18 and Peter's reason for quoting Joel 2:28-32 in Acts 2:16-21 are the same. Both of the literal Old Testament prophecies are quoted in the New Testament to demand a point of application. One more example concerning Matthew's reason for quoting Isaiah 53:4 in Matthew 8:17 will serve to demonstrate this principle. The Old Testament prophecy anticipated a fulfillment in the work of Christ on the cross when He would bear the "sickness" of the sins

---

139   Raymond E. Brown, *The Birth of the Messiah* (Garden City, NY: Doubleday, 1977), p. 222.

of the world, thereby making provision for the eradication of sin's results (death, sickness and demon possession). The healing that Christ provided in the atonement was from the "sickness" of sin (cf. 1 Pet. 2:24). A point of application is demanded from readers, in the quotation of Isaiah 53:4 (a literal prophecy fulfilled in the death of Christ). The application is to receive Jesus as Messiah and Savior because His healing ministry anticipated His work on the cross and undoubtedly He will inaugurate the conditions of the prophesied kingdom. Both Matthew and Peter quoted Old Testament prophecies to illustrate the nature of a literal prophecy that demands an application.

Literal Prophecy and Typical Fulfillment

The next example will demonstrate how the New Testament quotes the Old Testament for the purpose of a typical fulfillment.[140] By its simplest definition a type is predictive of something future (e.g., Leviticus and Hebrews). God predestined a type as representing the relationship that certain events, institutions or persons have that correspond to a specific person, institution or event in the future. According to Virkler, "Typology is based on the assumption that there is a pattern in God's work throughout salvation history. God prefigured His redemptive work in the Old Testament, and fulfilled it in the New; in the Old Testament there are shadows of things which shall be more fully revealed in the New."[141]

One must exercise caution in seeking to find an exact correspondence between something in the Old Testament and something similar in the New Testament. The danger of not exercising caution regarding types is not only allegorism, but also the credibility of the interpreter is in jeopardy. Not every characteristic of a type may be the Divine intent (one of the requirements of a legitimate type). Scripture must be the sole criteria for determining a Biblical type. Ramm listed three reasons for typological

---

140   Many of the quotations of Exodus and Leviticus in Hebrews fit this category.
141   Virkler, *Hermeneutics*, p. 184.

interpretation:[142] (1) "The general relationship which the Old Testament sustains to the New is the very basis for such a study;" (2) "Our Lord's own use of the Old Testament is His invitation to us to find Him in the Old Testament;" and, (3) "Even more specific is the vocabulary of the New Testament with reference to the nature of the Old." Scripture must be the sole criteria for determining a Biblical type.

Matthew's quotation of Hosea 11:1 in Matthew 2:15 is an example of a literal event that is typical of a future New Testament event. The passage in Hosea refers to the historical exodus of Israel from Egypt. Israel (the national son) is a type of the Lord Jesus Christ (*the* unique Son). Not only did He descend to Egypt but also (as Israel) Christ is called from that land. The King of Israel departed Egypt, even as Moses led Israel from Egypt. The intent of Hosea 11:1 is not changed in the New Testament. The prophecy is fulfilled in the life of Christ as He returned to Israel from Egypt.

Scripture does employ riddles and enigmatic sayings (similar to normal speech), but whenever they are used the historical-grammatical context will alert the interpreter to this fact. However, some interpreters assume enigmatic sayings in contrast to meticulous detail to the contrary. The interpreter is to abandon self of presuppositions and biases in order to understand the intended meaning of the Divine Author. Those who introduce a deeper sense and secondary meaning into the text, produce an element of confusion into Biblical interpretation.

Summation of Literal Old Testament Prophecies

The best example of literal Old Testament prophecies summarized in the New Testament is Matthew 2:23. The passage records prophecy fulfilled by Jesus Christ: "*This was* to fulfill what was spoken through the prophets: 'He shall be called a Nazarene.'"[143] Nowhere in the Old Testament can

---

142 Bernard Ramm, *Protestant Biblical Interpretation: A Textbook on Hermeneutics*, 3rd rev. ed. (Grand Rapids: Baker, 1970), pp. 215-17.

143 Jesus was called a Nazarene geographically not because of the Nazarite vow.

such a statement be found, yet Matthew did not assert that his summary statement was a prophecy given by one prophet. Mathew used the plural "prophets" to indicate the fulfillment is a summary of all that the Old Testament prophets spoke concerning the rejection of the Messiah. In the time of the New Testament, the Nazarenes were despised and rejected as a people. The term Nazarene was used shamefully (John 1:46). Since Isaiah 53 (especially) prophesied that Messiah would be despised and rejected, then the term Nazarene would best summarize the Old Testament concept.

Every citation of the Old Testament in the New Testament corresponds to one of the four categories just illustrated. Arnold Fruchtenbaum commented, "The procedure is not simply 'to interpret the Old by the New' as Covenant Theology insists. The procedure is first to see what the original quotation means in its own context. Once that is determined, then it can also be determined in just which of the four categories the quotation belongs. There is no need to conclude that the New Testament changes or reinterprets the Old Testament."[144]

CONCLUSION

Premillennialism and postmillennialism are the only millennial systems that are futurist. Although postmillennialists affirm the future aspect of the millennium, it does not have any special relationship to Israel. Individuals Jews and other peoples will be blessed as the church through faith in Jesus Christ. A major reason postmillennialism (and amillennialism could be included) deny that the Old Testament promises made with national Israel will be fulfilled with a future national Israel is the issue of testament priority (i.e., the New Testament changes Old Testament meaning).

---

144 Arnold G. Fruchtenbaum, *Israelology: The Missing Link in Systematic Theology* (Tustin, CA: Ariel Ministries Press, 1989), p. 845.

However, the establishing of the millennial (Davidic) kingdom was the longing of the prophet Isaiah (11:1-5; 55:1-3). The same yearning belongs to believers today: the second coming of Jesus Christ to fulfill the earthly, political promises of the Davidic covenant, and as the root and offspring of David to be seated on David's throne in Jerusalem to rule in peace and righteousness. The vision in Daniel 2 and 7 prophesies that human history will culminate in an everlasting dominion of King Jesus. The longing of an earthly kingdom characterized by faithfulness, peace and righteousness is an eternal promise based upon God's faithfulness.

CHAPTER 6

PROPHETIC TIMING
AND THE MILLENNIUM:
DISPENSATIONALISM

T
he present chapter will conclude the emphasis upon views of prophetic timing (preterism, historicism, idealism and futurism) with an emphasis upon dispensational premillennialism. All premillennialists are futurists (obviously) who believe that prophetic fulfillment regarding the rapture, tribulation, second coming and millennium will occur in an eschatological (future) period. Dispensational premillennialists, in particular, believe that prophecies concerning the tribulation, second coming and millennium are all future events pertaining to national Israel (the "rapture passages" have distinct reference to the church). The primary difference between premillennial and non-premillennial systems is hermeneutical (interpretive), that is, an understanding of the continuity and discontinuity between the Old and New Testaments. The procedure is

not to interpret the Old Testament by the New Testament; rather it is to interpret the meaning of an Old Testament passage in its context and to systematize prophetic doctrines from the priority of the Old Testament, as opposed to the New Testament changing the original meaning. The relationship between the Old and New Testaments is a primary emphasis of dispensational premillennialism.[145]

THE THEOLOGICAL SYSTEM OF DISPENSATIONAL PREMILLENNIALISM

In regards to the millennium, dispensational premillennialists believe the rapture of the church will precede the period of the tribulation. At the end of the tribulation, Jesus Christ will return in glory and power to establish His earthly kingdom from Jerusalem. The duration of the kingdom will be a literal 1,000 years.

Hermeneutics (Science of Biblical Interpretation)

In regards to the issue of eschatological events, dispensational premillennialists (if they are consistent in their hermeneutic) believe it is *possible* to witness signs of the times prior to God resuming His unconditional and eternal program with Israel in the tribulation and the millennium. Consistent futurism recognizes that current world events set the stage for eschatological events in relation to Israel. However, the only prophetic event for the church in the future is the rapture, which is imminent, and without any signs (this is why all attempts to predict the rapture inevitably resort to faulty application of prophecies to Israel by referencing those aspects in relation to the church).

---

145 John S. Feinberg, "Systems of Discontinuity," in *Continuity and Discontinuity: Perspectives on the Relationship Between the Old and New Testaments*, gen. ed. John S. Feinberg (Wheaton: Crossway, 1988), p. 74.

Even though the tribulational events will not occur during the present church age, this is not to imply that world events are not significant. If there are present signs of events that are setting the stage for the fulfillment of prophesies that relate to the tribulation, then it is appropriate to believe that the rapture of the church is drawing near since that blessed event will occur prior to the beginning of the tribulation. As already stated (in the opening chapter), tribulational events are not fulfilled in the present church age. Consistent (dispensational) premillennialists should not adopt an historicist interpretation of world events by quoting, as fulfillment, passages that undoubtedly refer to eschatological events in relation to the nation of Israel. Expositors must relate Biblical passages to their appropriate period in time (either the church or Israel). Commingling eschatological events for the church and Israel creates misunderstanding.

Biblical Covenants

Some Biblical prophecies obviously awaited fulfillment because a particular human response was required. For instance, the prophecies of the Assyrian Captivity (722 B.C.) and the Babylonian Captivity (586 B.C.) were conditioned on the response of Israel to the message of repentance the prophets preached to them. God, of course, already prophesied the response of Israel but this did not mean the nation was not responsible for her rejection of God's message. Although, it is true that some prophecies are conditioned on human response, other prophecies are clearly unconditional.

Dispensational premillennialists believe that four of the covenantal promises of the Old Testament between God and Israel are unconditional. During the tribulation, God will prepare Israel for the response He desires for fulfillment of those unconditional covenants. One should note that the Abrahamic covenant, from which all the covenants with Israel branch, is entirely conditioned upon God's faithfulness. He alone obligated Himself to the covenant by passing between the severed animals (Gen. 15:12-20).

There are no conditions required upon Israel for God to fulfill the covenant, which means there are no "if" clauses suggesting that fulfillment is dependent upon human effort (as in salvation by grace through faith in Jesus Christ). Conversely, non-premillenialists generally believe that Israel's rejection of the Messiah resulted in the cancellation of Old Testament promises, without regard for her response in the present or future.

Understanding Biblical Covenants

Two types of covenants are revealed in Scripture: conditional and unconditional. A *conditional covenant* is characterized by God making a promise to man—conditioned by "if you will"—whereby He then promises to accomplish the covenantal promises. An *unconditional covenant* is a sovereign act of God whereby He fulfills the covenantal promises made with an individual, without regard for the recipient's obedience or disobedience (i.e., promises are given without any conditions whatsoever, and remain unalterable in spite of human unworthiness). An unconditional covenant is characterized by "I will," which declares that God alone will accomplish the promises.

God made five covenants with the nation of Israel: the Abrahamic, the Mosaic, the Land, the Davidic and the New covenant. Of the five covenants made with Israel, only one of those is conditional: the Mosaic covenant. Three things are to be noted regarding the covenants with Israel: (1) The covenants are literal, which means that the contents of those covenants must be interpreted literally; (2) The covenants God made with Israel are eternal, that is, they are not restricted by time; and, (3) The covenants (except for the Mosaic covenant) are all unconditional. The covenants with Israel are not annulled because of her disobedience; it is because the covenants are dependent upon God for fulfillment that their literal fulfillment can be expected in the future.

All the Biblical covenants contain two types of promises: physical and spiritual. The physical promises are, and will continue to be, fulfilled by and limited to Israel. The Biblical covenants are literal, eternal and depend entirely upon God's sovereignty; they were made with a covenant people, Israel. Nevertheless, some of the spiritual blessings of the covenants will extend to the Gentiles. Since the death of Christ is the basis of salvation for all people (Tit. 2:11) —for all time—the church has become a partaker of the Jewish spiritual blessings. The church will not fulfill the Jewish covenants. For instance, only Israel will fulfill the new covenant (as promised in the Old Testament). The new covenant was given to Israel and will be fulfilled by Israel. The church participates in the promises (for in like manner as Israel in the future, Christians are forgiven, indwelt, regenerated and taught by the Holy Spirit) but she will not fulfill the covenants given to Israel (specifically the promises relating to Israel's restoration to the land, in addition to the blessings associated with that land).

One's ability to understand the Bible (and God's interaction with humanity in general) depends upon how one regards the conditioned response necessary for fulfillment of the Biblical covenants. Covenants are contracts given to define a relationship between individuals. The Biblical covenants between humanity and God are entirely unique to Christianity. Nowhere in the religions of the world does one find gods relating to humanity covenantally. In Scripture, the personal relationship between God and humanity is based upon and mediated through means of covenants. The purpose of the covenants is to reveal the following: (1) God's earthly agreements (covenants being contracts between individuals for the purpose of governing that relationship); (2) spiritual promises (God wants to bind Himself to His people so He is able to maintain His promises, and thereby demonstrate in history the kind of person He is); (3) earthly redemption (plan of redemptive unity); and, (4) the only hope for mankind (relationships in the Bible, especially between God and humanity), are legal (law) or judicial (court). Consequently, God's earthly agreements are mediated through covenants, which involve intent, promises and sanctions. God wants to bind Himself to His people, that is, to maintain His promises so that He can demonstrate His character.

Examples of Covenants

The royal grant treaty is an example of an unconditional covenant; it is a promissory covenant that arose solely from a king's desire to reward a faithful servant. Examples of this type of covenant are the Abrahamic and Davidic covenants. The suzerain-vassal treaty is a conditional covenant; this type of covenant bound a subordinate vassal to a superior vassal, and was binding only upon the one who swore it. The purpose of the covenant was to emphasize the goodness and kindness of the lord to his vassal in order that the vassal would gladly accept responsibilities and obligations. Examples of this type of covenant are the Noahic[146] and Mosaic covenants.

A parity treaty was a covenant binding two equal individuals in a relationship; it provided conditions that were stipulated by the participants. Examples of this type include: (1) Abraham and Abimelech (Gen. 21:25-32); (2) Jacob and Laban (31:44-50); (3) David and Jonathan (1 Sam. 18:1-4; 2 Sam. 9:1-13); and, (4) Christ and the church (John 15). The Abrahamic covenant is the greatest of redemptive covenants. All Divine blessings for both Jew and Gentile originate from this covenant (Gen. 12:1-3, 7;

---

146 The Noahic covenant was made not only with Noah, but also with "the sons of Noah who came out of the ark" (9:8, 18). The covenant would also include all people for God said, "I establish my covenant . . . and all flesh shall never again be cut off by the water of the flood, neither shall there again be a flood to destroy the earth" (9:11). The Noahic Covenant is eschatological and redemptive. The covenant is God's eschatological promise that He will never again destroy the earth with a flood. The covenant is God's redemptive promise that He will be merciful to "all flesh" by not destroying humanity by means of a worldwide flood. God's covenant with Noah will continue because it is an "everlasting covenant between God and every living creature of all flesh." The Noahic covenant is a grand example of a suzerain-vassal treaty. The Noahic covenant is not conditional, but it is "everlasting" since God is the one who gave the promise (9:16). The rainbow is God's token of the covenant (9:17). The rainbow will continue to give humanity assurance that God will never again destroy the Earth with a worldwide flood. The value of the Noahic covenant is that it is perpetual and continues to assure humanity even today.

13:14-17; 15:1-21; 17:1-21; 22:15-18). Regarding the unconditional covenants, Fruchtenbaum wrote:

> An unconditional covenant can be defined as a sovereign act of
> God whereby God unconditionally obligates Himself to bring
> to pass definite promises, blessings, and conditions for the cov-
> enanted people. It is a unilateral covenant. This type of covenant
> is characterized by the formula *I will* which declares God's de-
> termination to do exactly as He promised. The blessings are se-
> cured by the grace of God.[147]

The participants of the Abrahamic covenant are God and Abraham.
There are 14 provisions of the Abrahamic covenant. *First*, from Abraham
would come a great nation, Israel (12:2; 13:16; 15:5; 17:1-2, 7; 22:17).
Second, Abraham was promised a land, Canaan (12:1, 7; 13:14-15, 17;
15:17-21; 17:8). *Third*, Abraham would be greatly blessed (12:2; 15:6;
22:15-17). *Fourth*, Abraham's name would be great (12:2). *Fifth*, Abraham
will be a blessing to others (12:2). *Sixth*, those who bless the nation of Israel
will themselves be blessed (12:3). *Seventh*, those who curse the nation of
Israel will themselves be cursed (12:3). *Eighth*, all humanity will be blessed
through Abraham, including Gentiles (12:3; 22:18). *Ninth*, Abraham
will receive a son of promise by his wife Sarah (15:1-4; 17:16-21). *Tenth*,
Abraham's descendants would undergo the Egyptian bondage (15:13-14).
Eleventh, there will be other nations that would originate from Abraham
(17:3-4, 6). *Twelfth*, Abraham's name would be changed (17:5). *Thirteenth*,
the name of Abraham's wife would be changed. *Fourteenth*, circumcision
would be the token of the covenant (17:9-14).[148]

The Abrahamic covenant involves a promise of a land to Abraham and
Israel, a nation (seed), and a worldwide blessing. The implication is that the

---

147 Arnold G. Fruchtenbaum, *Israelology: The Missing Link in Systematic Theology* (Tustin: Ariel
Ministries, 1989), p. 570.

148 Ibid., pp. 574-75.

Abrahamic covenant will be fulfilled in the form of three sub-covenants: (1) the land covenant; (2) the Davidic covenant; and, (3) the new covenant. The Abrahamic covenant is literal (13:15, 17), eternal (13:15; 17:7, 8, 13, 19) and unconditional (15:1-18). The confirmation of the covenant would be through Isaac (26:2-5, 24). Although Isaac had two sons, the promise of the covenant would be through Jacob. Concerning the sons of Jacob, the covenant was confirmed through his 12 sons, who would father the 12 tribes of Israel.[149]

Concerning the promise of land, God promised that Israel would return to their land subsequent to being scattered throughout the world. The content of the covenant is found in Deuteronomy 29:1—30:10. The land covenant is distinct from the Mosaic covenant (Deut. 29:1). The covenant was made between God and the nation of Israel. There are eight provisions of the land covenant. *First*, the disobedience of Israel to the Mosaic Law and subsequent worldwide scattering was prophesied (29:2—30:2). *Second*, subsequent to her disobedience, Israel will eventually repent (30:2). *Third*, the Messiah will return (30:3). *Fourth*, subsequent to being dispersed, Israel will be regathered to her land (30:3-4). *Fifth*, Israel will possess the land promised to her (30:5). *Sixth*, Israel will be regenerated (30:6). *Seventh*, Israel's enemies will be judged. *Eighth*, Israel will receive the blessings of the Messianic (Davidic) kingdom (30:8-10).[150]

The land covenant was given to reaffirm the title deed of Israel to her promised land, as was originally given in the Abrahamic covenant. Since the land covenant is unconditional, the covenant cannot be canceled (despite Israel's disobedience). Disobedience does affect Israel's enjoyment of the land. The land covenant enlarges upon the original Abrahamic covenant, and this covenant was still in effect centuries later despite Israel's continued disobedience (Ezek. 16:1-63). The land covenant will be fulfilled in the coming Messianic kingdom.

---

149 Mal Couch, *God's Plan of the Ages* (Ft. Worth, TX: Tyndale Theological Seminary, n.d.), p. 36.
150 Fruchtenbaum, *Israelology*, p. 582.

The Davidic covenant is specified in two passages: 2 Samuel 7:11-17 and 1 Chronicles 17:10-15. The Davidic covenant was made between God and David. David endures as the representative head of his house and dynasty. The Davidic covenant amplifies the seed aspect of the Abrahamic covenant; it narrows the promise of a seed to one rightful claimant: David. There are seven main provisions given in this covenant. *First*, David was promised a house (dynasty) that would be eternal (2 Sam. 7:11; 1 Chron. 17:10). *Second*, David's son would be established on his throne following him (2 Sam. 7:12). *Third*, Solomon would build the Temple (7:13). *Fourth*, the throne of the Davidic and Solomonic kingdoms would be established forever (7:13, 16). *Fifth*, though Solomon would be judged for disobedience, God would not remove his lovingkindness from him (7:14-15). *Sixth*, the Messiah will come from the seed of David (1 Chron. 17:11). *Seventh*, the Messiah's throne, house and kingdom will be established forever (17:12-14).[151]

The Davidic covenant is a literal, unconditional and eternal covenant. The covenant still awaits fulfillment and is confirmed in numerous Biblical passages (Ps. 89; Isa. 9:6-7; 11:1; Jer. 23:5-6; 30:8-9; 33:14-17, 19-26; Ezek. 37:24-25; Hos. 3:4-5; Amos 9:11; Luke 1:30-35, 68-70; Acts 15:14-18). The eternal promises of the Davidic covenant will be mediated through the Messiah. The kingdom promised to David would be a people possessing a land that God promised. The throne is used to indicate authority, and it is only as David's seed that one will have the right to rule. The seed of David who will reign is the Messiah.[152] The importance of the Davidic covenant is to amplify the seed aspect of the Abrahamic covenant. According to the Abrahamic covenant, the seed would be from Abrahamic descent, which meant that the Messiah would be a Jew. The patriarch Jacob received revelation that the seed would be limited to the tribe of Judah, the family of David (Gen. 49:10).

---

151 Ibid., pp. 584-85.
152 Couch, *God's Plan*, p. 42.

The new covenant is recorded in Jeremiah 31:31-37 (cf. Isa. 55:3; 59:21; 61:8-9; Jer. 32:40; Ezek. 16:60; 34:25-31; 37:26-28; Rom. 11:25-27; Heb. 8:7-13; 10:16-17). There are eight main provisions of this covenant. *First*, it is an unconditional covenant between God and Israel (Jer. 31:31). *Second*, it is distinct from the Mosaic Covenant (31:32). *Third*, it promises the regeneration of Israel (Jer. 32:33; Isa. 59:21). *Fourth*, the regeneration of Israel would be universal among the Jews (Jer. 31:34; Isa. 61:9; Rom. 11:25-27). *Fifth*, it would provide a provision for permanent forgiveness of sin (Jer. 31:34). *Sixth*, the provision is the indwelling of the Holy Spirit (Jer. 31:33; Ezek. 36:27). *Seventh*, Israel is promised many material blessings (Jer. 32:41; Isa. 61:8; Ezek. 34:25-27). *Eighth*, it will provide for a new temple (Ezek. 37:26-28).[153]

The new covenant amplifies the blessing aspect of the Abrahamic covenant, particularly in relation to salvation. The covenant is not an elaboration of the Mosaic covenant since it ultimately replaced the law (Jer. 31:31-32; Rom. 6:14-15). The primary aspect of this covenant is the blessing of salvation that will include the national regeneration of Israel (Jer. 31:34; Ezek. 36:29; Rom. 6:22; 11:25-27). The national salvation of Israel will extend to every individual Jewish person, and this salvation will be true in succeeding generations from the time that the initial regeneration of Israel begins. Therefore, during the millennium the only unregenerate people will be Gentiles. In other words, during the entire millennium there will be no unsaved Jews, which is the reason why "'they will not teach again, each man his neighbor and each man his brother, saying, 'Know the LORD'" (Jer. 31:34).

The Church and the New Covenant

The relationship of the church to the new covenant has caused some confusion because the prophet Jeremiah specified that the covenant was made with Israel and not the church. Nevertheless, there are numerous

153 Fruchtenbaum, *Israelology*, pp. 586-87.

passages that relate the new covenant with the church (Matt. 26:28; Mark 14:24; Luke 22:14-20; 1 Cor. 11:25; 2 Cor. 3:6; Heb. 7:22; 8:6-13; 9:15; 10:16, 29; 12:24; 13:20). Scripture is unambiguous with regard to the following: Israel, and not the church, will fulfill the new covenant. However, the church does partake of the spiritual blessings of the Abrahamic and new covenants (Rom. 15:27).

Some have tried to teach that there are two new covenants: one made with Israel and one made with the church. Such teaching is quite difficult to defend from the Scriptures. Others have tried to teach that there is only one covenant, but that there are two aspects of the covenant. The solution to the problem can be found in Ephesians 2:11-16 and 3:5-6. The two passages teach that God made four unconditional covenants with Israel, and it is through these four covenants that all God's spiritual blessings will be mediated. However, the Mosaic covenant was the "diving wall" between Jew and Gentile. The law prohibited the Gentiles from experiencing the blessing of the four unconditional covenants. For a Gentile to experience the blessings of the four unconditional covenants, he or she had to submit himself or herself entirely to the Mosaic law, and since this was not possible as a consequence of the weakness of human flesh, the Gentiles were "excluded from the commonwealth of Israel."

When the Lord Jesus Christ died, the "dividing wall" was demolished. Christ ratified the new covenant. The church celebrates the new covenant and the ratifying of it through the death of Christ (1 Cor. 11:23-26). Although the church is partaking of the spiritual blessings of the covenant (Eph. 1:3), it is the nation of Israel who will receive the material and national promises. The relationship of the church to the new covenant is explained in Galatians 3:13-14. Through Christ, the church partakes of the covenant between God and Israel (Rom. 11:28-29; 11:17).

Summary Regarding the Covenants

All the Biblical covenants contain two types of promises: physical and spiritual. The physical promises are, and will continue to be, fulfilled by and limited to Israel. Nevertheless, some of the spiritual blessings of the covenants will extend to the Gentiles. Since the death of Christ is the basis of salvation for all people—for all time—the church has become a partaker of the Jewish spiritual blessings. The church is not the eschatological fulfillment of the Jewish covenants. Only Israel will fulfill the new covenant as promised in the Old Testament. The new covenant was given to and will be fulfilled by Israel. The church participates in the promises but she will not fulfill the covenants given to Israel. One's ability to understand the Bible (and God's relationship with humanity in general) depends upon how well that person understands the Biblical covenants.

The Old Testament refers to the millennial kingdom when referring to the Davidic kingdom, but it did not designate its length (Ps. 2:6-9; Isa. 2:2-4; 11:6-9; 65:18-23; Jer. 31:12-14; 31-37; Ezek. 34:25-29; 37:1-6; 40—48; Dan. 2:35; 7:13, 14; Joel 2:21-27; Amos 9:13, 14; Mic. 4:1-7; Zeph. 3:9-20; Zech. 14:9). The New Testament teaches that the length of the kingdom will be 1,000 years in length when the Lord Jesus Christ establishes His kingdom and reigns on Earth from David's throne in Jerusalem (Rev. 20:1-9). If the Biblical covenants are understood literally (on the basis of grammatical interpretation), then there must be a future, regenerate national Israel in the land under the rule of her Messiah-King. The covenants await fulfillment in the millennial kingdom.

ISRAEL AND THE CHURCH

Although the English word "church" is opulent in meaning, and used quite commonly and extensively, the Biblical meaning is often misunderstood.

The term has been used in reference to a building (whether a cathedral or storefront), corporation with tax-exempt status, denomination, national or state church, people who meet together corporately in obedience to Biblical commands, religion generally (i.e., "separation of church and state"), and the universal body of Christ. The word "church" is actually only vaguely related to the concept of the Greek word *ekklēsia* used in the New Testament.

> The English term *church*, along with the Scottish word *kirk* and German *Kirche*, is derived from the Greek *kuriakon*, which is the neuter adjective of *kurios*, "Lord," and means, "belonging to the Lord." *Kuriakon* occurs only twice in the New Testament, neither time with reference to the church as commonly used today. In 1 Corinthians 11:20 it refers to the Lord's Supper and in Revelation 1:10 to the Lord's Day.
>
> Its application to the church stems from its use by early Christians for the place where they met together, denoting it as a place belonging to God, or God's house.[154]

Usage Prior to the New Testament

The doctrine of the church is not based upon the English word, but rather upon the Greek word *ekklēsia* that is used 114 times in the New Testament (three in Matthew's Gospel, 23 in Acts, 62 in Paul's letters, six in non-Pauline letters and 20 in Revelation).

> There are words whose etymology it is interesting to watch, as they are transformed and consecrated by the Christian church—words that the church did not invent but has employed in a loftier sense than the world has ever used them. The very word by which the church is named is a key example of this type of transformation. For we have *ekklesia* in three distinct stages of meaning—the secular, the Jewish, and the Christian.[155]

---

154 Robert L. Saucy, *The Church in God's Program* (Chicago: Moody, 1972), p. 11.

155 Richard Chenevix Trench, *Synonyms of the New Testament* (Grand Rapids: Baker, 1989; reprint,

The Greek word in the New Testament for the English word *church* is *ekklesia*. It is derived from the verb *ekkaleo*, a compound of *ek*, "out," and *kaleo*, "to call or summon," which together mean "to call out." While often this etymological meaning is used to support the biblical doctrine of the church as a people called out, separated from the world by God, the usage of this term both in secular Greek and the Greek New Testament, which provides the background for the New Testament language, does not lend support to this doctrine from the word *ekklesia* itself.[156]

Usage in Classical Greek

Although *ekklēsia* was used to specify the formal Greek assembly (legislature), it was also used in reference to any assembly, regardless of who was included or how it was instituted. The classical Greek usage is used in only one passage of the New Testament (Acts 19:32, 39, 41). *Ekklēsia*, as demonstrated by the common understanding in the Acts passage, was a broad term which did not have a religious connotation; it merely referred to an assembly but is never once used absolutely of the people who composed the assemblage.

Usage in the Greek Old Testament

An investigation of the Septuagint [Greek Old Testament] use of the word *ekklesia* includes a consideration of the Hebrew words *qahal* and *edhah* (the two principal Hebrew words for "gathering" or "assembly") along with the related use of the Greek *sunagoge* to translate these words.

Both *edhah* and *qahal* refer to an assembly or gathering, yet *ekklesia* is never used to translate *edhah*.[157]

The two Hebrew words that refer to an "assembly" or "gathering" are *qahal* and *edah*. At times these words appear synonymous. However, the

Peabody, MA: Hendrickson, 2000), p. 17.

156 Saucy, *Church in God's Program*, pp. 11-12.

157 Radmacher, *Nature of the Church* (1972; reprint, Hayesville, NC: Schoettle, 1996), pp. 123, 127.

translators of the Septuagint differentiated *qahal* and *edah*. For instance, the Septuagint never uses *ekklēsia* to translate *edah*, rather, it will translate *qahal* as *ekklēsia*.[158] The translators used *sunagoge* to translate *qahal*.[159] Although *qahal* and *edah* did not have a technical meaning in the Hebrew Old Testament, the differentiation in the Septuagint led to a technical meaning in the New Testament as the synagogue and the church.

Discussion of the use of *ekklēsia* in the Septuagint carries significance not only to the study of any Biblical passage, but also to understanding a distinction between Israel and the church. For instance, *ekklēsia* in the Septuagint was never used to connote a spiritual verity that would be free of spatial and earthly confines. The simple meaning of *ekklēsia* is an assembly. There is absolutely no factual basis for attempts to find the church (as defined in the New Testament) referenced in the Old Testament on the basis of the usage of *ekklēsia*. The New Testament advanced and gave technical meaning to the usage of *ekklēsia*.[160]

Matthew's use of *ekklēsia* was a reference to the natural Jewish mindset of an "assembly;" it is even possible (although not likely) that Matthew referred to a Jewish "assembly" as the synagogue in 18:17. The following quote demonstrates the national Jewish understanding of the word.

> The word [*ekklēsia*] occur about 100 times in the LXX. . . . When there is a Heb. Equivalent, it is almost always *qahal* . . . In the LXX [*ekklēsia*] is a wholly secular term; it means "assembly," whether in the sense of assembling or of those assembled...The real point is who assembles, or who constitutes the assembly.[161]

---

158   The translation of *qahal* as *ekklēsia* is not exclusive since *qahal* is translated in the Septuagint with approximately seven other Greek words; it is even translated 25 times as *sunagoge*. Therefore, *qahal* was used quite broadly as an "assembly" or "gathering" in the Old Testament.

159   From Exodus to Proverbs, the Septuagint translates *edah* approximately 130 times as *sunagoge*.

160   Acts 7:38 and Hebrews 2:12 are the only New Testament passages which use *ekklesia* as a reference to Israel similar to that found in the Septuagint.

161   Karl Ludwig Schmidt, "ἐκκλησία," in *Theological Dictionary of the New Testament*, 10 vols., ed. Gerhard Kittel, trans. Geoffrey W. Bromiley (Grand Rapids: Eerdmans, 1964-76), 3:527.

Usage in the New Testament

Refinement and transformation from a generic (non-technical) term into a technical term—both unique and rich in meaning—awaited usage in the New Testament. There are only two verses, Acts 7:38 and Hebrews 2:12, which use *ekklēsia* as a reference to Israel such as used in the Septuagint.[162] Consequently, it is possible, though not likely, that Matthew 18:17 is also a reference to a Jewish gathering such as the synagogue.[163]

Usage determines meaning and the New Testament certainly uses *ekklēsia* in a manner that distinguishes it from both its Greek and Old Testament significance.[164] There is a significant reason for the New Testament usage of *ekklēsia* as opposed to *sunagoge*.

> This distinction resulted in the choice of *ekklēsia* by Christ (Matt. 16:18; 18:17) and his apostles as the more noble of the two words. It designated the new society of which Jesus was the founder, being as it was a society knit together by the closest spiritual bonds and altogether independent of space.[165]

The determined opposition of the Jewish religious leaders could be a reason why the New Testament never used *sunagoge* as reference to the church.[166]

> Customarily the concept of the church has focused on the universal and local church. Sometimes, erroneously, the categories are stated as invisible and visible. But even universal and local do not seem to cover all the facets of the concept. Universal serves well as a label for the body of Christ, whether on earth or in heaven (Hebrews 12:23). But local needs further defining. How local is the church?

---

162 Saucy, *Church in God's Program*, p. 13.
163 Radmacher, *Nature of the Church*, pp. 139-42.
164 Ibid., p. 132.
165 Trench, *Synonyms*, p. 19.
166 Ibid., pp. 19-20; Radmacher, *Nature of the Church*, p. 140.

Apparently we need more than the customary twofold organization of the church—universal and local. (1) There is the universal church—all believers in heaven or on earth. (2) There is the
visible church—local churches in various areas, especially those
I am acquainted with. (3) There is the local church—the particular assembly with which I have my primary and sustained relation. Every believer actually belongs to all these three aspects of
the church, and 1 Corinthians 10:32 applies to any of them with
which he has contact any time.[167]

Usage Not Found in the New Testament

The New Testament concept of the church is never used of a
building,[168] a particular denomination (Baptist, Lutheran, Presbyterian)
or of a territorial church (e.g., Church of England, Roman Catholic
Church)[169] or of the kingdom of God (or the kingdom of heaven).[170] The
church is never designated as Israel. Although it has been common for
some Christians to reference the church as the "new Israel," a concordance study in the New Testament will demonstrate contrariwise. In
each of the 66 occurrences of the word "Israel" in the New Testament,
the term always refers to the Jewish people.[171] Both the church and Israel
have special relationships with God, but they must be distinguished.
The distinction between Israel and the church is the natural result of
interpreting the Bible historically and grammatically (i.e. literal, plain
interpretation). One must interpret the words of the Bible in their
normal or plain meaning. The opposite would be a spiritualizing (allegorizing) of the Biblical text. Ryrie explained,

---

167   Charles C. Ryrie, *Basic Theology* (Wheaton: Victor, 1986), p. 395.
168   Radmacher, *Nature of the Church*, p. 161.
169   Ibid., 162; Saucy, *Church in God's Program*, p. 18.
170   Radmacher, *Nature of the Church*, p. 168; Ryrie, *Basic Theology*, p. 399.
171   Paul Enns, *The Moody Handbook of Theology* (Chicago: Moody, 1989), p. 352.

Use of the words Israel and church shows clearly that in the New Testament national Israel continues with her own promises and that the church is never equated with a so-called "new Israel" but is carefully and continually distinguished as a separate work of God in this age.[172]

Since Israel and the church are distinct entities, the unfulfilled prophecies to Israel of both blessing and curse have not been transferred to the church. Indeed, as the cursings to Israel were fulfilled literally, so will the future restoration blessings be fulfilled literally.

DEFINITIONS OF NEW TESTAMENT *EKKLESIA*

Classic definitions of the church are particularly deficient in terms of New Testament theology. Definitions of the universal church and the local church are often stated separately, and to the exclusion of either the universal or local church.

> The catholic or universal church, which is invisible, consists of the whole number of the elect. . . . The visible church, which is also catholic or universal under the Gospel, consists of all those throughout the world that profess the true religion, together with their children. . . . (Westminster Confession of Faith, Chapter XXV).

> The church is a company of visible saints, called and separated from the world by the Word and Spirit of God, to the visible profession of the faith of the Gospel; being baptized into that faith (Baptist Confession of Faith, Article XXXIII).

The *World Book Dictionary* expresses contemporary misunderstanding of the word *church* Biblically and theologically (some of the definitions are entirely inconsistent with the New Testament).

---

172   Charles C. Ryrie, *Dispensationalism*, rev. ed. (Chicago: Moody, 1995), p. 129.

1. a building for public Christian worship or religious services. 2. public worship of God in a church. 3a. Usually, Church. a group of persons with the same religious beliefs and under the same authority; denomination. b. that portion of the whole body of believers in Christ, or of one denomination of these, which belongs to a particular country, nation, state, or city. 4. a locally organized unit of a group of Christians for religious services; congregation. 5. Usually, the Church. all Christians; the whole body of believers in Christ collectively. 6. Also, Church. the organization of a church; ecclesiastical authority or power as embodied in the clergy and historically constituting one of the three estates. 7. the profession of a clergyman. 8a. any religious body other than Christian; a non-Christian creed or congregation. b. a building for public worship or religious services of such a body. 9. any building, group, or organization like a church.[173]

There is a minimum of 80 and as many as 100 descriptive terms used with reference to the church in the New Testament. Therefore, the essential elements for defining the church must incorporate the identity and function of the church.

> The nature of the church is far too broad to be exhausted in the meaning of the one word ekklesia. To describe its manifold meaning the New Testament writers employed numerous descriptive expressions. They explained the concept of the church both in literal terms and in rich metaphorical descriptions. This richness of description precludes a narrow concept of the church and warns against magnification of one aspect to the disregard of others.[174]

---

173 World Book Dictionary, version 2.0.1 (The Software MacKiev Company, 2005).

174 Saucy, *Church in God's Program*, p. 19.

Essential Elements of a Definition

Theologically, only one church exists as regards the body of Christ universally (1 Cor. 12:12-27; Eph. 4:4-6). The reason is that Christians are currently fellow citizens and saints of the household of God. The church is not the consequence of human organization; rather, it is built upon the foundation of the apostles and prophets. Furthermore, the church is God's workmanship (Eph. 2:10), created in accordance with His eternal purpose in Christ (1:4) so that God may demonstrate the exceeding riches of His grace (2:7).[175] The church is invisible only as regards those of the body who are already present with the Lord. The local gathering of believers in the service of Christ is as a part of the universal church. Consequently, it is essential to understand the universal and localized elements for a complete understanding of the New Testament doctrine of the church. Accordingly, the plural, "churches," is used in the New Testament as a description of multiple assemblies in a city or territory. Those who are Christians—by grace through faith in Christ alone—are expected to be members of both the universal and local church.[176]

The church includes all, and only those, who have been regenerated (born again). The new birth by the Holy Spirit results in faith and repentance in the completed redemptive work of Christ, and union with the Lord Jesus and with fellow believers (Acts 2:47; 20:28). The church is unique to this age (dispensation). The origin of the church was still future in Matthew 16:18. Members are placed into the body of Christ through the baptism of the Holy Spirit (1 Cor. 12:13). Subsequent to His resurrection, Christ said the baptizing work of the Holy Spirit was still future (Acts 1:4-5). The church excludes believers of the Old Testament and those who trust in Christ for salvation subsequent to the church having been raptured.

---

175   Geoffrey W. Bromiley, "Church," in *The International Standard Bible Encyclopedia*, rev. ed., 4 vols., gen. ed. idem (Grand Rapids: Eerdmans, 1979-84), 1:693.

176   Ryrie, *Basic Theology*, p. 395.

Unity of believers in a local church (community) is only a part, not all, of the universal church. The local church is a voluntary assembly of Christians and is the sphere where the Holy Spirit manifests His gifting and edifying, which makes Christ known to a lost world. The local church should be a microcosm of the unity and purity that is reality of the universal church. The universal church is instructed to evangelize/disciple, serve, teach and worship, but the expression of this instruction is fulfilled by the local assembly through the empowering of the Holy Spirit. The ordinances of baptism and the Lord's Supper are not the exclusive privilege of the local church, but are universal expressions of the believer's identity with and remembrance of Jesus Christ (Acts 2:41; 8:36-38; 18:8; 1 Cor. 11:23-26).

The church is the regenerate people of this age—both in heaven and on earth—who have been redeemed by grace through faith in the finished work of Christ, and are united with Him and each other by the baptizing work of the Holy Spirit, and who assemble voluntarily in any local community for the express purpose of edification, making disciples, worship and administration of the ordinances. The church has a holy calling distinct from Israel, as this is evident from an understanding of the foundation and origin of the church.

DISTINGUISHING ISRAEL AND THE CHURCH

Both the church and Israel have special relationships with God, but they must be distinguished. Interpretative views that confuse general terms like "elect" and "saints" (which apply to saints of all ages) with specific terms like "church" and those "in Christ" (which refer to believers in the church age only) are misinterpretations of Scripture. Ryrie also noted the importance of this distinction. "The nature of the church is a crucial point of difference between classic, or normative, dispensationalism and other doctrinal systems. Indeed, ecclesiology, or the doctrine of the church, is the touchstone of dispensationalism (and also of pretribulationism)."[177]

Within covenant theology,[178] however, the church and Israel are not distinguished Biblically, but combined as the one people of God. Covenant theology teaches that the New Testament church is a continuation of those of faith within Old Testament Israel. In terms of God's plan of salvation, they are both regarded as under the benefits of the new covenant of grace. Consequently, both the church and Israel comprise the one people of God. Berkhof described the teaching of covenant theology.

> After the exodus the people of Israel were not only organized into a nation, but were also constituted the Church of God. . . . The New Testament Church is essentially one with the Church of the old dispensation. As far as their essential nature is concerned, they both consist of true believers, and of true believers only. . . . The representation given in the preceding proceeds on the assumption that the Church existed in the old dispensation as well as in the new, and was *essentially* the same in both, in spite of acknowledged institutional and administrative differences. . . . The Church is essentially, as was pointed out in the preceding, the community of believers, and this community existed from the beginning of the old dispensation right down to the present time and will continue to exist on earth until the end of the world.[179]

Some covenant theologians perceive new privileges and new blessings in the New Testament church, but still regard the church and Israel as

---

177 Ryrie, *Dispensationalism*, p. 123.

178 Covenant theology is the system of theology that teaches God instituted the covenant of works and the covenant of grace in the history of creation. The covenant of works was made with Adam (as representative of all humanity) prior to the fall. God then established the covenant of grace, through the second Adam, Jesus Christ, in response to Adam's disobedience. The covenant of grace promises eternal life to all those who trust in Christ. Covenant theology also teaches that the true Israel, the church, is one people of God.

179 Louis Berkhof, *Systematic Theology* (Grand Rapids: Eerdmans, 1938), pp. 570-71.

constituting the one people of God. Grudem summarized this view within covenant theology.

> Therefore, even though there are certainly new privileges and new blessings that are given to the people of God in the New Testament, both the usage of the term "church" in Scripture and the fact that throughout Scripture God has always called his people to assemble to worship himself, indicate that it is appropriate to think of the church as constituting all the people of God for all time, both Old Testament believers and New Testament believers.[180]

Covenant theology, which *essentially* is replacement theology,[181] teaches that the promises made to the nation Israel in the Old Testament are now fulfilled spiritually in the New Testament church. Therefore, it is common to read covenant theologians who refer to the church as the "new Israel." Clowney, a covenant theologian, explained his view.

> Those who are united to Christ are heirs in him of all the promises of God. Christ fulfills the calling of Israel; those united to him are by that fact the new Israel of God (Gal. 3:29; 4:21; Rom. 15:8). The ethnicity of the new people is now spiritual rather than physical, making the bonds stronger and the brotherhood more intense (1 Pet. 1:22). Christians are not just born-again individuals, they are a family, 'spiritual ethnics', the new people of God in Christ.[182]

Covenant theology began late in the 16th century as a reaction to the strict predestinarianism of certain reformers in France and Switzerland. Not only is covenant theology unbiblical, but also it is teaching that is foreign to the early church. What is the result of covenant theology? Showers provided an answer.

---

180 Wayne Grudem, *Systematic Theology* (Grand Rapids: Zondervan, 1994), p. 854.

181 Theonomists are also covenant theologians who not only believe the church and Israel are combined, but also argue that the Mosaic law is still in effect. Therefore, one of the responsibilities of the church is to institute Mosaic law in society, which will then introduce the conditions of the millennial kingdom.

182 Edmund P. Clowney, *The Church* (Downers Grove, IL: InterVarsity, 1995), pp. 43-44.

It should be noted that the Covenant Theology view of the nature of the Church leads logically to several conclusions. Israel and the Church are the same; there are no distinctive groups of saints throughout history; all saints of all periods of history are members of the Church; since saints will be on earth during the Tribulation period, the Church will be on earth during the Tribulation, and there will be one general resurrection of dead saints at one time, not more than one resurrection of saints at different times.[183]

Dispensational theology teaches the Biblical distinction between Israel and the church.[184]

Negatively stated, it has been seen that it is improper to speak of the *ekklesia* ["church"] as a building, a denomination, or a state or national church. Also, it is imperative that it be recognized that the *ekklesia* ["church"] is not to be confused with Israel or the kingdom of God. The *ekklesia* ["church"] is a unique dispensational work of God in this age.[185]

Use of the words Israel and church shows clearly that in the New Testament national Israel continues with her own promises and that the church is never equated with a so-called "new Israel" but is carefully and continually distinguished as a separate work of God in this age.[186]

Since Israel and the church are distinct entities, the unfulfilled prophecies to Israel of both blessing and curse have not been transferred to the church.

[T]his doctrine of the church is a watershed in dispensationalism . . . Use of the words Israel and church shows clearly that

183 Renald E. Showers, *There Really is a Difference! A Comparison of Covenant and Dispensational Theology* (Bellmawr, NJ: Friends of Israel Gospel Ministry, 1990), p. 170.

184 Progressive dispensationalism teaches erroneously that the church is less distinct than Israel; rather this *essentially* non-dispensational view affirms Israel and the church as two embodiments of a single people in salvation history.

185 Earl Radmacher, *Nature of the Church*, pp. 185-86.

186 Ryrie, *Dispensationalism*, p. 129.

in the New Testament national Israel continues with her own promises and that the church is never equated with a so-called "new Israel" but is carefully and continually distinguished as a separate work of God in this age.[187]

CONCLUSION

The Old Testament promises made with national Israel will be fulfilled with a future, regenerate national Israel. Since Israel and the church are distinct entities, there is no sense in which the latter can fulfill promises to the former (unless, of course, one *wrongly* assumes priority of the New Testament, resulting in the meaning of the promises in their original context being changed or reinterpreted so that they were not unconditional or eternal; e.g., amillennialism and postmillennialism). God will be faithful to the unconditional covenants that He has made. God has a covenant relationship with Israel that will lead to future fulfillment of the Abrahamic covenant (and the sub-covenants of land, seed and blessing). Due to the current disobedience of the nation, she is experiencing the curses of the Mosaic covenant (and just as the cursings were literal so will be the blessings). When those curses have reached their culmination in the seven-year tribulation—resulting in a regenerate nation—God will fulfill the Biblical covenants with His chosen people. Since the church does not have any relation to the period of the tribulation, she will be removed prior to the start of that period; and when Christ returns to earth, the church will have already received glorified bodies to rule and serve with Him in the millennial kingdom.

---

187 Ibid., pp. 123, 129.

Amillennialists and postmillennialists understand the second coming of Christ as a single event that will be climaxed by a general resurrection and judgment of all people. Dispensational premillennialism is the only millennial view that consistently interprets Biblical prophecies in a literal manner. The other positions invariably spiritualize Old Testament prophecies and apply them to the church, which they understand to be the spiritual Israel. All the prophecies of Christ's first coming were fulfilled literally, thus common sense would dictate that prophecies of Messiah's second coming will be fulfilled in the same manner. To spiritualize the prophecies of the last days by denying a literal tribulation and Earthly millennial kingdom is inconsistent with the interpretative methodology already demonstrated in the prophecies of Christ's first coming. All premillennialists believe in the rapture of the church, yet there is notable disagreement regarding the timing of this event in relation to the tribulation period. The timing of the rapture will be examined in the subsequent chapters, as represented by the three principal viewpoints: midtribulationism (and pre-wrath rapturism as a variation), posttribulationism and pretribulationism.

CHAPTER 7

PROPHETIC TIMING AND THE RAPTURE: MIDTRIBULATIONISM

Midtribulationism is one of the primary views concerning the timing of the rapture in relation to the seven-year tribulation. Midtribulationists are premillennialists who believe the church will experience the first half of the 70th week and that the rapture will occur at the midpoint of the eschatological tribulation. The second half of the 70th week encompasses the wrath of God, so the midtribulational view teaches that God will remove the church from earth prior to the outpouring of His wrath. In contrast to God setting the stage for prophetic fulfillment, midtribulationism can allow for fulfillment of certain prophecies in the current age prior to the timing of the rapture, while also simultaneously affirming the blessed hope of the church, which posttribulationists deny unreservedly by having the church experience the entire tribulation period (i.e., the 70th week). The midtribulational view is relatively new and gained some prominence in 1941 with Norman B. Harrison's *The End: Rethinking the Revelation.*

Although other premillennialists refer to the view as midtribulational, midtribulationists do not use the term in reference to themselves. They prefer to classify themselves as pretribulational (or the midweek view)[188] since they believe the church will be raptured prior to the great tribulation—the wrath of God—which is the last half of the 70th week. Harrison wrote that he taught the "pre-Tribulation coming" of Christ.[189] The term midtribulationism, however, is an accurate classification for the belief of Harrison. For example, the entire seven years of the 70th week can be rightly classified as the tribulation period. Pretribulationists would agree with midtribulationists that only the last half of the 70th week is the great tribulation, but since Harrison would argue that the church is present during the first half of the tribulation period this would mean it is correct to classify the position as midtribulationism despite Harrison's objection.

DEFINING CHARACTERISTICS

Midtribulationism differs both exegetically and theologically from pretribulationism. The essential characteristics for this view are sixfold. *First*, the sounding of "the last trumpet" of 1 Corinthians 15:52 is taught to occur at the midpoint of the tribulation. The last trumpet in 1 Corinthians 15:52 is regarded as equivalent to the seventh trumpet of Revelation, which will begin the great tribulation.[190]

---

188 Gleason Archer, "The Case for the Mid–Seventieth-Week Rapture Position" in *The Rapture: Pre-, Mid-, or Post-Tribulational?* (Grand Rapids: Zondervan, 1984), pp. 115-45.

189 Norman B. Harrison, *The End: Re-thinking the Rapture* (Minneapolis: Harrison Services, 1941), p. 118.

190 The better approach would be to understand Scripture to teach that the sixth seal occurs at the

Second, the seventh trumpet of Revelation is interpreted as the last trumpet (mentioned in 1 Cor. 15:52) for the church. *Third*, the church is only exempted from the wrath of God during the great tribulation (Rev. 11:2; 12:6), which is the last half of the 70th week. The last half of the 70th week is regarded as more severe than the first half. *Fourth*, the resurrection of the two witnesses in Revelation 11:11 is regarded as a representation of the rapture of the church, and since this event occurs at the midpoint, then the rapture is thought to be midtribulational. *Fifth*, God's purposes for Israel and the church are interrelated to each other. The reason for this overlap is due to the belief that the church will experience at least one half of the 70th week, "the time of Jacob's distress," but not the last half (and most severe) of the 70th week. *Sixth*, the Biblical teaching concerning the imminency of the rapture is denied. In terms of the basic chronology of events, premillennial midtribulationism is similar to pretribulationism. The obvious contrast with midtribulationism is that it requires a radically different interpretation of the Scriptures regarding the coming of Christ for His church as opposed to Messiah's coming with His church to earth to establish the Davidic (Messianic) kingdom.

Midtribulationism does have some similarities with pretribulationism in certain fundamentals, such as the eschatological character of the 70th week. However, midtribulationism places the rapture at the midpoint of the tribulation, and not prior to the beginning of it. Of course, the chronological placement of the rapture at the midpoint distinguishes midtribulationism also from posttribulationism; it is best to understand midtribulationism as an intermediary of pretribulationism and posttribulationism.

---

midpoint of the tribulation. See Ron J. Bigalke Jr., "A Comparison of the Synoptic Eschatological Discourses and Revelation 6—20," *Chafer Theological Seminary Journal* 13 (Spring 2008): 60-78.

The adherents of midtribulationism are found generally to have abandoned pretribulationism or posttribulationism. For instance, Van Kampen was pretribulational and sought to find "the common denominator that made the biblical truths of pretribulationism and posttribulationism come together perfectly."[191] Although no mention was made of midtribulationism within the so-called "new" view of pre-wrath rapturism, it is quite similar to that system. Indeed, it is best to regard the prewrath view as a variation of midtribulationism.[192]

The Last Trumpet and Seventh Trumpet

Harrison understood the sounding of "the last trumpet" (1 Cor. 15:52) to occur at the midpoint of the tribulation. The last trumpet in 1 Corinthians 15:52 was thought to be the same as the seventh trumpet of Revelation 11, which midtribulationists believe will commence the great tribulation. Therefore, the seventh trumpet of Revelation would be the last trumpet for the church. The identification of the last trumpet in 1 Corinthians 15:52 with the seventh trumpet of Revelation 11 is essential for the midtribulational view to be correct.

Midtribulationism requires the seventh trumpet to begin the great tribulation. Therefore, the church will experience the first half of the tribulation, but not the great tribulation. The seven seals and the first six trumpet judgments occur in the first half of the 70th week, which means they do not occur during the great tribulation.[193] Pretribulationists would generally agree that the last half of the tribulation could be designated the "great tribulation" (cf. Matt. 24:19); however, the midtribulationist's conclusion that the last trumpet of 1 Corinthians 15:52 and the seventh trumpet of Revelation 11 are the same would be opposed resolutely, in addition to the midtribulational

---

191   Robert D. Van Kampen, *The Rapture Question Answered* (Grand Rapids: Revell, 1997), p. 47.

192   Mike Stallard, "An Analysis of the Use of Cosmic-Sign Passages by Proponents of the Pre-Wrath Rapture Theory" (paper presented at the Pre-Trib Study Group, Dallas, TX, 2002).

193   Harrison, *The End*, p. 54.

understanding of the wrath of God during the entire seven years of tribulation. Harrison wrote, "'Wrath' is a word reserved for the Great Tribulation—
see 'wrath of God' in [Rev.] 14:10, 19; 15:7; 16:1, etc."[194] Harrison cited
Revelation 11:18 ("Your wrath came") as proof that the wrath of God will
not be associated with the seven seals and first six trumpet judgments. Of
course, he did not reference 6:16-17 or 7:14 in his lists of "wrath" references in
Revelation since those texts obviously contradict the notion that the seventh
trumpet begins the time of Divine wrath.[195]

There is also a problem of context with midtribulationism in the
assertion that God connected the last trumpet of 1 Corinthians 15:52 with
later revelation. The Corinthians would have understood Paul to speak
concerning an imminent return ("in a moment, in the twinkling of an
eye") of their Lord "at the last trumpet." There is nothing in the context of
1 Corinthians that would indicate a time of intense tribulation upon the
whole world that would precede the return of their Lord. The interpretation
of the last trumpet in 1 Corinthians would be changed by the revelation of
the seventh trumpet in Revelation. Moreover, a primary matter is whether
or not "last" is limited only to a given chronological sequence.

Indeed, the usage of the word "last" is not limited to the last in a given
chronological sequence; it can also refer to the end of a specific period (or
epoch).[196] Therefore, "last" can refer to the end of something chronologically,
as in the seven trumpets of Revelation, or to the end of a specific period
(e.g., the dispensation of the church). Gerald Stanton rightly stated, "The
fact of subsequent trumpets is no problem" for a pretribulational interpretation of 1 Corinthians 15:52."[197] Even amillennialist Barnes noted,
"The word 'last' here does not imply that any trumpet shall have been
before sounded at the resurrection, but is a word denoting that this is the

---

194 Ibid., p. 91.

195 Ibid., pp. 91, 120. When he did interpret 6:16-17, Harrison regarded it as a future tense.

196 J. Dwight Pentecost, *Things to Come* (Grand Rapids: Zondervan, 1964), p. 189.

197 Gerald B. Stanton, *Kept from the Hour* (Miami Springs: Schoettle Publishing, 1991), pp. 194-95.

consummation or close of things; it will end the economy of this world; it will be connected with the last state of things."[198]

Although God's purposes for Israel and the church are distinct, the soteriological (redemptive) intents for both appear to end with the sounding of a trumpet; however, those trumpets are not identical. The "last trumpet" of 1 Corinthians 15:52 is not a reference to the last in any preceding sequence, but is related to the end of a specific age, namely, the dispensation of the church. The significance of the "last trumpet" in 1 Corinthians 15:52 may be twofold. First, the "last trumpet" may be a technical phrase denoting the end of the dispensation of the church. The word "last" is quite common when referring to events involving the end of the church age (Acts 2:17; 2 Tim. 3:1-5; Heb. 1:1; Jas. 5:3; 1 Pet. 1:5, 20; 1 John 2:18; Jude 18). Second, "last trumpet" may also be a technical phrase indicating the gathering together of the church. E. Schuyler English noted that the sounding of a trumpet in Numbers 10 was to gather an assembly of the people. Therefore, "last trumpet" would be a "rallying call" indicating that the church is changing locations, much like Israel changed camps in the wilderness (1 Cor. 15:23).[199]

The resurrection of Christ made Him "the first fruits" (1 Cor. 15:20, 23) the first resurrected from the dead. Christ's resurrection is the first fruits of many to be raised. The seventh trumpet of Revelation 11, however, announces the kingdom reign of Jesus Christ, which is why there is mention of the resurrection of the righteous dead from the Old Testament economy (11:18; cf. Dan. 12:2, 13). With the announcement of the kingdom in Revelation 11, the remaining bowl judgments will immediately precede the establishment of that kingdom.

---

198   Albert Barnes, *Notes on the First Epistle to the Corinthians* (London: Gall & Inglis, 1847), p. 386.

199   E. Schuyler English, *Re-Thinking the Rapture* (Neptune, NJ: Loizeaux Brothers, 1954), p. 109.

The Wrath of God

According to the midtribulational view, the church is only exempted from the wrath of God during the great tribulation (Rev. 11:2; 12:6), or the last half of the 70th week. Midtribulationists regard the last half of the 70th week as more severe than the first half. Indeed, Harrison described the first half as "'sweet' anticipation to John, as it is to them [Israel] under treaty protection, they will be 'sitting pretty,' as we say. But the second half—'bitter' indeed."[200] Pretribulationists could agree that the first half of the tribulation will be *relatively* peaceful for Israel, since this will be a time of protection for the nation (albeit deceitful). However, if midtribulationists intend to argue that the seven seal judgments and the first six trumpet judgments occur in the first half (i.e., because the seventh trumpet announces the rapture), it would be difficult indeed to imagine John thinking of the prophecies in 6:12–17, 8:11, and, 9:1–10:11 as "'sweet' anticipation."

Buswell believed that the first half of the tribulation will be characterized by general trials and troubles that the church would experience. He understood the first half to depict the wrath of man and not the wrath of God. Concerning "Jacob's distress" in Jeremiah 30:7 (Buswell correlated Dan. 11:31 and 12:1–2, 11 with this reference), he wrote:

> This most terrible time of trouble is *not to be identified with the wrath of God*. Both Matthew and Mark record the words of the Lord predicting cosmic upheavals *"immediately after the tribulation of those days . . ."* (Matthew 24:29; cf. Mark 13:24, 25; Luke 21:25, 26). The Lord proceeds to enumerate as definitely coming "after that tribulation," signs and portents which should be identified with the events which take place at the pouring out of the vials of God's wrath (Revelation 16:1–21). I take the reference to these portents, coming "after the tribulation of those days," to mean that the pouring out of the vials of God's wrath (a time which is commonly, but mistakenly, identified with "the great tribulation") will be definitely subsequent to this very brief but

very intense time of trouble. Tribulation is the common lot of the church in every age.

Tribulation is, generally speaking, from the wrath of man, and to undergo tribulation is the common lot of the church in all ages. But the wrath of God is not for the church. . . .[201]

The fact that unbelieving kings and rulers, rich and strong men as well as slaves, seek to hide "from the face of Him who sits upon the throne, and from the wrath of the Lamb," and that these unbelievers say, "The great day of His wrath has come,"— these reactions of unbelievers do not prove that the sixth seal is the day of wrath. This is but a reaction of the ungodly to cosmic disaster.[202]

Buswell attempted to make an artificial distinction (in opposition to Rev. 4—5) between the wrath of man and the wrath of God by citing passages like Acts 14:21 and 1 Thessalonians 3:3-4 as proof that "tribulation is the common lot of the church in all ages." Therefore, he argued, the first half of the tribulation cannot be identified as the wrath of God. As evident from the previous quotation, Buswell did not even regard the bowls of God's wrath as components of the great tribulation. He related the commencement of the millennial kingdom and the wrath of God (associated with the bowl judgments only). Commenting on the sounding of the seventh trumpet in Revelation 11:14–17, he wrote, "What has taken place is that He who is eternally and continuously the King of Kings and Lord of lords . . . has now ended the time of His 'longsuffering. . . .' True, He allows the Antichrist to continue for three and one half years but his continuance on earth is under the outpouring of the vials of the wrath of God."[203]

J. Oliver Buswell, *A Systematic Theology of the Christian Religion*, 2 vols. (Grand Rapids: Zondervan, 1962; reprint, 1976), 2:389.

202 Ibid., 2:435–36.

203 Ibid., 2:457.

Matthew 24:29 was cited to indicate the time of the wrath of God. In that verse, Jesus stated that cosmic signs would follow "immediately after the tribulation of those days." "Those days" are a reference to the great tribulation that commenced in 24:15. Buswell regarded the cosmic signs in Revelation 16 (cf. 11:13) as part of the bowls of God's wrath, yet he argued that special cosmic signs follow the great tribulation and herald the wrath of God. Whereas Buswell referenced the cosmic signs resulting from the opening of the bowls in Revelation 16 to argue for the time of the wrath of God, Harrison related the time of the wrath of God with the seventh trumpet in Revelation 11. Both Buswell and Harrison ignored the unequivocal references to Divine wrath in Revelation 6:16–17 and 7:14. For instance, Buswell disregarded the aorist (*ēlthen*) in 6:16–17 as "but a reaction of the ungodly to cosmic disaster."[204] Instead, he understood the seventh trumpet as the beginning of the wrath of God. "But not only does the seventh trumpet announce the beginning of the earthly reign of Christ, the voices of the twenty-four elders further announce, 'The nations were angry and Thy wrath has come and the time . . . to destroy those who are destroying the earth.' These words, I believe, refer to the outpouring of the vials of the wrath of God, and the destruction of the Beast and the False Prophet, and of the armies of the Beast."[205]

The promise of rewards for the saints in 11:16 was correlated with 1 Corinthians 15:51–52:[206] "From the point of view of God's own people, the most important announcement of the words of the twenty-four elders is, 'The time has come for the dead to be judged, even to give the reward to thy servants the prophets and to the saints and to those who fear thy name, to the small and to the great.' In other words, the seventh trumpet announces the time of rewards for the righteous dead."[207]

---

204 Ibid., 2:436.
205 Ibid., 2:457.
206 Ibid., 2:457–58.
207 Ibid.

Scripture, however, does not teach that the seventh trumpet begins the wrath of God. The truth of the Biblical teaching is that the tribulation commences with the outpouring of God's wrath in the seal judgments, followed by the trumpet judgments, and concluding with the bowl judgments. The judgments are progressive and sequential, which means there is no halting in the outpouring of God's wrath, and as they are cast upon the earth, they intensify. The progressive and sequential nature of the judgments is consistent with the analogy of birth pangs, since such pains do not occur at the beginning of pregnancy, but at the end.

The Two Witnesses

Harrison made the assertion that the resurrection of the "two witnesses" in Revelation 11:11 is a picture of the rapture of the church. His interpretation would require the ministry of the two witnesses to occur in the first half of the tribulation for the resurrection to occur at the midpoint. His tabulation on page 117 primarily confused the pretribulational rapture in 1 Thessalonians 4:13-18 with the resurrection of the two witnesses in Revelation 11. Harrison wrote, "all the elements of Coming are here."[208] Likewise, Buswell identified the rapture with the resurrection of the two witnesses, which was thought to occur subsequent to the seventh trumpet.

> In the Olivet discourse Jesus said that "immediately after the tribulation of those days" (Matthew 24:29; Mark 13:24,25) the cosmic disturbances, which I have sought to identify with the outpouring of the vials of God's wrath (Revelation, chapter 16), will occur. But Christ added, "And at that time (I understand this to mean, at the time of the conclusion of the terrible tribulation which He had described), there will appear the sign of the Son of Man in heaven, and at that time all the tribes of the land will mourn because of Him and they will see the Son of Man coming upon the clouds of heaven with power and great glory, and

---

208 Harrison, *The End*, p. 117.

> He will send forth His angels with a great trumpet and they will gather His elect from the four winds, from corners of heavens to corners thereof (Matthew 24:30,31; cf. Mark 13:26,27).
>
> It is my opinion that in the coming to life and Rapture of the two witnesses (Revelation 11:11 ff.) we have an exact synchronization of events. The two witnesses are caught up into heaven "in the cloud" at the same moment that the elect of God are caught up together in clouds to the meeting of the Lord in the air (I Corinthians 15:52; I Thessalonians 4:13-18).[209]

Apparently, the church remains in the clouds with Christ to view the unfolding of the tribulational events.

> John says [in Rev. 19:11-16], "I saw heaven standing open." Literally, the perfect passive participle, "having been opened," is harmonious with my speculative suggestion that Christ is visible with His glorified saints in heaven throughout the three and one half year period during which the Antichrist is allowed to prevail upon the earth.[210]

Midtribulationists erroneously conclude the "loud voice from heaven saying to them, 'Come up here'" is the rapture of the church. Nothing in the context supports the conclusion that Revelation 11:12 is the rapture; rather, only the two witnesses are resurrected. Furthermore, Revelation 11:14-15 places the seventh trumpet subsequent to the events of 11:3-14 when "the second woe is past." The second woe is still the sixth trumpet that was opened (cf. 9:13). If Revelation 11:12 is the rapture, then midtribulationists would have to accept the opinion that the rapture occurs at the sixth trumpet as opposed to the last trumpet in Revelation. The seventh trumpet actually occurs near the time of the end of the tribulation, somewhat prior to the second coming of Christ.

---

209 Buswell, *Systematic Theology*, 2:456.
210 Ibid., 2:483.

The seventh angel does not sound the seventh trumpet until a time subsequent to the resurrection of the two witnesses. However, in 1 Corinthians 15:52 the trumpet for the rapture sounds "in a moment, in the twinkling of an eye" (cf. 1 Thess. 4:13-18). In the sense that the seventh trumpet is the seven bowls of wrath, the seventh trumpet sounds for a continuous period of time. (The verb, *esalpisen*, "sounded," indicates the trumpet will begin to sound.)

God's Purposes for Israel and the Church

The midtribulational view interrelates God's program for Israel and the church with each other. The reason for this overlap is due to the belief that the church participates in at least one half of the 70th week, "the time of Jacob's distress," but not in the last half (and most severe) of the 70th week. Both Harrison and Buswell must place the church into the context of the Olivet Discourse. Harrison argued the existence of the temple in A.D. 70 is proof that God's program for Israel and the church overlap. Buswell's overlap of the programs for Israel and the church is obvious in his understanding of the Olivet Discourse, as the following quote demonstrates.

> The next section in the Olivet discourse begins again with tote, "at that time." This word does not mean "then" in the sense of "subsequently." That meaning would be indicated by eita or epeita. Tote means "then" in the sense of "at that time." In other words, the rapture of the church is not said to come subsequently to the time of the wrath of God, but is said to come "at that time."
>
> This particular section of the Olivet discourse is given almost identical words in Matthew and Mark, and in almost identical words in Luke as far as Luke goes in this section. Matthew says, "And at that time there will appear the sign of the Son of Man in heaven and at that time all the tribes of the land will weep [Zechariah 12:10-14; cf. Revelation 1:7] and they shall see the Son of Man coming upon the clouds of heaven with power and great glory. And He will send

forth His angels with a great trumpet [I Corinthians 15:52; I Thessalonians 4:16; Revelation 11:15-19] and they will gather together His elect from the four winds from corners of heaven unto corners thereof" (Matthew 24:30,31).

I have indicated above that the Apostle Paul alludes to these words of Christ in II Thessalonians 2:1 taking the noun, "gathering together," in the phrase, "our gathering together unto Him," from the very verb which Jesus used in saying, "They will gather together His elect."

Luke (ch. 21:27,28) uses the same words employed by Matthew and Mark in reference to the coming of the Son of Man "in a cloud," "with power and great glory." Luke does not include the statement with reference to the great trumpet and the angels and the gathering together of the elect, but Luke adds, "When these things begin to come to pass, look up and lift up your heads, because your redemption is near." In my opinion, the words, "these things," refers back to the material in Luke 21:25,26, namely, the cosmic disturbances which are to come after the brief tribulation. In other words, although Luke does not specifically refer to or describe the rapture, yet his words, "your redemption draweth near," are the equivalent of it.[211]

Midtribulationists ignore the obvious by introducing the church into the context of the Olivet Discourse, and hence, the first half of the tribulation. The tribulation is the 70th week of Daniel, which, fundamentally, is the period that the Olivet Discourse addresses. The dispensation of the law ended with the crucifixion of Christ (2 Cor. 3:11; Gal. 3:25; Col. 2:14) and the beginning of the dispensation of the church on the day of Pentecost (Acts 2). Since the 69th week of Daniel's prophecy (9:24-27) was fulfilled prior to the crucifixion of Christ, and the church was not instituted until Pentecost, then God's purposes for Israel have been postponed until the dispensation of the church is completed.

---

211   Ibid., 2:398-99.

Once the rapture occurs, God will resume His salvific purposes with Israel *as a nation*, which will begin the 70th week. The overlap of the two purposes for Israel and the church is not a Biblical teaching, but it is a necessary doctrine for midtribulationism.

The Doctrine of Imminency

Midtribulationists vigorously deny the Biblical teaching concerning the imminency of the rapture. Midtribulationists must deny imminency. If the rapture is midtribulational, then it is possible to set a date for its occurrence. Indeed, date-setting is quite characteristic of Harrison.[212] If the rapture occurs at the midpoint of the tribulation, then believers would merely count three-and-one-half years from the signing of the peace treaty with Israel, which certainly would become international news, yet such teaching clearly denies imminency of the rapture. Christians are not looking for the Antichrist, but the imminent appearing of Jesus Christ. God provided Israel with numerous signs that would precede the second coming. In light of such signs, Israel was to live in expectancy of the coming of Messiah to fulfill the Biblical covenants and establish His millennial reign.

CONCLUSION

The sounding of the seventh trumpet at the beginning of the great tribulation is essential to the midtribulational viewpoint. Rationale for such a perspective is based upon regarding the "last trumpet" (1 Cor. 15:52) and the seventh trumpet (Rev. 11:15-19) as synonymous. While the purposes of God for both Israel and the church are distinct, the Lord's soteriological intents for both entities appear to end with the sounding of a trumpet, yet those proclamations are not identical for the "last trumpet" is not sequential as it simply denotes the conclusion of the ·

212 Harrison, *The End*, pp. 20, 42-43, 218.

church age. Midtribulationism understands the rapture to occur at the midpoint of the seven-year tribulation for the wrath of God is thought to commence in association with the seventh trumpet. Scripture, however, reveals that God's wrath is outpoured in the seal judgments at the very beginning of tribulation. The judgments, then, of the trumpets and bowls are sequential and progressive, which means there is no interval in the outpouring of God's wrath, from the beginning to the end of the tribulation. Furthermore, to regard the two witnesses as symbolic of the rapture is to argue by analogy as opposed to Biblical exegesis for the simple fact that as "two olive trees" (Rev. 11:4), they are related to Israel (Zech. 4:2-3) and thus could not represent the church. Moreover, the sounding of the seventh trumpet does not result in translation for the church; rather, the result is triumph for Christ as the kingdoms of the world become His. If the church were to be raptured at the midpoint of the tribulation, it would necessitate that the church look for the signs of that period (particularly the first half), which would be contrary to the doctrine of imminency. Consequently, the examination of midtribulationism has demonstrated that the essential characteristics of the view are contrary to the Biblical revelation.

CHAPTER 8

PROPHETIC TIMING AND THE RAPTURE: PRE-WRATH RAPTURISM (MIDTRIBULATIONISM REDUX)

Pre-wrath rapturism is a variation of the midtribulational view of the rapture, and has thus revived much of the argumentation of that viewpoint, in addition to developing some unique distinctives. Only the nomenclature "pre-wrath rapture" is recent in origin. The major works on the subject include: Marvin J. Rosenthal, *The Pre-Wrath Rapture of the Church* (1990); Robert D. Van Kampen, *The Rapture Question Answered* (1997); and, Robert D. Van Kampen, *The Sign* (1992). Rosenthal also publishes a bimonthly publication entitled *Zion's Fire*.

DEFINING CHARACTERISTICS

Pre-wrath rapturism is the teaching that the church passes through approximately three-fourths of Daniel's 70th week (the seven-year tribulation) prior to being raptured. The initial period of the tribulation is termed "man's wrath" since humanity and Satan are regarded as the agents causing the prophesied events. Pre-wrath rapturists are adamant that the entire period of Daniel's 70th week should not be regarded as *the* "tribulation." Only the final one-fourth of Daniel's 70th week includes the wrath of God. Since God does not outpour His wrath until three-fourths of the 70th week has transpired, and the church is allegedly raptured prior to the last one-fourth of the period when God outpours His wrath, then the originators of this view regard themselves as "pre-wrath."

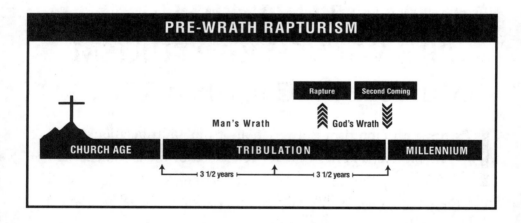

Rosenthal provided the basic tenets of the pre-wrath rapture view.

1. The Rapture of the church will occur immediately prior to the beginning of the Day of the Lord.
2. The Day of the Lord commences sometime within the second half of the seventieth week.

3. The cosmic disturbances associated with the sixth seal will signal the approach of the Day of the Lord.

4. The Day of the Lord will begin with the opening of the seventh seal (Rev. 8:1).[213]

There are, at least, four additional tenets that are imperative for the pre-wrath viewpoint. *First*, the opening three and one-half years of the 70th week commences with the Antichrist signing the peace covenant with Israel; it is called the beginning of sorrows. The first three-and-one-half years only comprise the trials and tribulations of life; therefore, pre-wrath rapturism does not recognize the wrath of God during the beginning of sorrows. Rosenthal believes that any designation of the first half of Daniel's 70th week as the tribulation "has no biblical justification."[214]

Second, the Antichrist will commit the abomination of desolation at the midpoint of Daniel's 70th week, and will thereby reveal his true nature. The abomination of desolation is the beginning of the "great tribulation." Although the great tribulation begins at the midpoint of the seven-year week, it does not actually continue until the end of the last three-and-one-half years. The majority of Rosenthal's charts illustrate that the great tribulation only comprises half of the last three-and-one-half years.[215]

Third, the first six seals cover the time span of approximately five-and-one-quarter years of Daniel's 70th week. The opening of the sixth seal results in "the cosmic disturbances," which signal the sign of Christ's coming. The sixth seal follows the great tribulation but precedes the end of the last three-and-one-half years.[216]

Fourth, the seal judgments are "man's wrath through Antichrist." Approximately five-and-one-quarter years will comprise the seal judgments.

---

213 Marvin J. Rosenthal, *The Pre-Wrath Rapture of the Church* (Nashville: Thomas Nelson, 1990), p. 60.
214 Ibid., p. 103.
215 Ibid., pp. 104-10.
216 Ibid., pp. 110-11.

The trumpet judgments are "God's wrath on all mankind (Israel and the nations)." Approximately one-and-three-fourth years will comprise the trumpet judgments. The bowl judgments are "God's wrath upon the nations for persecution of Israel." The bowl judgments will endure 30 days and will occur subsequent to Daniel's 70th week.[217]

Rosenthal does believe correctly that the Olivet Discourse is "a central text" in determining the chronology and sequence of Daniel's 70th week. His next statement, however, "that the seventieth week of Daniel has three major, distinct, and identifiable periods of time: the 'beginning of sorrows,' the Great Tribulation, and the Day of the Lord [the sole time of God's wrath]—all found in the Olivet Discourse"[218] is to be challenged.

The Tribulation Period

According to Rosenthal's chronology, the rapture occurs subsequent to the great tribulation and prior to the Day of the Lord. The notion that the Day of the Lord is the beginning of the wrath of God is the reason why the view is called "pre-wrath." Pre-wrath rapturists do not identify the entire seven years of Daniel's 70th week with the wrath of God. The distinctions in terminology for the pre-wrath view are central to arguments for that perspective. In Chapter 8, "And What of the Tribulation Period?" of *The Pre-Wrath Rapture of the Church*, Rosenthal argued,

> The designation *the tribulation period* should properly be omitted from any honest consideration of the time of the Rapture of the church. The term *tribulation period* is normally used by pretribulation rapturists as a synonym for the seventieth week of the book of Daniel (Dan. 9:27); that is, to describe the seven years that immediately precede Christ's physical return to the earth to

217 Ibid., p. 147.
218 Ibid., p. 61.

establish His millennial kingdom. Although popular and used by many competent preachers, teachers, and theologians, such a designation has no biblical justification.[219]

A clear fact emerges from an examination of the word *tribulation* as used in the Bible. In a prophetic context, it is used to describe only the period of time that begins in the *middle* of Daniel's seventieth week—never of the first half of it. *Based on that indisputable fact, to call the entire seven-year time frame the tribulation period is to coin a technical phrase and superimpose it upon the Scriptures, reading into the biblical text that which it does not itself declare.*[220]

One can admit unreservedly that the phrase "tribulation period" does not appear in the Bible, yet to accuse pretribulationists with the "coining" of the phrase and superimposing it on the Scriptures with "no biblical justification" is an argument that will also betray the pre-wrath view. For instance, using Rosenthal's logic, to conceive a technical phrase such as "pre-wrath rapture" would be superimposing a designation that the Bible does not use. Rosenthal desires to designate the period covering the three septet judgments and wrath of God as the "70th week of Daniel." Although the Bible does not use the phrase "tribulation period," its meaning is indeed Biblical, and hence, its usage may be used widely as an effective term in contrast to the awkwardness of the expression *70th week of Daniel* that Rosenthal prefers.[221] Furthermore, Rosenthal's expression does not occur in Scripture either. The reason that Rosenthal does not want to use the term *tribulation period* is due to the fact that its usage will not support his threefold division of Daniel's 70th week into the "beginning of sorrows," "Great tribulation" and "Day of the Lord."

---

219   Ibid., p. 103.

220   Ibid., p. 105.

221   For promotional clarity, Rosenthal's publisher even uses the expression "Tribulation" period *twice* on the back cover on his own book.

Θλῖψις (*thlipsis*) is used in the first half of the 70th week. "Then they will deliver you to tribulation [θλῖψιν, *thlipsin*], and will kill you, and you will be hated by all nations because of My name" (Matt. 24:9). Obviously this θλῖψις ("tribulation") occurs in the first half since it precedes the abomination of desolation at the midpoint (24:15-21). Θλῖψις is also used in relation to the second half of the 70th week. "For after all it is *only* just for God to repay with affliction [θλίβουσιν, *thlibousin*] those who afflict [θλῖψιν, *thlipsin*] you, and *to give* relief to you who are afflicted [θλιβομ-ένοις, *thlibomenois*] and to us as well when the Lord Jesus will be revealed from heaven with His mighty angels in flaming fire, dealing out retribution to those who do not know God and to those who do not obey the gospel of our Lord Jesus" (2 Thess. 1:6-8).

The timing "when the Lord Jesus will be revealed from heaven" is certainly the second coming; this return of the Lord will bring the fulfillment of 2 Thessalonians 1:6, which would be chronologically prior to the second coming. In other words, the θλῖψις (*thlipsis*) is also within the second half of the 70th week. Both Matthew 24:9 and 1 Thessalonians 1:6-8 provide Biblical support for the expression "tribulation period" to describe the entire seven years of the 70th week of Daniel. Indeed, the terms can be used synonymously. The only reason for not using them synonymously is to lend support to the pre-wrath, threefold division of the same time period.

The Length of the Great Tribulation

Already it has been demonstrated that Rosenthal does not believe that the entire seven years of Daniel's 70th week should be regarded as the tribulation period. Citing Matthew 24:21, 29 and Mark 13:19, 24, he wrote, "Of the four times the Lord spoke of tribulation in prophetic context, He was speaking of the Great Tribulation which begins in the middle of Daniel's seventieth week—precisely three and one-half years into it."[222]

---

222 Rosenthal, *Pre-Wrath Rapture*, p. 105.

The shortening of the Great Tribulation to less than three and one-half years is one of the most important truths to be grasped if the chronology of end-time events is to be understood. It literally is the key that reveals the sequence to Matthew 24-25 and the chronology of the book of Revelation with the opening of the seals, trumpets, and bowls.[223]

Rosenthal agrees with the majority of pretribulationists that the great tribulation should be reserved for the second half of the 70th week. However, his contention with pretribulationists is that the great tribulation "begins in the middle of the seventieth week, but it does not run until the end of the seventieth week."[224] Rosenthal's error is easily discerned when reading Daniel 12:1 ("Now at that time Michael, the great prince who stands *guard* over the sons of your people, will arise. And there will be a time of distress such as never occurred since there was a nation until that time; and at that time your people, everyone who is found written in the book, will be rescued"). Daniel's words are the same as Matthew 24:21, which clearly occurs at the midpoint of the 70th week.

Both Daniel 12:1 and Matthew 24:21 refer to the time known as the great tribulation. Daniel 12:6-7 prophesies the length of this period. "And one said to the man dressed in linen, who was above the waters of the river, 'How long *will it be* until the end of *these* wonders?' I heard the man dressed in linen, who was above the waters of the river, as he raised his right hand and his left toward heaven, and swore by Him who lives forever that it would be for a time, times, and half *a time*; and as soon as they finish shattering the power of the holy people, all these *events* will be completed."

Furthermore, Revelation 12:14 ("But the two wings of the great eagle were given to the woman, so that she could fly into the wilderness to her place, where she was nourished for a time and times and half a time, from

---

223 Ibid., pp. 111-12.
224 Ibid., p. 109.

the presence of the serpent.") prophesies of the same time as Daniel 12:7 and Matthew 24:21. "Michael, the great prince who stands *guard* over the sons of your people, will arise" with the heavenly angels to battle with Satan and the fallen angels who will persecute Israel, "the woman." Those who flee "into the wilderness" will be protected by God "for a time and times and half a time" (Rev. 12:14).

The length of the period is qualified in Revelation 12:6 as "one thousand two hundred and sixty days," and in 13:5 as "forty-two months." Therefore, the great tribulation is the entire second half of the 70th week. The period of "time and times and half a time" is 1,260 days, or 42 months, which is exactly three and one-half years. The time designated as the great tribulation will be unprecedented in its dreadfulness (Dan. 12:1; Matt. 24:21). If Christ did not return to the earth, "no life would have been saved; but for the sake of the elect those days will be cut short" by the second coming of Christ (Matt. 24:22).

The Seal Judgments

Both Rosenthal and Van Kampen gave attention to the similarities between the events of Matthew 24:5-9 and the first five seals of Revelation 6:1-8. However, their argument is that the first five seals (Rev. 6:1-11) are not the wrath of God, but that of humanity through the Antichrist.[225] Rosenthal and Van Kampen were correct in asserting that the seal judgments are opened at the start of the tribulation. The difference with pretribulationism is not primarily the chronological placement of the seal judgments after the opening of the first seal, but the "pre-wrath" contention that the first five seals are the wrath of humanity through Antichrist as opposed to all the seal judgments occurring as the wrath of God.

Rosenthal interpreted the first seal correctly as describing the rise of the Antichrist. He rejected the first seal as Divine wrath since "God alone must take direct responsibility for a counterfeit religious system"

---

225   Ibid., pp. 147-51; Van Kampen, *Rapture Question*, pp. 139-52.

and "to attribute the emergence of the Antichrist to God is obviously preposterous."[226] What is unreasonable is the minimizing of God's sovereignty by pre-wrath rapturists.

The pre-wrath view is part of an increasing trend within the church that argues contrary to the Biblical revelation of God's sovereignty. For instance, Isaiah 10:5-12 records the sovereignty of God in using an evil nation, Assyria ("the rod of My anger"), to accomplish His purposes for Judah.[227] Judah was "a godless nation" and would be plundered and trampled by Assyria (10:6). However, even though God used Assyria as the rod of His anger, He would still judge them as responsible for their wickedness. The Lord "will punish the fruit of the arrogant heart of the king of Assyria and the pomp of his haughtiness" (10:12b). Assyria was responsible for her arrogance and haughtiness, even though God used the nation as an evil instrument to accomplish His purposes for Judah. The Isaianic passage demonstrates the sovereignty of God in the affairs of history, yet also does not excuse the wicked for their actions.

The prophet Habakkuk also needed clarity regarding God's sovereignty, particularly in how the Lord used wicked Babylon to punish Judah (Hab. 1:12—2:20). While it may appear paradoxical to the human mind that God is sovereign and people are responsible, it is not an antinomy for the Lord. The psalmist writes,

> For the wrath of man shall praise You;
> With a remnant of wrath You will gird Yourself. (Ps. 76:10)

The book of Job also demonstrates that God will allow evil to occur under His sovereign control in order to accomplish His purposes and to

---

226 Ibid., p. 142.

227 Interpreters disagree whether Judah was a reference to the northern kingdom of Israel or the southern kingdom of Judah. H. C. Leupold believed it was the northern kingdom (*Exposition of Isaiah*, 2 vols. [Grand Rapids: Baker, 1968-1971], 1:200-01), while Edward J. Young believed it was the southern kingdom [*The Book of Isaiah*, 3 vols. [Grand Rapids: Eerdmans, 1965-72], 1:359). Since verse 12 refers to God's "work on Mount Zion and on Jerusalem," it is most likely the southern kingdom of Judah that was being addressed.

glorify Himself. A classic example of the perfect symmetry between the sovereignty of God and the responsibility of humanity is Acts 2:23. Peter said, Jesus was "delivered over by the predetermined plan and foreknowledge of God," who was "nailed to a cross by the hands of godless men and put .. . to death." God predestined the death of Jesus, yet the wicked people who "put *Him* to death" are responsible for their actions. Likewise, 2 Thessalonians 2:3-7 says the Antichrist, "the man of lawlessness," "the son of destruction," will be restrained "so that in his time he will be revealed." While the "mystery of lawlessness is already at work . . . he who now restrains *will do so* until he is taken out of the way." The Restrainer withholds the Antichrist from being revealed. Obviously, the restraint is within God's sovereign power.

According to 2 Corinthians 12:7, God gave the Apostle Paul "a thorn in the flesh" as a means of preventing the apostle "from exalting" himself due to "the surpassing greatness of the revelations" he had received. God sent "a thorn in the flesh" as "a messenger of Satan." In like manner to the previous examples referenced (as to how God used evil), so will He use the Antichrist to accomplish His purposes for Israel, tribulation saints and the unbelieving world. God is sovereign over the affairs of humanity while holding individuals accountable for sinning of their own nature. God used the wicked as instruments of judgment upon His people for His own purposes.

In Revelation 5:1, the Apostle John "saw in the right hand of Him who sat on the throne a book written inside and on the back, sealed up with seven seals." "A strong angel" proclaimed loudly, "'Who is worthy to open the book and to break its seals?'" "No one was found worthy to open the book or to look into it" except "the Lion that is from the tribe of Judah, the Root of David," the Lamb that was slain, comes forth (5:2–5). The "Lamb" was found worthy to break the seals, and such authority proves the judgment comes from Him (5:5, 9; 6:1). When each seal is broken, there is a description in Revelation 6 of the judgment to occur on Earth, thereby indicating the successive nature of the judgments. The judgment is from the sovereign Lord, even though from humanity's perspective the seal judgments demonstrate the depravity of fallen mankind.

Nevertheless, both Rosenthal[228] and Van Kampen[229] argued that God's wrath does not begin until after the sixth seal. Subsequent to the cosmic signs of Revelation 6:12-14, verses 15-17 provide the reaction of "the kings of the earth and the great men and the commanders and the rich and the strong and every slave and free man." They will cry "to the mountains and to the rocks, 'Fall on us and hide us from the presence of Him who sits on the throne, and from the wrath of the Lamb; for the great day of their wrath has come, and who is able to stand?'" A plain reading of Scripture here should cause one to conclude that "the great day" of God's wrath has already appeared and is present during the sixth seal.

Since pre-wrath rapturists do not believe God's wrath begins until the seventh seal, they must argue, "the aorist tense ["has come"] is, generally speaking, timeless."[230] Rosenthal wrote, "the phrase, 'the great day of his wrath is come' refers, not to a past event, but to an event about to occur, and that in concert with the opening of the seventh seal."[231] Following the sixth seal, God's wrath "is an event that is on the threshold of happening—a future event soon to occur."[232] The aorist, ἦλθεν (*ēlthen*), in 6:17 is in the indicative mood, which would confirm the reality of the action (God's wrath) from the standpoint of the world leaders. However, the reader does not need the perspective of the world leaders in order to determine if God's wrath has occurred. The sealed book in Revelation 5 contained God's judgment and the breaking of the seals by Jesus Christ released the Divine wrath.

Furthermore, the aorist is not timeless as the pre-wrath view requires; rather, the time of action is past. Non-indicative moods may indicate the

---

228   Ibid., p. 167.
229   Van Kampen, *Rapture Question*, p. 164.
230   Ibid., p. 153.
231   Rosenthal, *Pre-Wrath Rapture*, p. 167.
232   Van Kampen, *Rapture Question*, p. 154.

kind of action as opposed to the time of action. Greek grammarians Dana and Mantey stated, "It has no essential temporal significance, its time relations being found only in the indicative, where it is used as past and hence augmented. . . . The aorist signifies nothing as to completeness, but simply presents the action as attained. It states the *fact* of the action or event without regard to its *duration*."[233] Robertson concurred, "It is true that in the expression of past time in the indicative and with all the other moods, the aorist is the tense used as a matter of course. . . ."[234] Wallace acquiesced, "In the *indicative*, the aorist usually indicates *past* time with reference to the time of speaking (thus, 'absolute time'). . . . Outside the indicative and participle, time is not a feature of the aorist."[235]

The Elect and the Church

Another crucial argument for the pre-wrath rapture is the contention that the elect in the Olivet Discourse (Matt. 24:22, 24, 31) is the church. Pre-wrath rapturists attempt desperately to prove that the church will endure suffering during the tribulation, and especially during the great tribulation. Van Kampen wrote,

> It will be the church in general that will fall away into apostasy in the last days. It is the elect of God (the saints) who will endure Antichrist's persecution. That is precisely why terms such as "the elect" and "the saints" are used instead of the word church to describe the faithful who will choose death over compromise![236]

In a desperate attempt to prove the church is referenced in the Olivet Discourse, Rosenthal contended, "Not once in the New Testament is Israel

233　H. E. Dana and Julius R. Mantey, *A Manual Grammar of the Greek New Testament* (New York: Macmillan, 1927), p. 193.

234　A. T. Robertson, *A Grammar of the Greek New Testament in the Light of Historical Research* (Nashville: Broadman Press, 1934), p. 831.

235　Daniel B. Wallace, *Greek Grammar Beyond the Basics* (Grand Rapids: Zondervan, 1996), p. 555.

236　Van Kampen, *Rapture Question*, p. 81 (emphasis original).

ever called the 'elect.'"[237] The statement is entirely inaccurate. *First*, the Gospels were written during the Mosaic dispensation so it would be natural for the Jews to understand the words of Jesus concerning His coming to mean the deliverance of Israel. *Second*, קָהָל (*qahal*)—one of the principal Hebrew words for "gathering" or "assembly"—was used frequently in the Old Testament to describe Israel. The natural Jewish understanding of elect in the Olivet Discourse would be based on the use of קָהָל (*qahal*) within the Old Testament dispensation.[238]

Third, context determines whether elect is referring to Israel, the church or both. The elect in Matthew 24 refers to the Jewish remnant of the tribulation period who will come to believe in Jesus as Messiah and Savior. The context of Matthew 24 supports the conclusion that elect refers to the Jewish remnant. Terms such as "this gospel of the kingdom" (24:14), "the holy place" (24:15), "a Sabbath" (24:20) and "the Christ" (24:23-24) indicate that Israel as a nation is principal.

The Coming of Christ in Matthew 24

Rosenthal's interpretation of Matthew 24:29-31 is a peculiar one. Generally, the coming of Christ "with power and great glory" is understood to occur at the end of the seven-year tribulation and preceding the establishment of His millennial kingdom (25:31, 34). Rosenthal and Van Kampen interpreted "the sign of the Son of Man" in Matthew 24 as manifested following the cosmological signs of the sixth seal and the cosmological signs preceding the Day of the Lord.[239]

---

237   Marvin J. Rosenthal, "The Great Tribulation," *Zion's Fire* (May-June 1998): 9.

238   Despite their transgressions, God will never cast away the nation of Israel (Rom. 11:1-6). There is always a godly "tenth" (the remnant) that shall "return and be healed" (Isa. 6:10-13), and this remnant is referenced in Isaiah 65:7-16, and contrasted with the unbelieving Jews of the nation. God called the godly remnant, "My chosen ones" (65:9). In contrast to the unbelievers who will not be allowed entrance into the future millennium, God's "chosen ones" will be blessed in the earth (65:17-25).

239   Rosenthal, *Pre-Wrath Rapture*, p. 153; Van Kampen, *Rapture Question*, p. 164.

Such an interpretation forces the sixth seal and the events of the Olivet Discourse into an artificial pattern created by the pre-wrath rapturists.[240] Rosenthal interpreted the coming of Christ in 24:30 as the rapture, which he believes will occur prior to the opening of the seventh seal "after the Great Tribulation but long before the end of the seventieth week."[241] What this means is there is "only one *parousía* of Christ and one Day of the Lord, both occurring when Christ comes to rapture the faithful and then begins his systematic destruction of the wicked who remain (the Day of the Lord)!"[242] Such an interpretation denies the Biblical teaching of Christ coming for His church in the rapture to take them to His Father's house (John 14:2-3), and His coming with His church to Earth to deliver Israel and establish His kingdom.

Pre-wrath rapturists also confuse the coming of Christ in Matthew 24:40-41 and Luke 17:20-37. Commenting upon a classic text of the second coming of Christ to Earth to deliver Israel, Rosenthal reinterpreted as follows:

> . . . the Lord taught, "For as the lightning, that lighteneth out of the one part under heaven, shineth unto the other part under heaven, so shall also the Son of man be in his day" (Luke 17:24). The phrase "in his day" is a clear reference to the Day of the Lord.... The point of the Lord's teaching is clear. Noah entered the ark, then the judgment began—on the same day. For emphasis, the Lord gave another illustration of the same truth: "But the same day that Lot fled Sodom, it rained fire and brimstone from heaven, and destroyed them all" (Luke 17:29). . . . . *Deliverance of the righteous immediately precedes judgment of the wicked. To postulate a period of time between rapture (deliverance) and wrath (judgment) is to contradict the Scriptures.*[243]

---

240   Mal Couch, "A Review of the Book 'The Rapture Question Answered Plain and Simple'," *The Conservative Theological Journal* 3 (December 1997): 243-45.

241   Rosenthal, *Pre-Wrath Rapture*, p. 153.

242   Van Kampen, *Rapture Question*, p. 100.

243   Rosenthal, *Pre-Wrath Rapture*, p. 140.

Rosenthal cited Luke 17:26-27 as proof of a "same day" rapture associated with the Day of the Lord. The problem is there is nothing in Scripture indicating judgment began on the very day that Noah entered the ark. According to Genesis 7:7 and 10, the flood waters did not begin until seven days after Noah and his family entered the ark. Even though Rosenthal wrote, *"Biblically, no extended period of time can separate the two events of rapture and wrath,"*[244] there is in reality an interval between the entering of the ark and the judgment. One should note that much of the pre-wrath argument depends upon the absence of an interval, which cannot be supported by Scripture.

Rosenthal also referred to the Lord's deliverance of Lot prior to the destruction of Sodom and Gomorrah as proof for no interval. Genesis 19:15-24 seems to suggest that an interval did occur between Lot's deliverance from Sodom, until he arrived in Zoar ("Hurry, escape there, for I cannot do anything until you arrive there."). Lot left Sodom "when morning dawned" (19:15), but it was not until "the sun had risen over the earth" (19:23) that "the LORD rained on Sodom and Gomorrah brimstone and fire from the LORD out of heaven" (19:24).

The pre-wrath view also confuses those "taken" and those "left" in Matthew 24:40-41. Rosenthal reversed the teaching of Scripture to mean "one will be taken" in the rapture and "one will be left" to experience the wrath of God. In the days of Noah and Lot, and the second coming of Christ, "one will be taken" in judgment and "one will be left" to enter the millennial kingdom (cf. Luke 17:34-37; Rev. 19:17-18). The unbelievers in the days of Noah "did not understand until the flood came and took them all away" (Matt. 24:39a). Matthew said the judgment would be the same: "So will the coming of the Son of Man be" (24:39b).

The first half and the second half (a great tribulation) of the tribulation will span a period of seven years of Divine wrath. The rapture will not only preclude the church from God's wrath during the last quarter of the tribulation (what

---

244 Ibid., p. 196.

Rosenthal called the Day of the Lord), but also from the entire seven years of Divine wrath. Furthermore, even if Rosenthal could prove the Day of the Lord begins during the last quarter of the tribulation it still would not make the pre-wrath view correct since the entire 70th week includes the Divine wrath. Once the Lord Jesus, the one who is worthy "to open the book and its seven seals" (Rev. 5:5), breaks the sixth seal even the world leaders recognize the wrath of God. Indeed, if the rapture is to be "pre-wrath" it must be pretribulational, which of course, is the teaching of Scripture.

CONCLUSION

Fundamental to the pre-wrath viewpoint is the division of the tribulation into "three major, distinct, and identifiable periods of time: the 'beginning of sorrows,' the Great Tribulation, and the Day of the Lord."[245] Scripture, however, reveals that two parts distinguish the tribulation, and both are equally three-and-a-half years in length (cf. Dan. 7:25; Rev. 12:6, 14; 13:5). Pre-wrath advocates seek to avoid using the term "tribulation" in reference to the first half of the 70th week, yet it is obvious that tribulation is an appropriate designation for that time period, and also for the second half (cf. Matt. 24:15-21; 2 Thess. 1:6-8). Moreover, the day of the Lord cannot be separated from the entire time of tribulation (cf. Jer. 30:7; Dan. 12:1; Joel 2:1-2; Zeph. 1:14-15; Matt. 24:21). The length of the tribulation is the entire seven years of Daniel's 70th week, and the evidence of Scripture is that the wrath of God encompasses the entire tribulation period; and, the Great Tribulation is "cut short" (Matt. 24:22) only in the sense that if the intense judgment of that period continued for any longer than the prescribed time, no human being would be able to survive. Consequently, the examination of pre-wrath rapturism has demonstrated that the essential characteristics of the view are contrary to the Biblical revelation.

---

245 Ibid., p. 61.

CHAPTER 9

PROPHETIC TIMING
AND THE RAPTURE:
POSTTRIBULATIONISM, PART I

The doctrine of the rapture in the history of the church is essentially a history of pretribulationism. Although there are other historic doctrines related to this history, there is not differentiation between the rapture and second coming. Consequently, midtribulationism and pre-wrath rapturism have minimal history (and perhaps it would be accurate to state that church history of those doctrines is entirely absent). Posttribulationists will often refer to their view as "historic premillennialism." The term is not accurate though, since the eschatological system of the early church is difficult to classify, and this difficulty is the consequence of frequent contradictory perspectives on the part of the early church, without any conscientious regard on their part for consistency.

The early church was principally premillennial;[246] rather than adhering to a contemporary form of posttribulationism, the term "imminent intratribulationism"[247] is more accurate. In the midst of continual persecution, the early church believed the tribulation was presently upon them and they anticipated the imminent return of Jesus Christ within this context. Although indeterminate, the climax of the tribulation would be the rapture of the church. Therefore, the rapture was an imminent event. The belief in the imminent return of Jesus Christ by the early church fathers is a primary aspect of pretribulational thought. The absence of any systematic eschatology by the early church fathers is the consequence of the lack of consistency by them regarding the exact chronology of the premillennial return of Jesus Christ.

DEFINING CHARACTERISTICS

Interestingly, posttribulationists such as Robert H. Gundry and George Eldon Ladd deny imminency, yet reference the church fathers frequently for alleged proof of their eschatological system. Any references to the church fathers would seem to necessitate that one explain how they could believe in imminency, yet also thought they were experiencing the tribulation. While it is understandable why the early church did not give systematic thought to eschatological doctrines,[248] it is not evident why the

---

246 With the exception of Caius, there is no church father who opposed premillennialism until the advent of Origen's allegorical method of interpretation, which then dominated eschatological thought through the spiritualized (and gnostic) interpretation of Revelation 20 by Augustine, and as a consequence of the legalization of Christianity by Constantine.

247 Larry V. Crtuchfield, "The Blessed Hope and the Tribulation in the Apostolic Fathers," in *When the Trumpet Sounds*, gen. eds. Thomas Ice and Timothy Demy (Eugene, OR: Harvest House, 1995), pp. 91-94, 101. John F. Walvoord referred to the Biblical understanding of the early church fathers "that the coming of the Lord could occur any hour" (*The Return of the Lord* [Grand Rapids: Dunham Publishing, 1955], p. 80).

248 As Walvoord stated, "The church soon became involved in problems other than the study of prophecy, however, and church councils in the fourth century and in following centuries were concerned primarily with the doctrine of the Trinity, the doctrine of sin, and various controversies. Paganism and ritualism engulfed the church after the fourth century, and it was not until

majority of modern posttribulationists deny imminency. Although post-tribulationists make frequent appeals to the church fathers for defense of their view, it is apparent that there is a lack of continuity between the early church and posttribulationists today. The early church simply did not articulate a systematized form of eschatological doctrine.

> The situation in the Christian church, immediately following the apostles, did not require an extensive literature of its own. Men were expecting important changes in the world. The authoritative teaching of the apostles was, of course, still fresh in memory, and the struggle between Christianity and paganism had not yet assumed any large proportions. It was the twilight period, before the literature of the early church philosophers had developed. Their first writings were not so much history, expositions, or apologies, as simply letters.[249]

Another common feature of modern posttribulationism is the teaching that the church is the true Israel, which includes saints of all ages. Scripture unmistakably teaches there will be a redeemed group of people in the future tribulation. The replacement theology of the more common forms of posttribulationism believes this teaching to mean the church must experience the period of future tribulation. For this reason, Israel and the church are understood as a single covenant community who experience the same eschatological events.

Another typical characteristic of posttribulationism is to make their position a matter of orthodoxy since it was a view held by the Protestant Reformers. Since posttribulationists believe their view to be that of the

---

the Protestant Reformation in the sixteenth century that Biblical doctrines began to be restored" (*Return of the Lord*, p. 81). The systematic teaching of premillennial pretribulationism is a consequence of the Protestant Reformation. Amillennial and postmillennial theologies essentially deny the principle of *sola Scriptura* by not applying the Reformation hermeneutic consistently. Due to their own historical context, the Protestant Reformers themselves cannot be *directly* accused of this deficiency.

249   Leroy Edwin Froom, *The Prophetic Faith of Our Fathers*, 4 vols. (Washington, DC: Review and Herald Publishing, 1950), 1:205.

early church fathers and the Protestant Reformers, any deviation from the system is a departure from historic, orthodox Christianity. One should not neglect to recognize that the church fathers held to a *form* of posttribulationism because of the Roman persecution that they believed was proof they were experiencing the eschatological tribulation (yet one cannot discount their belief in imminency). The Reformers likewise believed they were in the tribulation because of persecution from the Roman Catholic Church. Both were wrong since their eschatological thought was subjugated by their persecution. The four prevailing varieties of modern posttribulationism include: (1) classic posttribulationism; (2) semiclassic posttribulationism; (3) futuristic posttribulationism; and, (4) dispensational posttribulationism.

VARITIES OF POSTTRIBULATIONISM

Classic Posttribulationism (J. Barton Payne)

Payne is perhaps the only writer of the 20th century who held to the same form of "historic premillennialism" as the early church fathers. He wrote *The Imminent Appearing of Christ* to promote what he believed was the position of the early church. Payne believed the perspective of the early church was both posttribulational and premillennial. The classic view spiritualizes the tribulation and relates it with current tribulations of Christianity. Payne is even critical of posttribulationists, such as Ladd, who defended a future tribulation. Although Payne's view is not popular among posttribulationists, the proclivity to spiritualize the tribulation is quite characteristic of other posttribulationists.

The Doctrine of Imminency

Unlike modern posttribulationists, Payne defended the imminency of the second coming, which he believed would occur simultaneously with the rapture. Imminency was defined as "an event 'almost always of danger,' which is 'impending threateningly;' hanging over one's head; ready to befall or overtake one; close at hand in its incidence; coming on shortly."[250] To support his definition, Payne cited the following verses: Matthew 24:38-39, 42; 25:13; and Revelation 22:7, 12; cf. 3:11, 22:20. He concluded, "It should therefore be clear at the outset that imminency does not mean that Christ's coming *must* be soon. All forms of date-setting (which generally is so executed as to bring on the end-time in the contemporary generation!) are forever ruled out. The day of Christ's appearing rests in the hands of God, 'which in its own times *he* shall show' (I Tim. 6:15)."[251] Payne's arguments for imminency were his most important contribution to posttribulationism.

> Finally, the "blessed hope," as it has been interpreted by the classical view of the church, is one the full accomplishment of which is imminent. Each morning, as the Christian casts his glance into the blueness of the sky, he may thrill with the prayerful thought, "Perhaps today!" Or, if his particular skies be shrouded in gloom, still the blackest moment comes just before the dawn. His very prayer of petition may be cut short by "a great earthquake" (Rev. 6:12). Then, "Look up, and lift up your heads; because your redemption draweth nigh" (Luke 21:28).[252]

Payne's defense of imminency is appreciated, for it should not be difficult to understand why the doctrine is cherished among those who study the numerous New Testament passages that encourage Christians to anticipate—with eagerness—the return of Christ for His church.

250 J. Barton Payne, *The Imminent Appearing of Christ* (Grand Rapids: Eerdmans, 1962), p. 85.
251 Ibid., p. 86.
252 Ibid., p. 161.

However, Payne wrongly applied imminency to the second coming of Christ to Earth rather than the rapture prior to the tribulation. He believed many of the prophesied events of the New Testament are already fulfilled in church history or in modern problems of Christianity. Payne's defense of an imminent second coming required him to spiritualize the period of the tribulation. "For the great tribulation, as classically defined, is potentially present, and perhaps almost finished: Look up! Your redemption may be today!"[253]

Semiclassic Posttribulationism (Alexander Reese)

The semiclassic view is the most common form of posttribulationism. The view can be difficult, at times, to summarize, as there is an ample diversity of interpretations among posttribulationists.[254] However, some common details can be ascertained. Most posttribulationists affirming the semiclassic view could be considered amillennial historicists because this variety of posttribulationists believe the current age is the tribulation so that discussions of a pretribulational rapture are impossible. The semiclassic view could not be termed amillennial preterism because they do not insist that the majority of Bible prophecy has already been fulfilled. The principal argument they emphasize is an historicist view of the present-day nature of the tribulation. The semiclassic view understands the church already to be in the great tribulation.

Although semiclassic posttribulationists believe the church is already in the tribulation, they do believe some events of the tribulation are eschatological; it is because some events of the tribulation are regarded as unfulfilled that semiclassic posttribulationists anticipate specific events and persons dominant throughout the tribulation as eschatological. Since the classic

---

253 Ibid., p. 133.

254 The assertion here should not be missed since pretribulationists are often charged with disagreement among themselves, whereas posttribulationists also disagree on some of the particulars of their own view.

view spiritualizes portions of the tribulation, it can anticipate the second coming as imminent. However, the semiclassic view cannot consistently affirm the imminency of the second coming since certain events and persons must still be revealed in fulfillment of all eschatological prophecy.

In 1962, J. Barton Payne described Alexander Reese's work as "Pre-tribulationism's most detailed refutation."[255] Reese's arguments in his work *The Approaching Advent of Christ* certainly influenced posttribulational authors such as Norman F. Douty,[256] Alexander Fraser,[257] Robert Gundry,[258] George Eldon Ladd,[259] Dave MacPherson[260] and George L. Rose.[261] His thought has significantly influenced other posttribulationists, who have further developed his arguments.

The foremost argument of Reese concerned the timing of the resurrection of the saints. Reese believed the resurrection of the saints would occur simultaneously with the resurrection in Revelation 20. He wrote, "the Coming of the Lord synchronises with the resurrection of the saints. The latter follows immediately upon the former. Nothing disputes this. . . . The time of the Rapture must stand or fall with the time of the saints' resurrection. . . ."[262] Reese believed the rapture was "approaching," but rejected the doctrine of imminency.[263]

Reese gave much emphasis to words such as "appearing," "the day," "the end" and "revelation" as technical terms, which made the rapture and second coming the conclusion of the current age. He believed certain aspects of the book of Revelation were fulfilled in the past and some fulfilled in the present

---

255 Payne, *Imminent Appearing*, p. 185.

256 Norman F. Douty, *Has Christ's Return Two Stages?* (New York: Pageant Press, 1956).

257 Alexander Fraser, *The Return of Christ in Glory* (Scottdale, PA: The Evangelical Fellowship, 1953).

258 Robert Gundry, *The Church and the Tribulation* (Grand Rapids: Zondervan, 1973).

259 George Eldon Ladd, *The Blessed Hope* (Grand Rapids: Eerdmans, 1956).

260 Dave MacPherson, *The Incredible Cover-Up* (Medford, OR: Omega Publications, 1975).

261 George L. Rose, *Tribulation till Translation* (Glendale, CA: Rose Publishing, 1942).

262 Alexander Reese, *The Approaching Advent of Christ* (London: Marshall, Morgan and Scott, 1932), p. 154.

263 Ibid., pp. 225-61.

day, but still anticipated the fulfillment of all prophecies in an eschatological manner. The first chapter of his work was an excursus on the 70 weeks of Daniel. Reese adopted the chronology of Sir Robert Anderson's *The Coming Prince*, and even affirmed "an undetermined interval" between the 69th and 70th weeks.[264] Nevertheless, it is because he believed that a literal 70th week of seven years was yet to be fulfilled—prior to Christ returning to Earth—that an "approaching advent" was the most Reese defended.

The Nature of the Tribulation

There is general confusion regarding the nature of the tribulation among posttribulationists. Some believe the church is already in the tribulation. For example, Rose equated the "great persecution" of Acts 8:1-3 with the "great tribulation" in Matthew 24:21 since θλῖψις (*thlipsis*) is used in both passages.[265] Since "great persecution" began in the early church, and this is the same as the great tribulation, then the church could be understood as already in the great tribulation. Such novel methods of interpretation ignore the plain teaching of Scripture by spiritualizing language that is unmistakably literal in meaning.

According to Daniel 12:11, the abomination of desolation will begin the 1,290 days, or 42 months (Rev. 13:5), of great tribulation, which is given as a definite sign (in Matt. 24:15-30) that the second advent of Christ is approaching. Furthermore, Daniel 12:1 teaches this period "will be a time of distress such as never occurred since there was a nation until that time." The church has always endured persecution since its inception, but this cannot be compared to the period that Daniel described. The great tribulation will end the current age prior to the second coming of Christ.

Reese did not teach that the current age is the great tribulation. He taught the 70th week of Daniel was eschatological. He wrote, "the

---

264 Ibid., p. 31.
265 Rose, *Tribulation till Translation*, p. 68.

eschatological character of the Seventieth Week is assumed throughout this volume."[266] Reese would rightly agree with pretribulationists and post-tribulationists (such as Gundry and Ladd) concerning the eschatological character of the time prior to the second coming of Christ. However, Reese's eschatology was not entirely characteristic of a futurist. He rejected "the extravagances of the Historical School," but still believed some of the seven seals of Revelation have already been fulfilled (or, at least, some have been opened) throughout church history.

Israel and the Church

A common argument among posttribulationists is to interpret the elect in Matthew 24:31 as referring to the church. Since the prophesied events of Matthew 24:31 will occur during the time of the tribulation, then the church would experience the tribulation period (as posttribulationists understand this verse). Reese described this group as follows:

> In the Gospels, a people ignorant of the first principles of Christ, ignorant of redemption, devoid of the Spirit, guided by select beatitudes and other snippets from the Sermon on the Mount, and by the Imprecatory Psalms; fulfilling Matt. xxviii. 18-20 in 1260 days; converting countless millions of the heathen to Christ during the absence of the Holy Spirit, yet, though preaching the Gospel of that Kingdom [Matthew 24:14] whose very essence is "righteousness and peace and joy in the Holy Ghost," they invoke terrible curses upon their enemies, and their enemies' children. *Elect* indeed!
>
> To refute such supreme rubbish requires either a volume or a page; we can only give it a page, which will be sufficient for those ingenuous readers who have followed us so far, and have seen that the saints are raised at the Day of the Lord; that the Blessed Hope is none other than the Glorious Appearing; that

---

266 Reese, *Approaching Advent*, p. 30.

the Appearing, the Revelation and the Day of Christ are for the Church; that the Parousia is not in secret; but in triumph.[267]

His description is not an argument though; it is encumbered with emotion and also depends upon circular reasoning to assert the conclusion that the elect is the church. Reese assumed at the onset of his argument that the church is the elect in order to argue the very point he was attempting to prove. He stated the church is the elect; therefore, the elect in Matthew 24 has to be the church. The term elect is not a technical term though; it is a general term used to refer to the saved of all dispensations. The context will reveal whether it is referring to Israel or the church.

Tribulation saints are the elect of God, but this is not to say that because they are elect, then they must also be members of the church. The two principal Old Testament words for "gathering" or "assembly," *qahal* and *edah*, and the New Testament word for "church," *ekklēsia*, indicate an assembly of believers. Expressions such as "in Christ" or "the body of Christ" are particular to the church, as a unique group of the elect, who are not the same as the saints of all dispensations. The use of the term "elect" in Matthew's gospel could just as easily be understood generally of those who are gathered at the end of the tribulation and who will enter the millennial kingdom. Nevertheless, the fact that there is no mention of resurrection, and the context of the Olivet Discourse in its entirety, demonstrates the elect to be Israel.

Who Is Taken and Who Is Left?

From the Biblical standpoint, the day and hour of Christ's second coming is uncertain. In the Olivet Discourse, Christ compared His second coming to the skepticism rampant in the days of Noah. Keeping the analogy between the flood and the second coming would mean there will be signs

---

267   Ibid., pp. 206-07.

before Christ returns to earth. However, as in the flood, the unbelievers will continue living their lives as if there was no judgment to come. Similar to the flood, the second coming will be preceded by warnings of its approaching but the day and hour is known only to the Lord. Those left behind will be saved and those taken will experience judgment.

Since the time of the rapture is unknown, and the time of Christ's return in Matthew 24:40-41 is uncertain, posttribulationists feel justified in emphasizing similarities to argue that the time of both events will occur at the end of the tribulation. Reese was aware of the majority interpretation of dispensationalists: "[They] have a shift to get rid of these damaging facts: they interpret the Rapture in Matt. xxiv. 41, and Luke xvii. 34-5, as a seizure to *judgement*; the leaving as a leaving for blessing, in the kingly rule of the Son of Man."[268] Reese argued against the idea of "taking away" to judgment by contrasting the Greek word *airō* in Matthew 24:39 with *paralambanō* in Matthew 24:40–41. However, the following statement by Reese demonstrates that he did not sufficiently consider the contextual continuity: "The use of this word in the N.T. is absolutely opposed to this; it is a good word; a word used exclusively in the sense of 'take away with' or 'receive,' or 'take *home.*'"[269]

Reese was wrong in asserting that *paralambanō* is always "a good word." Although the word can refer to a blessed event (John 14:3), it can also refer to a "taking" to judgment. For example, John 19:17 used it of the religious leaders who "took" Jesus to be crucified. Likewise, Matthew 27:27 records that the soldiers of the governor "took" Jesus before the Roman cohort who proceeded to mock and beat Him. Such usages can hardly justify the notion that *paralambanō* is always "a good word." Contextually, *airō* and *paralambanō* are equivalent within the Olivet Discourse.

---

268 Reese, *Approaching Advent*, pp. 214-15.
269 Ibid., p. 215.

Futuristic Posttribulationism (George Ladd)

The futuristic view is the form of posttribulationism advocated by George Eldon Ladd. Similar to Reese, Ladd demonstrated that the great tribulation is an eschatological event. His work, *The Blessed Hope,* is an adept defense of the posttribulationism. Ladd informed his readers, "The central thesis of this book is *the Blessed Hope is the second coming of Jesus Christ and not a pretribulation rapture.*"[270] Whereas classic posttribulationism, and some semiclassic posttribulationists, could embrace the doctrine of imminency, Ladd (similar to Reese) believed in a literal seven-year tribulation as fulfillment of the 70th week in Daniel 9:27. Since he believed the rapture and second coming occur at the end of the tribulation, it was not possible for Ladd to teach an imminent return of Christ. The return of Christ can only occur subsequent to the 70th week prophecy being fulfilled in a seven-year eschatological tribulation.

Some aspects of Ladd's eschatology are similar to covenant theology. For instance, he believed the covenantal promises in the Old Testament to Israel would be fulfilled not only by Israel, but also by the church. However, he differed from covenant theology in teaching the great tribulation and major aspects of the book of Revelation are still future. Ladd attributed the rise in futurist interpretation of Bible prophecy to John Nelson Darby and the Plymouth fellowship,[271] and adamantly rejected any dispensational interpretation.[272] He ignored the primary reason for a return to futurism as the restoration of a literal method of interpretation.

A significant argument that Ladd employed was that posttribulationism is the orthodox position of the church throughout the centuries. He devoted two chapters to the history of posttribulationism, but it should be noted that his view of a literal eschatological tribulation is unique to the history of the

---

270   Ladd, *Blessed Hope*, p. 11.
271   Ibid., pp. 40-41.
272   Ibid., pp. 130-36.

doctrine. Furthermore, he never addressed imminency as a common teaching among the early church. A puzzling aspect of Ladd's work is why he subtitled it, "A Biblical Study of the Second Advent and the Rapture," yet one-third of his "Biblical study" was devoted to historical arguments for posttribulationism.

Vocabulary of the Blessed Hope

Although written by an Adventist, the following quote could just as easily have been written by Ladd. "So, the vocabulary of the Blessed Hope provides no basis whatsoever for a two-phase distinction of Christ's return. Its terms are used interchangeably to describe a single, indivisible, post-tribulational advent of Christ to bring salvation to believers and retribution to unbelievers."[273] Ladd's argument of the vocabulary attempted to render *parousia* ("coming"), *apokalupsis* ("revelation") and *epiphaneia* ("appearance") as technical terms that must always refer to one single coming of Christ at the end of the tribulation. However, there is no grammatical support that any of the three Greek words should be considered technical terms. Depending upon the context, the words can describe either the rapture or the second coming.

The first (and only) indication of the rapture in the gospels is John 14:1-3. The passage anticipated the birth of the church in Acts 2, so it could have occurred at any moment. The passage is an intimate description, since the house is heaven, and there is no mention of judgment there. John 14:1-3 is similar to 1 Thessalonians 4:17, where the emphasis is upon being with Christ. Whereas there are many signs for the second coming of Christ in the Olivet Discourse and the book of Revelation, there are none for the rapture. The usage of same terms in the New Testament for the rapture and second coming does not prove they are the same event. Context will always determine which event the writer had in mind.

---

273 Samuele Bacchiocchi, "What the Bible Says About the Rapture," *Signs of the Times* Special Issue (2000): 10.

Dispensational Posttribulationism (Robert Gundry)

The fact that Robert Gundry denied the doctrine of imminency makes his eschatological beliefs similar to the other three posttribulational systems already examined. However, the uniqueness of his posttribulationism is that Gundry interpreted prophetic passages with an entirely original methodology than previous posttribulationists. His eschatology, as presented in *The Church and the Tribulation*, is based on a threefold thesis.

> (1) direct, unquestioned statements of Scripture that Jesus Christ will return after the tribulation and that the first resurrection will occur after the tribulation, coupled with the absence of statements placing similar events before the tribulation, making it natural to place the rapture of the Church after the tribulation; (2) the theological and exegetical grounds for pretribulationism rest on insufficient evidence, *non sequitur* reasoning, and faulty exegesis; (3) positive indications of a posttribulational rapture arise out of a proper exegesis of relevant Scripture passages and derive support from the history of the doctrine.[274]

Although Gundry listed the above threefold thesis as the basis of his view, there are other aspects of his posttribulationism which need appraisal in critiquing his eschatological system. Gundry considered himself a dispensationalist, but he distinguished Israel and the church in a manner that is entirely original. Even though Gundry employed a typical posttribulational response, his premise concerning Israel and the church differentiates his argument significantly from other posttribulationists.

---

274 Gundry, *Church and the Tribulation*, p. 10.

CHAPTER 10

PROPHETIC TIMING
AND THE RAPTURE:
POSTTRIBULATIONISM, PART II

T he first part of the emphasis upon posttribulationism critiqued and explained three variations of posttribulationism: classic, semiclassic and futuristic. Part two of this concentration will provide an extended critique and discussion of dispensational posttribulationism, which is an entirely unique (but persuasive) doctrine. The view was articulated first by Robert H. Gundry in *The Church and the Tribulation* (1970). The importance of understanding the distinctive features of Gundry's eschatology is due to his use of arguments that have never been employed in defense of posttribulationism.

DISTINCTIVE FEATURES OF GUNDRY'S ESCHATOLOGY

Gundry is a respected New Testament scholar, who is scholar-in-residence at Westmont College in Santa Barbara, Calif. Several decades ago, Gundry's resignation from the Evangelical Theological Society was demanded in response to his enthusiastic use of redaction criticism (and his use of the Jewish literary genre called *midrash*). Assuming the validity of posttribulationism, he has presented basic premises in his works in such a manner that only his view could be correct. Gundry has several fundamental aspects of his arguments in defense of dispensational posttribulationism.

The Doctrine of Imminence

Gundry's *first* premise was to redefine the doctrine of imminence. He wrote:

> We should first of all note a lack of identity between belief in imminence on the one hand and pretribulationism on the other. By common consent imminence means that so far as we know no predicted event will *necessarily* precede the coming of Christ. The concept incorporates three essential elements: suddenness, unexpectedness or incalculability, and a possibility of occurrence at any moment. But these elements would require only that Christ *might* come before the tribulation, not that He must. Imminence would only raise the possibility of pretribulationism on a sliding scale with mid- and posttribulationism.[275]

The problem with Gundry's definition of imminence is the two words "necessarily" and "possibility."[276] According to Gundry, imminence

---

275   Robert H. Gundry, *The Church and the Tribulation* (Grand Rapids: Zondervan, 1973), p. 29.

276   Gundry attempted to offer an alternative definition of imminence that, in essence, argued against the rapture as an imminent (hence pretribulational) event, but still he sought to describe the

means that Christ will return "at any moment" subsequent to the tribulation. Jesus declared, "But of that day and hour no one knows, not even the angels of heaven, nor the Son, but the Father alone" (Matt. 24:36).[277] Gundry had to reinterpret this verse to mean, "The element of uncertainty is there, but it is slight."[278] Believers will know the approximate time, not the exact time of Christ's return. "The shortening of the tribulation thus enables us to resolve general predictability and specific unpredictability without rending the exhortations to watch from their posttribulational context and without minimizing the function of signaling events by resorting to the historical [preterist] view with its vagaries."[279] Even when such events occur, believers "shall not know exactly;" rather the attitude is to "know approximately." Imminence is redefined to "expectancy."[280]

coming of Christ as imminent. By limiting imminence to mean "belief in necessarily preceding events" prior to the Lord's return he only confuses issues. Basically, the definition that Gundry provided would only make posttribulationism correct. The attack upon the return of Christ as "not imminent, yet imminent" is hardly understandable. Gundry's argument against imminence is not uncommon among non-imminence writers. For instance, D. A. Carson's view of imminence is similar to Gundry because his definition can mean "at any moment" subsequent to the tribulation, or "at any time" but not "at any moment." Carson wrote, "The other problem concerns the meaning of the word 'imminent' itself as used in theological—especially evangelical—discussion. A dictionary defines it as 'impending': as applied to Christ's return, an 'imminent return of Christ' would then mean Christ's return was near, impending. Hardly anyone uses 'imminent' that way but understands it in a specialized, theological sense to mean 'at any time': 'the imminent return of Christ' then means Christ may return at any time. But the evangelical writers use the word divide on whether 'imminent' in the sense of 'at any time' should be pressed to mean 'at any second' or something looser such as 'at any period' or 'in any generation'" (D. A. Carson, "Matthew," in *The Expositor's Bible Commentary*, 12 vols., ed. Frank E. Gaebelein [Grand Rapids: Zondervan, 1984], 8:490).

277 Of course, if the rapture of the church is not even mentioned in the Olivet Discourse, and the prophecies of those chapters are teaching truths concerning the tribulation and second coming only, which culminate in the millennial kingdom, then Gundry's argument here is entirely meaningless.

278 Gundry, *Church and Tribulation*, p. 43.

279 Ibid.

280 The reasoning is similar to the pre-wrath rapture argument: "The Lord's coming is not imminent—any moment. It is expectant—it could happen in any generation" (Marvin J. Rosenthal, "The Church's Trojan Horse" [article online] [*Zion's Fire*, March-April 1997, <http://www.zion-shope.org/zionsfire/articles/trojan_horse.html>; Internet; accessed 13 June 2017.

Redefining the Tribulation

The *second* premise upon which Gundry bases his posttribulationism is the belief that the tribulation is the wrath of Satan, not the wrath of God. His argument is one of the most critical arguments that must be true for non-pretribulational systems. To prove his point, Gundry focused attention upon Divine wrath and the tribulation, and Revelation 3:10. Gundry believes Revelation 3:10 to teach that God will "preserve [believers] through" the tribulation. In the case of Gundry, this would mean, "preserve through" the seal and trumpet judgments, or Satanic wrath of the tribulation. Gundry wrote, "There is no difficulty for posttribulationism, however, when we properly understand τηρέω ἐκ [*tēreō ek*] as protection issuing in emission."[281]

The promise given to the church at Philadelphia was that Christ would keep them "from the hour of testing" (or "tribulation," cf. Matt. 13:21; Mark 4:17; Luke 8:13). The promise is noteworthy since many pretribulationalists refer to it. Although it is common to hear Revelation 3:10 cited as proof of a pretribulational rapture, there are problems with such references. However, such issues do not prove a posttribulational rapture. Robert Thomas explained:

> The statement does not refer directly to the rapture. What it guarantees is protection from the scene of the "hour of trial" while that hour is in progress. This effect of placing the faithful in Philadelphia (and hence, the faithful in all the churches; cf. 3:13) in a position of safety presupposes that they will have been removed to another location (i.e., heaven) at the period's beginning.[282]

The best understanding of Revelation 3:10 is to understand it as promising the church in Philadelphia a first-century deliverance from the tribulation period, but also extending that promise in a general manner to

---

281   Gundry, *Church and Tribulation*, p. 59.
282   Robert Thomas, *Revelation 1—7* (Chicago: Moody Press, 1992), p. 288.

the church throughout the centuries (cf. Rev. 3:13). Thomas was correct that the passage does not *directly* teach the pretribulational rapture. However, this is not to say that the passage does not relate to the rapture of the church. Walvoord stated accurately, "If the rapture had occurred in the first century preceding the tribulation which the book of Revelation described, they were assured of deliverance."[283]

The phrase kept "from the hour of temptation" is significant for several reasons. For instance, *hōras* ["hour"] designates deliverance not only from the "trial" but also deliverance from the period of time in which the trial exists. Ryrie commented, "In the Septuagint translation the *ek* ["from"] indicates an external, not internal preservation. *Ek* also is used in the same way of external protection in Joshua 2:13 and in Psalm 33:19; 56:13."[284] If the author of Revelation had intended to teach preservation through (rather than from) the tribulation, the correct grammar would be to use the Greek preposition *en* ("in"). Significantly, John stated, *ek tēs hōras* (ἐκ τῆς ὥρας). Gundry wrote, "First, if ἐκ [*ek*] ever occurs without the thought of emergence, it does so very exceptionally. This fact incapacitates Revelation 3:10 as a *proof*-text for pretribulationism."[285]

Indeed, the issue concerning the temporal force of *ek* is repeated often as a posttribulational argument. Gundry contended that the preposition *ek* must mean emergence. Gundry asserted his argument as follows: "Ἐν [*en*] would have placed all the emphasis on presence within. Διά [*dia*, "through"] would have distributed the emphasis between entrance, presence within, and emergence. As it is, ἐκ [*ek*] lays all the emphasis on emergence, in this verse on the final, victorious outcome of the keeping-guarding."[286] Although he provided several reasons for his case of a posttribulational emergence in Revelation 3:10, the primary imposition of his

---

283 John Walvoord, *The Revelation of Jesus Christ* (Chicago: Moody Press, 1966), p. 87.
284 Charles Ryrie, *Come Quickly, Lord Jesus* (Eugene, OR: Harvest House, 1996), p. 133.
285 Ibid., p. 56.
286 Ibid., p. 57.

view is a twofold grammatical argument. Gundry wrote, "Essentially, ἐκ [*ek*], a preposition of motion concerning thought or physical direction, means *out from within*."[287] Two pages later, he wrote, "the preposition ἐκ [*ek*] appears in John's writings approximately 336 times, far more often than in the writings of any other NT author. There is not a single instance where the primary thought of emergence, or origin, cannot fit, indeed, does not best fit the thought of the context."[288]

Gundry has disregarded the collective thought of the entire semantic structure by making the usage of *ek* the nucleus of his attention. His limited semantic consideration of *ek* is evident in the statement that it is essentially "a preposition of motion concerning thought or physical direction."[289] Gundry's statement is correct generally; *however*, if ἐκ [*ek*] is used in relationship to a noun or if it is controlled by a verb that does not contain motion, then the preposition would be governed by a non-motion verb (e.g., τηρέω [*tēreō*, "to keep"] in Rev. 3:10); it will not essentially indicate motion. The problem is that Gundry accepted a far too simplistic view of ek without giving complete attention of the connection to τηρέω (which does not contain motion). His analysis of *ek* is used in separation of its verb.

As a matter of example, the preposition *eis* ("into") is the spatial opposite of *ek*. In his section of "Motion, State, Prepositions, and Verbs," Wallace wrote, "εἰς [*eis*] generally has the meaning of movement *into from without*. However, when it is used with a stative verb, such as τηρέω [*tēreō*, 'to keep'], κάθημαι [*kathēmai*, 'to sit'], εἰμι [*eimi*, 'I am'], etc., the idea of *motion* is negated by the stative nature of the verb [cf., e.g., τηρέω εἰς [*tēreō eis*, 'kept in'] in Acts 25:4; κάθημαι εἰς [*kathēmai eis*, 'sitting on'] in Mark 13:3. . . . *Stative verbs override the transitive force of prepositions.*

---

287 Ibid., p. 55.
288 Ibid., p. 57.
289 Ibid., p. 55.

Almost always, when a stative verb is used with a transitive preposition, the preposition's natural force is neutralized; all that remains is a stative idea."[290]

The point is that a non-motion verb, such as τηρέω, used with *ek* in Revelation 3:10 truly argues in opposition to Gundry's posttribulationism. However, even if a motion verb, such as *sōzō* ("to save"), were used with *ek* in Revelation 3:10 this usage still would not prove Gundry's position because it cannot be said that *ek* means emergence "*out from within*" definitely.[291] If the Apostle John meant to teach a posttribulational rapture, he would have used a motion verb rather than a stative verb or he would have changed the usage of *ek* to *en* ("in") or *dia* ("through") (with genitive). The stative verb, *tēreō*, used with *ek* indicates that the individuals addressed in Revelation 3:10 will be kept "out of, from" *the hour of testing*. In other words, the promise includes exclusion not only "out of, from" the hour, but also "into" the hour.

The individuals addressed will be in a state that is "out of, from" *the hour of testing*. Gundry's argument that every Johannine usage of *ek* is a primary meaning of emergence, or origin, is far too myopic. Indeed, the normal usage of *ek* conveys the thought of emergence. However, Gundry's assertion that this meaning is the primary meaning in every Johannine passage is an overstatement.[292] Robertson provided six usages of *ek* as follows (all of which are Johannine usage): (1) to designate place; (2) to designate time; (3) to designate separation; (4) to designate origin or source; (5) to designate cause or occasion; and, (6) to designate partitive usage.[293]

Even if Gundry were correct with regard to the usage of *ek*, his argument would still be of no consequence to the interpretation of Revelation 3:10.

---

290   Daniel B. Wallace, *Greek Grammar Beyond the Basics* (Grand Rapids: Zondervan, 1996), p. 359.

291   Second Corinthians 1:10 is a good example. The motion verb, *rhuomai*, is used with *ek*, and refers to God's deliverance of Paul from death.

292   See John 9:24; Revelation 2:10; 3:9; John Beverage, "The Preposition jEk in Johannine Literature," Th.M. thesis, Dallas Theological Seminary, 1953; Ludwig Radermacher, *Neutestamentliche Grammatik*, 2nd ed. (1911; reprint, Tübingen: Mohr, 1925).

293   A. T. Robertson, *A Grammar of the Greek New Testament in the Light of Historical Research* (Nashville: Broadman Press, 1934), pp. 596-99.

For Gundry's statement to be correct, several other factors would also have to be true. If *ek* is to mean "emergence" then the church in Philadelphia must be placed into the reach of "the hour of testing" prior to Christ removing them from that period. Gundry's view is that Christ will preserve the church within the tribulation before He removes them from "the hour of testing." For Gundry to maintain his position of emergence ("out from within"), he would have to believe some rather extreme events must occur. For instance, at some future period, Christ will resurrect the first-century church at Philadelphia, which have long since died, and place them into the tribulation for the purpose of bringing them *out from within* "the hour of testing." Indeed, the pretribulational view is consistent with the grammar. The promise of Revelation 3:10 is that every generation of the church, including the church at Philadelphia, will be kept "out of, from" the reach of the tribulation.

The Day of the Lord

Gundry's basic argument concerning the Day of the Lord is that it will begin at the battle of Armageddon when God outpours his wrath upon the unsaved and raptures the saints.[294] The Old Testament teaches that there would be a time of wrath in the future prior to Israel turning to faith in the Messiah, and God upholding her to a place of glory in the world. Deuteronomy 4:30 said that when Israel was in tribulation even "in the latter days," that she would turn to God and be obedient unto the Lord's voice. The word "distress" or "tribulation" is the same as that used by Zephaniah. The prophet spoke of the period as a time of God's wrath.

> A day of wrath is that day,
> A day of trouble and distress,
> A day of destruction and desolation,
> A day of darkness and gloom,

---

294 Gundry, *Church and the Tribulation*, p. 94-95.

A day of clouds and thick darkness.

Neither their silver nor their gold
Will be able to deliver them
On the day of the LORD's wrath;
And all the earth will be devoured
In the fire of His jealousy,
For He will make a complete end,
Indeed a terrifying one,
Of all the inhabitants of the earth. (Zeph. 1:15, 18)

Jesus described the last three-and-one-half years of this period as "great tribulation, such as has not occurred since the beginning of the world until now, nor ever will" (Matt. 24:21). Daniel called it "a time of distress such as never occurred since there was a nation until that time" (12:1b). The same Hebrew word (*tsārāh*) that contains the concept of tribulation or trouble is used for both Daniel's description and the Day of the Lord in Zephaniah 1:15.

The New Testament equivalent of "trouble" and "tribulation" (*tsar* and *tsārāh*) is the Greek word *thlipsis*, which is translated "wrath" or "tribulation" in 1 Thessalonians 1:10. Isaiah called the Day of the Lord the time of the Lord's strange work, which means it is an alien or foreign deed because it is God's wrath against His people (Isa. 28:21). The suffering will ultimately end in deliverance though. The deliverance is compared to "birth pangs" which birthed (brought) deliverance at the end of a process (Isa. 21:3; 26:17-18; 66:7; Jer. 4:31; 30:6; Mic. 4:10). The concept of "birth pangs" bringing forth what was promised is familiar in Matthew and Mark's gospel.[295] Joel (2:1-2, 11) also identifies the Day of the Lord as a time of judgment. Jeremiah referred to the Day of the Lord, or tribulation, as "the time of Jacob's distress" (30:7). Paul associated the period of the tribulation with "the day of wrath and revelation of the righteous judgment of God" (Rom. 2:5; cf. 2:6-9).

---

295   J. Randall Price, "Old Testament Tribulation Terms" in *When the Trumpet Sounds*, eds. Thomas Ice and Timothy Demy (Eugene, OR: Harvest House, 1995), p. 61.

The Reward of Believers and Great White Throne Judgment

Another of Gundry's arguments was to equate "the reward of believers with the second coming."[296] The simple manner to answer this proposition is that the church is already adorned in robes in order to descend with Christ at His return to earth (Rev. 3:5, 18; 19:8). The rewarding of believers would have to occur somewhere between the rapture and the second coming, which should be understood as the judgment seat of Christ (cf. Rom. 14:10; 1 Cor. 3:10-15; 2 Cor. 5:10). When "the armies which are in heaven" (Rev. 19:14) follow Christ, they are adorned as Christ's bride "clothed in fine linen." Jude 23 exhorts the church to hate "even the garment polluted by the flesh." The emphasis is upon motivation and the excellence of things done in the body. The passage refers not to the righteousness of Jesus Christ with which believers are clothed for salvation (Isa. 61:10). The garments mentioned are those of good works (fruitfulness) in the life of a Christian who has persevered with a profitable result. Just as rewards may be gained, there may also be loss of rewards to the Christian's shame when Christ returns for His church in the rapture (1 Cor. 3:11-16; 4:1-5; 9:24-27; Tit. 3:8; 1 John 2:28; 2 John 1:8). Following the judgment seat of Christ will be the marriage of the Lamb, and this event will occur in heaven prior to the second coming of Christ to earth and subsequent to the rapture of the church, as this is apparent in Revelation 19:7 ("His bride has made herself ready"). John the Baptist declared, "He who has the bride is the bridegroom" (John 3:29). The bride "has made herself ready," which is apparent by the "fine linen" of good works.

---

296   Gundry, *Church and the Tribulation*, p. 169.

Inadequate Application of the Olivet Discourse

As already stated, Gundry rejected the imminency of the rapture by equating it with the second coming of Jesus Christ. He demanded that the three essential elements of possibility, suddenness and unexpectedness of a prophetic event at any moment ought to occur simultaneously in a Biblical passage for an event to be imminent. Gundry contended that the words for expectancy alone would not resolve questions of imminence (or non-imminence) so that the contexts are the deciding factor.

Concerning admonitions to watch, he wrote, "The phraseology [of watchfulness] and the parables are almost identical to those in the Olivet Discourse. . . . The strongest and most extensive warnings to watch in the entire NT appear in the Olivet Discourse (Matt. 24:32-25:30; Mark 13:28-37; Luke 21:28-36)."[297] Rejecting the distinctive Jewish nature of the Olivet Discourse, Gundry believed that it is primarily applicable to the church. He wrote, "There Jesus gives not the slightest hint of a pretribulational rapture in the chronological outline of events which occupies the first section of His discourse. Yet a very full description of the posttribulational Parousia forms the climax."[298] While one can agree with the statement that there is no mention of a pretribulational rapture in the Olivet Discourse and a posttribulational coming of Christ to earth "forms the climax," Gundry assumed that an imminent coming prior to the tribulation is not possible since the same admonitions to watch in the epistles are similar to those in the Olivet Discourse. Similarities of admonition for the rapture and the second coming do not prove sameness.

---

297   Ibid., p. 33.
298   Ibid., pp. 33-34.

Entering the Millennium

A major problem for posttribulationists is who will enter the millennium, since they equate the rapture with the second coming. If the rapture occurs at the end of the tribulation then all believers will receive glorified bodies prior to Christ ever setting foot on Earth. In this scenario, there will be no believers on the Earth, but unbelievers only. The unbelievers certainly will not enter the millennium, which means there will be no believers to enter the millennium in their natural bodies. Since there are no people to enter the millennium in natural bodies then no one will be capable of procreation, which means there would be no unbelieving offspring to participate in the final rebellion at the end of the millennium. If the judgment was at the beginning of the millennium, this would not serve a purpose either since the sheep and goats would have already been separated in the rapture. Douglas Moo admitted the problem "that a posttribulational scheme cannot explain how nonglorified individuals enter the Millennium." He continued, "I find this argument the most difficult to handle—not only because the argument presents a difficulty for the posttribulational view, but also because the relevant evidence is both sparse and complex."[299] The problem does not only corroborate pretribulationism, since even Gleason Archer used this argument in favor of a midtribulational rapture.[300]

Gundry attempted to solve the problem by moving the sheep and goat judgment to the end of the millennium.[301] With this shift, unbelievers can enter the millennium with natural bodies. The proposal does not provide any solutions to the posttribulational system; rather, it brings more problems. For instance, Matthew 25:35-40 commends those who minister to "these brothers

---

299   Douglas J. Moo, "Response," in *The Rapture: Pre-, Mid-, or Post-Tribulational*, ed. Richard R. Reiter (Grand Rapids: Zondervan, 1984), p. 161.

300   Gleason A. Archer, "Mid-Seventieth-Week Rapture," in ibid., pp. 120-22.

301   Gundry, *Church and the Tribulation*, p. 166.

of Mine" (the Jews) when they were "hungry . . . thirsty . . . naked . . . [and] in prison." The actions would certainly be an odd experience for the Jews during the millennium since Isaiah (60:5-7, 11, 13-17) prophesied that the Gentiles will bring "the wealth of the nations" to Israel. Furthermore, Matthew 25:31 states that this judgment will occur "when the Son of Man comes in His glory," which is an obvious reference to the second coming at the beginning of the millennium.

Gundry assumed he solved the problem by allowing unbelieving Jews to enter the kingdom in natural bodies. "Thus, the 144,000 will include both men and women who will populate and replenish the millennial kingdom of Israel."[302] He believes the 144,000 will be unbelievers (orthodox Jews) and "the reason for their sealing" is for "special protection from the wrath of God and the persecution of the Antichrist."[303] When Christ returns to earth, the 144,000 will be saved in order to enter the millennium in their natural bodies and will father children in the millennium. Contrary to Gundry's position, Revelation 7:3 states that the 144,000 are "the bond-servants of our God." Revelation 14:4 adds even more conspicuous details that make it impossible for the 144,000 to be unbelievers ("These are the one who have not been defiled with women, for they have kept themselves chaste. These *are* the ones who follow the Lamb wherever He goes. These have been purchased from among men as first fruits to God and to the Lamb"). Since it is obvious that the 144,000 are believers, they would then experience the supposed posttribulational rapture, which would subsequently provide them with glorified bodies and make it impossible for them to father children.

Posttribulational Rapture

Scripture declares that the instantaneous change at the rapture will occur "at the last trumpet" (*en tē eschatē salpingi*; 1 Cor. 15:52). The

---

302 Ibid., p. 82.
303 Ibid., pp. 82-83.

only indication of time regarding this translation is "at the last trumpet." Interestingly, the Jewish understanding regarding the last trumpet is that it will be seventh in a series of trumpet blows, resulting in the dead being raised and clothed with immortality in order to stand before the "Throne of Glory."

> In the future the Holy One, blessed be He, will resurrect the dead. How will He do it? He takes the Great Shofar and blows it seven times. At the first blast, the whole world shakes and suffers pangs like a woman in childbirth. At the second, the dust is scattered and the graves open. At the third, the bones gather together. At the fourth, the limbs are stretched out. At the fifth, skin comes into being. At the sixth, spirits and souls enter the bodies. At the seventh, they live and stand up on their feet in their clothes [Rabbi Akiba, *Pesiqta Hadta, BhM* 6:58].[304]

The noun "trumpet" (*salpingi*) is used 11 times in the New Testament (Matt. 24:31; 1 Cor. 14:8; 15:52; 1 Thess. 4:16; Heb. 12:19; Rev. 1:10; 4:1; 8:2, 6, 13; 9:14) and the verb "to sound a trumpet" (*salpizō*) is used twelve times in the New Testament (Matt. 6:2; 1 Cor. 15:52; Rev. 8:6, 7, 8, 10, 12, 13; 9:1, 13; 10:7; 11:15). The four noun usages and 10 verb usages in Revelation 8—11 are in reference to the seven trumpet judgments of the tribulation. The noun usage in Matthew 24:31 is in reference to a great sound of the trumpet subsequent to Christ's coming in the clouds at the end of "the tribulation of those days." The trumpet mentioned in the Olivet Discourse gathers the elect who have survived the tribulation and have been scattered throughout the Earth as a result of the horrors of the tribulation period. In the previously mentioned passages (Matt. 24:31; Rev. 8—11), there is no mention of translation or resurrection in connection with the trumpets. First Corinthians 15:52 and 1 Thessalonians 4:16, conversely, do not have any reference to judgment; rather, they refer to the resurrection and translation, which proves an obvious dissimilarity.

304   As quoted in Raphael Patai, *The Messiah Texts* (Detroit: Wayne State University Press, 1979), p. 203.

First Thessalonians 4:16 emphasizes the "trumpet of God" that would seem to be equated logically with the "last trumpet" in 1 Corinthians 15:52. Both passages are in reference to the resurrection of believers who are united in Christ Jesus. The purpose of this coming of Christ is not to judge and then reign, but rather for the Lord Jesus to meet His saints in the air and to have them "changed" (1 Cor. 15:51). Therefore, it is perfectly logical to understand that this last trumpet is referring to the end of the dispensation of the church. The trumpet would be best identified as referring to the rapture of the church prior to the tribulation, since the trumpets mentioned in the tribulation relate to the coming of Christ in judgment to establish His visible kingdom on Earth.

Some equate the "last trumpet" with the seventh trumpet in Revelation 11:15 and the trumpet in the Olivet Discourse (Matt. 24:29-31). One of the arguments given by posttribulationalists is that the resurrection passages make no reference to an earlier, separate resurrection of all believers, but place the resurrection of all believers at a point prior to the millennium (cf. 1 Cor. 15:23-24; Rev. 20:1-4). The simplest explanation is that this is because the rapture of the church is "a mystery" (1 Cor. 15:51). In the New Testament, the sense of "mystery" is that of a doctrine not revealed in the Old Testament (cf. Matt. 13:11; Mark 4:11; Luke 8:10; Rom. 11:25; 16:25-27; 1 Cor. 2:1, 7; 4:1; 13:2; 14:2; Eph. 1:9-10; 3:1-12; 5:22-33; 6:19-20; Col. 1:24-29; 2:2-3; 4:3; 2 Thess. 2:7; 1 Tim. 3:9, 16; Rev. 1:20; 10:7; 17:5, 7). The second coming was not "a "mystery" (something unrevealed in the Old Testament); therefore, the rapture and the second coming are distinguished in Scripture.

Gundry determinedly believes the last trumpet of 1 Corinthians "might have looked back to the trumpet at the end of the age in the oral tradition of Jesus' discourse on the Mount of Olives." According to Gundry, "the superintendence of the Holy Spirit would have brought about a harmony of meaning" between the trumpet references in the Olivet

Discourse, 1 Corinthians 15:52, and the seven trumpets of Revelation.[305] Certainly, it is theoretically possible that the last trumpet of 1 Corinthians 15 could later be connected with the seven trumpets of Revelation. God does, indeed, reveal things progressively.

The problem in arguing that God associated the last trumpet of 1 Corinthians with later revelation has to do with the context. The Corinthians would have understood Paul as speaking in regards to an imminent return ("in a moment, in the twinkling of an eye") of their Lord "at the last trumpet." There is nothing in the context of 1 Corinthians that would indicate a time of intense tribulation upon the whole world that would precede the return of their Lord. Posttribulationalists interpret the passage by forcing the content of Revelation into what is apparently a rapture passage. The interpretation of the last trumpet in 1 Corinthians would be changed by the later revelation of the seventh trumpet in Revelation.

The issue concerns whether or not "last" is limited only to a given chronological sequence. The usage of the word "last" is not limited to the last in a particular sequential progression; it can also refer to the end of a specific period (age, epoch or dispensation).[306] Therefore, "last" can refer to the end of something chronologically, as in the seven trumpets of Revelation, or to the end of a specific period (i.e., the dispensation of the church). Gerald Stanton rightly stated, "the fact of subsequent trumpets is no problem" for a pretribulational interpretation of 1 Corinthians 15:52.[307] Even amillennialist Barnes noted, "The word 'last' here does not imply that any trumpet shall have been before sounded at the resurrection, but is a word denoting that this is the consummation or close of things; it will end the economy of this world; it will be connected with the last state of things."[308] Although God's purposes for Israel and the church are distinct, both appear to end

---

305 Gundry, *Church and the Tribulation*, pp. 149-50.

306 J. Dwight Pentecost, *Things to Come* (Grand Rapids: Zondervan, 1964), p. 189.

307 Gerald B. Stanton, *Kept from the Hour* (Miami Springs: Schoettle Publishing, 1991), pp. 194-95.

308 Albert Barnes, *Notes on the First Epistle to the Corinthians* (London: Gall & Inglis, 1847), p. 386.

with the sounding of a trumpet; these trumpets, however, are not identical. The "last trumpet" of 1 Corinthians 15:52 is not a reference to the last in any preceding sequence, but is related to the end of a specific age, namely, the dispensation of the church.

The significance of the "last trumpet" in verse 15:52 may be twofold. *First*, the "last trumpet" may be a technical phrase denoting the end of the dispensation of the church. The word "last" is quite common when referring to events surrounding the end of the church age (Acts 2:17; 2 Tim. 3:1-5; Heb. 1:1; Jas. 5:3; 1 Pet. 1:5, 20; 1 John 2:18; Jude 18). *Second*, "last trumpet" may also be a technical phrase indicating the gathering together of the church. E. Schuyler English noted that the sounding of a trumpet in Numbers 10 was to gather an assembly of the people. Therefore, "last trumpet" would be a "rallying call" indicating that the church is changing locations, much like Israel changed camps in the wilderness (1 Cor. 15:23).[309] The resurrection of Christ made Him the "first fruits," that is, the first resurrected from the dead. Christ's resurrection is the firstfruits of many to be raised. Consequently, "those who are Christ's at His coming" can be divided into four groups: (1) the resurrection of church age saints ("the dead in Christ" and those "who are alive and remain") at the rapture (1 Thess. 4:16-17); (2) the resurrection of all martyred (Jewish and Gentile) tribulation saints in connection with the second coming (Rev. 20:4); (3) the resurrection of Old Testament (Jewish and Gentile) saints in correlation with the second coming (Dan. 12:2; Isa. 26:19); and, (4) the resurrection of all millennial believers subsequent to that period (Rev. 20:5).

CONCLUSION

In contrast to other rapture views, pretribulationism is the only teaching consistent with the doctrine of imminence. Posttribulationism

---

309   E. Schuyler English, *Re-Thinking the Rapture* (Neptune, NJ: Loizeaux Brothers, 1954), p. 109.

must deny that doctrine for a multitude of signs (in that scheme) must occur for the Lord to return. Scripture abounds with prophecies concerning the necessity to purge the nation of Israel in preparation for Messiah's return and the establishment of His kingdom. As the Bible distinguishes Israel and the church, the prophecies revealing tribulation for Israel cannot be forced to teach that the church will also experience the tribulation. Consequently, the examination of the four prevailing varieties of posttribulationism has demonstrated that the essential characteristics of the view are contrary to the Biblical revelation.

CHAPTER 11

PROPHETIC TIMING AND THE RAPTURE: PRETRIBULATIONISM, PART I

P retribulationism is the belief that the rapture of the church occurs prior to the commencement of the seven-year tribulation. The rapture will result in church saints receiving glorified bodies—the living through translation and the deceased through resurrection—and forever being with the Lord Jesus Christ. Since amillennialists and postmillennialists regard the coming of Christ as a single event that will culminate in a general resurrection and judgment, the issue of the timing of the rapture in relation to the tribulation is a premillennial concern.

Within the gospels, the only mention of the rapture is John 14:1-3. By contrast, there are several references to the second coming in the gospels.[310] The rapture is a prophesied event for the church only. Logically, then, the Old Testament does not reveal the rapture because this is an event for the church. Christ first gave the promise of the rapture in the New Testament. However, the Old Testament promised the coming of Messiah to earth as the sovereign King. The epistles primarily emphasize the rapture. The gospels emphasize the second coming. Christ's disciples expected fulfillment of the Old Testament prophecies of Messiah, who will reign on David's throne in Jerusalem. The gospels would logically and contextually emphasize Christ's coming to national Israel for the purpose of fulfilling the covenantal promises and establishing His earthly kingdom. The church was a mystery "hidden from the *past* ages and generations" (Col. 1:26) and, therefore, the rapture of the church was also a mystery (1 Cor. 15:51-54).

Distinct Prophetic Emphases

OLD TESTAMENT	GOSPELS	EPISTLES	REVELATION
Millennial Reign	Second Coming	Rapture	Tribulation

The mystery concerning the resurrection of church saints is that some would not die (1 Cor. 15:51). All church saints will receive glorified bodies either by translation of the living or resurrection of the deceased at the coming of Christ. A mystery is a truth that had not been previously revealed by God; it is not something that God intended to withhold as a secret; rather, in due course of time God revealed something previously unknown

---

310 The author presented a paper entitled "Consistent Pretribulationism and Jewish Questions of the End" at the annual meeting of the Pre-Trib Study Group, Dallas, Texas, 11 December 2002, which argued that the rapture of the church is not within the context of the Olivet Discourse. A rough draft of the paper is available at http://www.pre-trib.org/article-view.php?id=121. The final draft of the paper was published as "The Olivet Discourse: A Resolution of Time," *Chafer Theological Seminary Journal* 9 (Spring 2003): 106-40.

(e.g., the rapture). There are various "mysteries" revealed in Scripture so that the idea itself is frequent.

Scripture refers to the mystery of the kingdom of heaven or kingdom of God (Matt. 13). Paul used the Greek word *mustērion* ("mystery") 20 times. According to 1 Corinthians 15:51, there is a mystery regarding the resurrection and translation of church saints (cf. 1 Thess. 4:14-17). The mystery of the church as being composed of both Jew and Gentile in equality was a mystery (Eph. 3:1-11). The incarnation was a mystery (1 Cor. 2:7; Col. 2:2, 9). Second Thessalonians 2:7 refers to the mystery of lawlessness. Israel's present blindness is a mystery (Rom. 11:25). The book of Revelation refers to the mystery of the seven stars (1:20) and of the harlot (17:5, 7). Scripture even refers to the mystery of "Christ in you, the hope of glory" (Col. 1:27). Regarding the use of *mustērion* in 1 Corinthians 15, amillennial commentator Albert Barnes noted:

> The word here does not mean anything which was in its nature unintelligible, but that which to them had been hitherto un-known. This commences the *third* subject of inquiry in this chap-ter—the question, what will become of those who are alive when the Lord Jesus shall return to raise the dead? This was an *obvious* inquiry, and the answer was, perhaps, supposed to be difficult, and says that they will undergo an instantaneous change, which will make them like the dead that shall be raised.[311]

The mystery that Paul communicated in 1 Corinthians 15 is "we will not all sleep" (i.e., die). The Greek there is the future passive indica-tive, *koimēthēsometha*, which means that believers "will not all sleep" in the future. In other words, some believers shall not die physically prior to the eschatological resurrection of the saints. When Paul wrote, "we will not all sleep" he was certainly referring to physical death.[312] The *mustērion* is that

---

311 Albert Barnes, *Notes on the First Epistle to the Corinthians* (London: Gall & Inglis, 1847), p. 383.

312 William F. Bauer, William F. Arndt, and F. Wilbur Gingrich, *A Greek-English Lexicon of the New Testament and Other Early Christian Literature*, 2nd ed., rev. F. Wilbur Gingrich and Frederick W.

when the resurrection occurs there will be believers who are still living. The use of the first person plural for "sleep" would mean that Paul included himself with those anticipating the possibility of being translated while living.[313] The apostle anticipated this resurrection as an imminent event that could occur in his own lifetime.[314]

Paul certainly expected the conclusion of his ministry would not be death but "the presence of our Lord Jesus at His coming" (1 Thess. 2:19); it is due to the fact that there were no events preceding this coming that Paul included himself as one who may experience the blessed event (cf. Tit. 2:13). Radmacher commented, "There may be delay, but there would be no necessary prophesied event before the coming of Christ for His church."[315] Morris would reply that this is an illegitimate conclusion: "The plain fact is that Paul did not know when these events would take place, and nowhere does he claim to know. When he says *we* he means 'we believers,' 'Christians alive at that day.'"[316] In response, if the passage could mean "Christians alive

---

Danker (Chicago: University of Chicago Press, 1979), p. 437.

313 For some who disagree regarding the possibility that Paul included himself as being alive at the resurrection, see Charles Hodge, *Commentary on the First Epistle to the Corinthians* (Grand Rapids: Eerdmans, 1980), pp. 354-55; and, A. T. Robertson, *Word Pictures in the New Testament*, 6 vols. (Nashville: Broadman, 1931; reprint, Grand Rapids: Baker, n.d.), 4:198.

314 How did Paul's expectation of the rapture as imminent affect the statement that Peter would "grow old" (John 21:18) and that Paul "must witness at Rome" (Acts 23:11)? God's promise to Peter may be regarded as a general description of his future (i.e., Peter could have died some time subsequent to the Lord's ascension and could be regarded as one grown old). Given the date for the composition of the gospel of John (A.D. 85-95), the prophecy would not have been circulated widely among the early church to dissuade belief in the imminency of the rapture. Secondly, by the time the book of James was composed, which may have been the first writing of the New Testament (it is possible that the gospel was written as early as A.D. 45, and therefore, the book of James was either the first or second book in the New Testament canon, since the gospel of Matthew was written approximately A.D. 45-55), Peter would have grown old in age and his death could be regarded as imminent. Moreover, understanding the progress of revelation, the doctrine of imminency was not revealed completely until the writing of the Pauline epistles (A.D. 48-64). The fulfillment of the prophecy concerning Paul's witness in Rome should be understood as probable if the Lord Jesus did not return sooner, as Christians today often say for something to be accomplished "if the Lord wills."

315 Earl Radmacher, "The Imminent Return of the Lord," in *Issues in Dispensationalism*, gen. ed. Wesley R. Willis and John R. Master (Chicago: Moody Press, 1994), p. 258.

316 Leon Morris, *1 Corinthians*, 2nd ed. (1958, 1985; reprint, Grand Rapids: Eerdmans, 1993), p. 227.

at that day" then this would include the Apostle Paul, which is the point. Without doubt, Paul regarded the imminent translation of living church saints as an incentive for holy living (1 Cor. 15:51; Phil. 3:20; 1 Thess. 4:17; Tit. 2:13) that could occur in his lifetime.

The other truth that Paul communicated to the Corinthians is "we will all be changed." Either a believer's body will be dead or living at the time of the resurrection (1 Thess. 4:13-18), but irrespective of the present state, all will be translated (changed).[317] The translation of church saints at the rapture answers Paul's preceding statement in verse 50: What will occur to believers who do not die prior to the resurrection? How shall they take part in the resurrection of the body? "Flesh and blood cannot inherit the kingdom of God," so there must be a transformation (1 Cor. 15:50; Phil. 3:21).

The transformation for some will be while they are still living; it must be stated that the doctrine of the resurrection of the body is not a mystery, since it was taught in the Old Testament (Job 14:14). The mystery truth is not all church saints will experience physical death. The resurrection *and* translation occurring for some still living is a mystery previously unknown. There will be a group of believers that will not experience the intermediate state, which follows physical death and precedes the resurrection of the body (2 Cor. 5:10).

---

317   Since Paul stated, "we will all be changed" (1 Cor. 15:51) and "God will bring with Him those who have fallen asleep in Jesus" (1 Thess. 4:14), such statements would negate partial rapturism (the belief that only "spiritual" Christians who are watching for the rapture will experience the event). Moreover, 1 Thessalonians 5:10 teaches that whether watching ("awake") or not watching ("asleep"), the rapture will be experienced by all church saints. (The Greek word translated "asleep" in 1 Thess. 5:6, 10 is different than the word for "asleep" in 1 Thess. 4:13-15. The former context is that of watchfulness, whereas the latter context is physical death.)

RAPTURE PASSAGES

John 14

The Lord God commanded the first man, Adam, "saying, 'From any tree of the garden you may eat freely; but from the tree of the knowledge of good and evil you shall not eat, for in the day that you eat from it you will surely die'" (Gen. 2:16-17).[318] Adam's disobedience[319] regarding God's prohibition resulted in the origin of death. God declared,

> For you are dust,
> And to dust you shall return. (3:19)

Not only would humanity experience physical death but also spiritual death (cf. 3:8-10, 21, 22-24). Even the "ground" was cursed because of Adam's sin, and therefore, death originated in the natural world at the time of his disobedience (3:17-18). As a consequence of the origin of death, the redeemed will experience "a resurrection of life," whereas those who are dead in trespasses and sins (Eph. 2:1) will experience "a resurrection of judgment" (John 5:29). The nature of the resurrection body for the redeemed is entirely different than that of those not redeemed by God (1 Cor. 15:35-49; Rev. 20:5-15).

The blessedness of the resurrection of life is well attested in Scripture. For instance, David exclaimed,

> With Your counsel You will guide me,
> And afterward receive me to glory. (Ps. 73:24)

---

318 The Hebrew verb form in Genesis 2:17 is the infinitive absolute, and to express emphasis it is used with the Qal imperfect, which would translate literally as "dying you shall die." (New Testament parallels of this idiom may be identified in Mark 4:41 and Luke 22:15.) Adam and Eve began to die physically the very moment that they disobeyed God (cf. Rom. 6:23). If they had not disobeyed, they would be living today upon the Earth and would have continued to live eternally. The grammar of Genesis 2:17 indicates that death was inevitable and does not refer to two aspects of death (i.e., spiritual death will culminate in physical death).

319 The conjunction and the Qal active participle in Genesis 3:5 indicates that there was never an instance in which Adam did not know the consequences of eating the forbidden fruit.

Even the book of Job, the oldest Biblical writing, references the doctrine of resurrection. Job inquired,

> If a man dies, will he live *again*?
> All the days of my struggle I will wait
> Until my change comes. (14:14)

Job anticipated a change of the condition of his body.[320] He rejoiced that upon death God would call and he would answer because the Creator "will long for" His creation (14:15). Job knew that because his "Redeemer lives" his "flesh" would "see God." The reality of resurrection caused Job to express the fainting of his heart (19:25-27). The blessedness of the resurrection of life instilled comfort and peace within Job:

> For I know that You will bring me to death
> And to the house of meeting for all living. (30:23)

Having been redeemed, Job anticipated receiving a resurrection body.

Resurrection is a fundamental doctrine of Scripture. The timing of the resurrection of life in relation to the return of Christ and specifically in relationship to His church will be the focus of these remaining chapters.[321] Passages such as John 14:1-3, Philippians 3:20-21, 1 Corinthians 15:23-58, 1 Thessalonians 4:13-18, 5:1-11 and 2 Thessalonians 2:1-12 (and an extended exegesis of the Olivet Discourse and Revelation 3:10) will be examined in relation to Christ's coming. The return of the Lord Jesus Christ resulting in the translation of living church saints and resurrection of dead church saints is called the rapture.[322] The issue is whether certain Biblical passages only teach the doctrine of blessed resurrection, and not the

---

320 C. F. Keil and Franz Delitzsch, *Commentary on the Old Testament*, 10 vols. (Edinburgh: T. & T. Clark, 1866-91; reprint, Peabody, MA: Hendrickson, 1996), 4:370.

321 The foundation and origin of the church indicates a holy calling distinct from Old Testament saints. For instance, see Ron J. Bigalke Jr., "God's Purpose for the Church – Part I," *Midnight Call* (February 2008): 16-23.

322 The Greek word for "caught up" in 1 Thessalonians 4:17 is ἁρπάζω (*harpazō*), which was translated as *rapiemur* in the Latin Vulgate. Depending upon the translation, the word "rapture" is specified in the Bible.

translation of *living* church saints and resurrection of *deceased* church saints prior to the beginning of the Day of the Lord.[323] The timing of the rapture in relation to the tribulation is, of course, relative only to premillennialism.

The Background of John 14

The gospel of John contains much narrative that is not contained in the synoptic gospels,[324] and serves as an invaluable supplement since John provided details and discourses of the ministry of Jesus (especially in Jerusalem and Judea) that would have otherwise been unavailable (thereby forming a fourfold gospel as opposed to four isolated works). The upper room discourse (John 13—17; cf. Matt. 26:20-30; Mark 14:17-26; Luke 22:14-30, 39) was given on Thursday of the Passion Week.[325] Whereas the Olivet Discourse (Matt. 24—25; Mark 13:1-37; Luke 21:5-36) given on Wednesday afternoon was focused upon the national future of Israel, this last of Christ's major discourses was focused upon addressing not only the state of the disciples but also other believers during the period of Jesus' absence[326] (John 13:33; 16:5-7).[327]

---

323 The "Day of the Lord" is primarily an Old Testament term referring to the seven years of tribulation (Daniel's 70th week); the term is never used in reference to the millennial kingdom. "That day" is an Old Testament term that may reference either the tribulation or millennium.

324 "Synoptic" (in reference to the gospel of Matthew, the gospel of Mark and the gospel of Luke) means "to represent the same point of view" or "to view together."

325 Later that evening, Jesus entered the garden of Gethsemane with His disciples where He suffered in agony (Matt. 26:36-46; Mark 14:32-42; Luke 22:39-46; John 18:1) and was betrayed and arrested (Matt. 26:47-56; Mark 14:43-52; Luke 22:47-53; John 18:2-12). He was also tried that day, first by Annas and later by Caiaphas (Matt. 26:57-75; Mark 14:53-72; Luke 22:54-65; John 18:13-27)

326 One could say the Olivet Discourse gave attention to the Old Testament, whereas the discourse in the upper room was given with attention to New Testament history and teaching that was then unwritten.

327 Some commentators believe Jesus delivered the discourse and intercessory prayer of John 15:1—18:1 after departing the upper room. Jesus' statement to "Get up, let us go from here" (John 14:31) may have simply expressed His intent to depart soon from the upper room and not the actual departure in Matthew 26:30; Mark 14:26; Luke 22:39; and John 18:1.

Comfort and Promise in John 14:1-3

On the night in which the specific events leading to His crucifixion would begin, Jesus was "troubled" in soul (John 12:27) and spirit (13:21). As the supreme servant, however, Jesus provided comfort and promise to His disciples who were "troubled" in heart (14:1). The disciples were not troubled because of *their* impending death but because they were confused regarding Jesus' references to *His* impending death and departure. In response, Jesus promised that for those who believe in Him, He will "go and prepare a place" for them in His "Father's house" that where He is, there they "may be also" (14:1-3). The disciples were not to let their hearts be troubled but to trust in God, which is related directly to trust in His Son (14:1). Jesus was telling His disciples to trust in Him the same as they trusted in the Father since His words and actions are those of God.

The reason why the disciples were to trust Jesus was due to His promise for them. In the context of the crucifixion, Jesus would indeed depart from them but He was going to prepare a place for them (14:2). Whereas there is general agreement concerning the interpretation of John 14:1-2, commentators disagree concerning Jesus' promise to "come again and receive" His disciples to be with Him (14:3). One interpretation is that Jesus was referring to coming again to His disciples to receive them after His resurrection. Although two resurrection appearances of Jesus could be called a coming again (John 20:19, 26), the comfort and promise of John 14:3 is related to an eternal dwelling place and that when Jesus does "come again and receive" His disciples it is permanent.

Another interpretation is that Jesus was referring to the coming of the Holy Spirit following His ascension and glorification. There is the promise of the coming of the Holy Spirit in John 14:18-20, which is evident by the structuring of verses 18-20 by two passages (14:16-17 and 14:25-26), but it is conjecture to think that the coming of the Holy Spirit is synonymous with the coming of Jesus in 14:3 (cf. 14:19-20; 16:16-30) because the coming of the Holy Spirit is conditioned upon Jesus' death and resurrection. The least possible interpretation is that the coming in 14:3 is a reference to the death of a Christian and Jesus receiving them into heaven. The death of Jesus is the only death in the context of the upper room discourse (not the Christian). Scripture does undoubtedly refer to the Christian *going* to be with the Lord (2 Cor. 5:1-8; cf. Luke 16:22; Acts 7:56).

The details of John 14:1-3 indicate that it is the rapture of the church when Jesus will "come again and receive" His own to be with Him forever. Of course, some commentators believe the coming in 14:3 is the coming of Christ in glory (at the end of the tribulation). For instance, posttribulationists interpret the coming in 14:3 as occurring at the end of the tribulation, which would mean believers are prevented from entering the Father's house since they return to Earth with Christ as He descends from heaven in glory. Such a view does not harmonize with the teaching that Christ will receive Christians when He comes again to take the believers to His Father's house.

Furthermore, if premillennialism is true, which this writer does believe Scripture to teach *unambiguously*, the Father's house would not be present upon the Earth in the millennial kingdom. Jesus is *currently* preparing the eternal dwelling place, which is likely the new Jerusalem that will descend from heaven to the new Earth, and will be the future and eternal dwelling place of the redeemed (Rev. 21:10-27). The departure to prepare the dwelling places is reason for coming again and receiving believers into His Father's house. The receiving of the believer is to heaven at the time of the coming in John 14:3, and not the time in which Christ descends to Earth with believers at the second coming.

John 14 introduces a new and distinctive revelation, as the promise is not something that any prophet promised or would have the ability to promise. There is no reference in John 14:1-3 to Messiah coming again and receiving His own into an earthly Jerusalem. The comfort and promise of the Lord Jesus Christ is to come again to receive His own into the Father's house where He abides presently. The Lord Jesus Christ promised, "I will come again and receive you to Myself," with no reference to the deliverance of the Jewish remnant, nor to His coming to establish His earthly kingdom reign upon the Earth. There is no reference in John 14:1-3 to Messiah judging the nations either, but only His coming for His own. The comfort and promise of John 14:1-3 is being with Jesus Christ in heaven, as the result of His coming again and receiving His own, which will result in the instantaneous glorification and resurrection of the body.

Philippians 3

According to Acts 16:11-40, the Apostle Paul visited Philippi on his second missionary journey. He traveled from the island of Samothrace to Neapolis (modern Kavalla), which was the seaport utilized by the Philippian residents. The city of Philippi was approximately nine miles northwest of the seaport. The city was named in honor of King Philip II of Macedonia (the father of Alexander the Great). Philippi became a Roman military colony in 42 B.C., following the defeat of Brutus and Cassius in battle by the triumvirs (Antony, Lepidus and Octavian). The citizens benefited from an autonomous government, immunity from taxation and conduct as if living in Italy.[328] The first convert of the missionaries in Philippi was "a woman named Lydia" whose heart was opened graciously and sovereignly by the Lord "to respond to the things spoken by Paul" (Acts 16:14). The church at Philippi was founded through the faithful ministry of Luke, Paul, Silas and Timothy (16:1, 10, 12, 19; 20:6).[329]

---

328 F. J. Foakes Jackson and Kirsopp Lake, eds., *The Acts of the Apostles*, 5 vols. (reprint, Grand Rapids: Baker, 1979), 4:187-90.

329 Although he is not mentioned specifically in Acts, the "we" sections in the narrative are understood as references to Luke, the "beloved physician" (cf. 16:10-17; 20:6—21:18; 27:1—28:16) (cf. Richard Belward Rackham, *The Acts of the Apostles* [London: Methuen & Co., 1901], xv-vii).

The epistle to the Philippians was written during Paul's first Roman imprisonment. Epaphroditus was sent from the church at Philippi to bring a monetary gift to the apostle, which occasioned the writing of Philippians as an expanded letter of thanks (Phil. 4:10-20; cf. 1:3, 5; 2:25, 30).[330] Epaphroditus became "sick to the point of death" (Phil. 2:27) in Rome, which was cause for the Philippians' expression of concern. Consequently, the Apostle informed the church with regard to Epaphroditus' return to Philippi (2:25-28). Paul also reported the status of his trial before the Roman imperial court (1:7, 13-17), and even attempted to reconcile a church conflict (4:2).

The theme of Philippians is "joy," which is used 13 times. Christ is also mentioned 38 times, and therefore, "rejoicing in the Lord" is a prominent emphasis. The epistle contains significant revelation concerning Christ's kenosis (2:7), which means His self-emptying of the prerogatives and powers that were His eternally by virtue of His Divine attributes. The passage concerning His humiliation explains that by not asserting His Divine prerogatives and powers, the Lord Jesus took the form of a servant (while never emptying Himself of His divinity) to become true humanity (2:5-11). The epistle may be outlined quite basically as follows: (1) rejoicing in prison (1:1-30); (2) rejoicing in others (2:1-30); (3) rejoicing in the future (3:1-21); and, (4) rejoicing in all things (4:1-23). The focus of this section will be upon the third division ("rejoicing in the future"), especially Philippians 3:20-21.

The Context of Philippians 3:20-21

Philippians 3:15-21 focuses upon an attitude of life that is pleasing to God. Paul urged his readers to know the truth of what had been written previously. Moreover, he promised that those who were not living as they

---

330   Peter T. O'Brien, *The Epistle to the Philippians* (Grand Rapids: Eerdmans, 1991), p. 513.

ought (i.e., "forgetting what *lies* behind and reaching forward to what *lies* ahead," v. 13) would have this "different attitude" revealed to them by God. Christians should always live consistently with an understanding of the truth and not postpone a life of maturity. The immature, for instance, were not living maturely; rather, as the result of incomplete understanding of what God has revealed, they were postponing maturity as opposed to living in accord with the truth that they did understand. Therefore, the apostle urged his readers to pursue maturity in Christ (vv. 15-16).[331] The life that pleases God must always focus attention upon the person and work of Jesus Christ as the believer is transformed into His likeness.

Paul concluded his admonition by exhorting believers to watchfulness (vv. 17-19) and hopefulness (vv. 20-21). For a second time (cf. v. 15), Paul exhorted his readers to follow his example. Not only was it necessary to pursue maturity in Christ, but also it was crucial to be watchful because many live as "enemies of the cross of Christ, whose end is destruction" (vv. 18–19). These false teachers are described threefold: (1) their "god is *their* appetite" (i.e., fleshly and sensual); (2) their "glory is in their shame" (i.e., disgraceful living); and, (3) they "set their minds on earthly things" (i.e., the material and physical as opposed to the eternal and spiritual) (v. 19). Therefore, the believer is to be watchful (observant) of those who live according to the standard of Christlikeness and to imitate such behavior, in contrast to those whose lifestyle indicated them as enemies of God (cf. Gal. 4:3, 9-11; Col. 2:21-22).

The reason to pursue maturity in Christ and to be watchful is related to the hope of the believer (Phil. 3:20-21). Christians do have citizenship on Earth, but also have citizenship in heaven (v. 20). Maturity in Christ is the goal of the Christian life because heavenly citizenship is eternal as opposed to the earthly life that is but a vapor (Jas. 4:14; cf. Gal. 4:26; Heb. 11:10). Paul's

---

331 Although the NASB translates *teleios* as "perfect" (3:15), it would be better rendered as "mature" (NIV).

exhortation is an obvious contrast to those whose minds are focused upon "earthly things" and destiny "is destruction." One challenge of the Christian life is learning to live as "strangers and exiles on the earth" (Heb. 11:13; cf. 1 Pet. 2:11).[332] Consequently, the believer is to "eagerly wait for a Savior, the Lord Jesus Christ" (Phil. 3:20).

The Coming of the Savior in Philippians 3:20-21

Philippians 3:20 first asserts that the believer's "citizenship is in heaven." Regarding the meaning of the Greek (*to politeuma*), *The Expositor's Greek Testament* is noteworthy. "This world has a characteristic spirit of its own. Worldliness is the common bond of citizenship in it. There is another commonwealth,[333] not of the world (John xviii. 36), which inspires its members with a different tone of life. They 'seek the things above where Christ sitteth at the right hand of God'. . . . The stability and security of the *pax Romana* (one of the most favorable influences for Christianity) filled the thought of the time with high conceptions of citizenship and its value. This would specially appeal to the Philippians," who would have greatly esteemed the right to possess all the privileges of Italian citizens (i.e. *jus Italicum*)[334] (Acts 16:12, 21).

The believer eagerly waits for the Savior's return from (*ex ou*) heaven. The believer's citizenship is in heaven and, therefore, the Christian may "have a claim on the Saviour, just as the Philippians might rightfully look for protection to Rome [as saviour]."[335] The double compound (*apekde-chometha*) translated "eagerly wait"[336] indicates anticipation and eagerness

---

332   John A. Witmer, "The Man with Two Countries," *Bibliotheca Sacra* 133 (October 1976): 338-49.

333   The author noted Tertullian's reading as "*municipatus*," and "*conversatio*" in Cyprian and Irenaeus.

334   H. A. A. Kennedy, "The Epistle to the Philippians," in *The Expositor's Greek Testament*, 5 vols., ed. W. Robertson Nicoll (reprint, Grand Rapids: Eerdmans, 1979), 3:462.

335   Ibid.

336   For other usages of the Greek word, see Romans 8:19, 23, 25; 1 Corinthians 1:7; Galatians 5:5; and Hebrews 9:28.

for the return of the Lord Jesus Christ as the habitual perspective of the Christian whose citizenship is in heaven. The normal attitude of the Christian is eager anticipation of the Lord's return (and Paul, of course, included himself in that anticipation). The longing for the coming of the Savior is also an incentive for holy living (cf. Tit. 2:13; 1 John 2:28). One should note that no other events are mentioned that must precede the coming of the Lord.[337] Indeed, if the rapture of the church were understood to occur at any time other than pretribulationally, it would be difficult to have such eager anticipation. For example, if Scripture revealed the rapture of the church as occurring midtribulationally or posttribulationally, then the eager anticipation would be for the commencement of the seven-year tribulation, for then and only then could the believer "eagerly wait" for the Lord's return. The expectation of the Lord's return as imminent and personal is cause for great joy and hope to the early church and the church throughout the ages.

The Lord Jesus Christ will come from heaven as Savior to "rescue" His saints "from this present evil age" (Gal. 1:4) and take His church to His "Father's house" (John 14:2). Coinciding with the Lord's return, the body of the believer's "humble state" will be transformed "into conformity with the body of His glory" (Phil. 3:21). The transformation of the believer's body will be into a glorified body just like the Son of God (1 John 3:2). The distinction is between the "the body of our humble state" and "the body of His glory." In this earthly life, the believer's body is humbled by death, disease, persecution and sin. The body is earthly, perishable, weak, natural and mortal (1 Cor. 15:35-58), so that believers "groan within ourselves, waiting eagerly for *our* adoption as sons, the redemption of our body" (Rom. 8:23). At the Lord's return, the transformation will occur whether by

---

337 The various views regarding the timing of the rapture are *primarily* (sc. there are always exceptions) among those who affirm premillennialism as true, which means amillennialists and postmillennialists would respond to the doctrine of imminency in a manner different than premillennialists since they believe the second coming of Christ is a single event.

resurrection of the dead or by the rapture of the living (cf. 1 Cor. 15:50-58; 1 Thess. 4:13-18; 5:9-10). The glorified and resurrected body will be just like the Son of God ("the body of His glory," Phil. 3:21), and the believer's sanctification will be ultimate. The expectation of the Lord's return should produce a purifying hope as a citizen of heaven while sojourning on earth (1 John 3:1-3). The transformation will occur "by the exertion of the power that He has even to subject all things to Himself" (Phil. 3:21). The same power that will ultimately subject all things in the universe to the authority of the Lord Jesus Christ is what accomplishes the transformation.

Philippians 3 concludes with an exhortation to "press on toward the goal for the prize of the upward call of God in Christ Jesus" (v. 14). The believer will demonstrate this persevering attitude by pursuing maturity in Christ (vv. 15-16), watching for those who imitate the Biblical standard (and follow their example) and being aware of those who are "enemies of the cross of Christ" (vv. 17-19), and "eagerly" waiting for the "Savior, the Lord Jesus Christ" (vv. 20-21). The heavenly citizenship of the believer parallels Jesus' words in John 14:1-3, and challenges every Christian to live with an eternal perspective. The hope of the Lord's imminent and personal return has sustained the church throughout the present evil age. The expectation of the Lord's return should stimulate the church to live holy and pure lives "so that when He appears, we may have confidence and not shrink away from Him in shame at His coming" (1 John 2:28).

First Corinthians 15

Regarding the resurrection of all humanity, the Bible states each will be raised "in his own order" (1 Cor. 15:23). The resurrection of the righteous (Luke 14:14; John 5:29) is distinguished from the resurrection of the unrighteous (Rev. 20:5, 11-15). The translation of living believers and the resurrection of deceased believers receives much attention in 1 Corinthians 15. The 15th chapter begins with an introduction of the gospel, which "first argues the resurrection of Christ as an essential of Christian faith and hope, and then links this with the resurrection of men in general."[338] "The grand exception to the doctrine of resurrection"[339] is the translation (rapture) of living believers. Until that joyful day occurs, God's people are to remain faithful and true, "always abounding in the work of the Lord" (1 Cor. 15:58).

Resurrection and Translation

The instantaneous resurrection and translation of believers is "a mystery" (1 Cor. 15:51). Consistent with the other Pauline usages of *mustērion*, certain doctrines were not previously revealed in the Old Testament. While the resurrection of the righteous dead from the Old Testament economy was revealed (Dan. 12:2; cf. John 5:29; 11:24), the rapture of the church was not (nor could it be since the church age was a mystery).

What is stated in 1 Corinthians 15:51-52 regarding "sleep" does find a parallel in 1 Thessalonians 4:13-17. In both texts, "sleep" is a euphemism for death (cf. 1 Cor. 11:30; 15:6, 18, 20). All believers "will be raised imperishable, and we will be changed" (15:52). The imminency of the change is evident in the fact that Paul included himself among those to be raptured (cf. "we" in 15:51-52; 1 Thess. 4:13-17) because there are no events preceding this event (cf. Tit. 2:13). The translation of believers—"those who have fallen asleep in Jesus" and "we who are alive and remain until the coming of the Lord" (1 Thess. 4:14-15) —will be "in a moment, in the twinkling of an eye" (1 Cor. 15:52). While the Thessalonians passage mentions "the trumpet of God" (4:16), the Corinthians text indicates the trumpet is "the last," in the sense of the end of a specific period (the dispensation of the church).

As already stated, "the last trumpet" is not equivalent to the trumpet in Matthew 24:31 and the seventh trumpet of Revelation 11:15. Certainly,

---

338 John F. Walvoord, *The Return of the Lord* (Grand Rapids: Dunham, 1955), p. 52.
339 Ibid.

the trumpets in the rapture passages should be equated, yet not regarded as corresponding to the trumpet prior to the return of Christ in Matthew 24:31 or the seventh trumpet in Revelation. The reasons for the distinction are fivefold. *First,* the seventh trumpet in Revelation was unknown to the Apostle Paul when the Lord revealed the Apocalypse because Paul was martyred at the end of Nero's reign (A.D. 65-68). *Secondly,* the "last trumpet" in 1 Corinthians is not the last chronologically; rather, it is last in sequence, referring to the conclusion of the church dispensation. *Third,* the "last trumpet" is God's own trumpet, while the seventh trumpet belongs to an angel.[340] *Fourth,* the "last trumpet" "issues in blessing, in life, in glory, while the trumpet in Revelation issues in judgment upon the enemies of God."[341] *Fourth,* the sixth seal appears to be the midpoint of the tribulation,[342] and thus the seven trumpets of Revelation occur in the second half of that period, which means the trumpet prior to Christ's return (Matt. 24:31) is subsequent to the trumpet judgments in Revelation. *Fifth,* the trumpets in Matthew 24:31 and Revelation 11:15 do not reference an unequivocal depiction of the resurrection of the dead.

Understanding the "last trumpet" within a pretribulational context is clarified by considering the first usage of trumpet in Scripture. The first trumpet reference is found in Exodus 19[343] when a "very loud trumpet" sounded for the purpose of assembling the people of Israel "to meet God" at the base of Mount Sinai (vv. 10-20), which resulted in their receiving the law of God and thus began the ministry of death (cf. 2 Cor. 3:7-9; Heb. 12:18-21). The "last trumpet" will have "the opposite purpose of that to which the first trump of God called people. It thereby will signal the

---

340   J. F. Strombeck, *First the Rapture* (Moline, IL: Strombeck Agency, 1950; reprint, Grand Rapids: Kregel, 1992), p. 109.

341   J. Dwight Pentecost, *Things to Come* (Grand Rapids: Zondervan, 1964), p. 190.

342   Ron J. Bigalke Jr., "A Comparison of the Synoptic Eschatological Discourses and Revelation 6—20," *Chafer Theological Seminary Journal* 13 (Spring 2008): 60-78.

343   James Strong, *The New Strong's Exhaustive Concordance of the Bible* (Nashville: Thomas Nelson, 1990), p. 1,121.

beginning of the end of death, the last enemy of mankind to be destroyed or abolished, and will fulfill another use of the trumpet in ancient times—that of terrifying an enemy or issuing a warning of coming danger or judgment."[344] Similar to how Scripture contrasts the first Adam and the last Adam, the trumpet of God can be called the "last trumpet" because it is distinguished from the first trumpet mentioned in the Bible.[345]

Moreover, trumpets were used for war, both in the Old Testament and the Greco-Roman world (cf. 2 Sam. 18:16; 20:22). Whereas the first trumpet assembled the soldiers for battle, the last trumpet was sounded to dismiss the troops and send them home from the warfare. The "last trumpet" at the rapture will bring to completion the spiritual battle that the church has been waging (cf. Rom. 13:12; 2 Cor. 6:7; 10:3-4; Eph. 6:10-18; 1 Thess. 5:8; 1 Tim. 1:18; 1 Pet. 5:8-9), and commission the saints to their "citizenship . . . in heaven" (Phil. 3:19-20). Similar to how Roman armies signaled the beginning and ending of "a guard's watch" with trumpets, so may the "last trumpet" at the rapture sound the end of the church's watch (cf. Acts 20:31; 1 Cor. 16:13; Eph. 6:18; Col. 4:2; 1 Thess. 5:6; 2 Tim. 4:5; 1 Pet. 4:7; Rev. 3:2).[346] At the rapture, the dead in Christ will be raised incorruptible never to die again. Those church saints who are alive and remain at the rapture will never experience death. Both the dead in Christ and the living saints at the rapture will be raised immortal at the sound of the "last trumpet," "and as such are now partakers of the future life."[347]

Titus 2

Godly living—according to Scripture—necessitates that the church maintains wise attitudes toward the world in which we live, specifically with regard to the *temporal* values of the world in which we live, and the

---

344 Renald E. Showers, *Maranatha: Our Lord, Come!* (Bellmawr, NJ: Friends of Israel, 1995), p. 263.
345 Ibid., p. 262.
346 Ibid., pp. 266-67.
347 Bauer, *Greek-English Lexicon*, p. 125.

eternal values of our faith in God and His holy Word. For instance, as a reason for the teaching concerning moral obligations, such as the moral duty of a slave not to steal from his master (2:10), we find attention upon "the grace of God that brings salvation" which "has appeared" (NKJV), a reference that is with respect to the first coming of Jesus Christ. The grace of God is here conceived as a dynamic that manifests in Christian ethical obedience and not merely the forgiveness of sins. One evidence of godly living is awaiting the "blessed hope" (2:11-14).

Awaiting the "Blessed Hope"

The exhortation to await the blessed hope is stated in the words that nearly conclude the sentence (begun in verse 11), which is "looking for the blessed hope and the appearing of the glory of our great God and Savior, Christ Jesus" (2:13). As the Greek verb translated "looking for" is in the present tense it signifies a characteristic attitude, that is, the church is always ready to meet the returning Lord. First Thessalonians 4:13-18 makes it evident that this "blessed hope" is indeed what is called the rapture: the translation of living church saints and resurrection of dead church saints, and meeting of both parties in the clouds to meet Christ in the air. The concept of the imminent coming of Christ may only be harmonized with the belief that Christ will rapture His church prior to the 70th week of Daniel 9, or what is more commonly termed "the tribulation" of seven years length. (Oddly, some individuals regard the doctrine of the rapture as too supernatural; however, to correct such a mentality, it would be best to review Old Testament history, in addition to the history of the gospels and the early church.)

The teaching of 1 Thessalonians 4:13-18 is that "we who are alive and remain"—in contrast to "those who have fallen asleep in Jesus"—always have the hope of instantaneous translation into the presence of our Lord and Savior Jesus Christ without intervening death and separation from the body. Of course, the same hope of receiving a new body ultimately (and seeing and being with Christ in the meantime) prevails for those Christians who die prior to that time. The anticipation of this translation, which is not merely desired but what is assured, is to affect the manner in which Christians live in expectation of the blessed hope, because they are to have a continual expectation of its occurring, even today. When it does occur, we may be certain that our Lord wants us to be doing something that is honoring to Him who we will suddenly greet. We do not want to feel ashamed when we meet our Lord and Savior face to face (1 John 2:28; 3:3).

In Titus 2:13, the Greek text uses the definite article "the" to introduce both "blessed hope" and "glorious appearing" (*tēn makarian elpida kai epiphaneian tēs doxēs*). Only one article (*tēn*) closely unites the two substantives, which suggests that the reference is with regard to one event from two aspects. The blessed hope is the glorious appearing of our God and Savior. Moreover, the appearing and the glory is of one person, our great God and Savior Jesus Christ. Most students of New Testament Greek are familiar with the Granville Sharp Rule. Stated simply, the rule is that when two nouns of the same case, which are not proper names (e.g., Titus) and are describing a person, and the two nouns of the same case are connected by the conjunction "and" (*kai*), if the first noun has the definite article ("the") and the second does not, then both nouns refer to the same person. In Titus 2:13, this is demonstrated by the words "God" and "Savior." (The King James Version was translated previous to Sharp's rule, which was written late in the 18th century, and therefore, regrettably, is probably not quite as dynamic in translation for it reads: "glorious appearing of the great God and our Saviour Jesus Christ.") However, the article is used with respect to God, and followed by the conjunction "and," and the word "Savior" does not have the article. Therefore, both nouns are being applied to the same person, Jesus Christ. The phrase "great God" is an application of an Old Testament description for the Savior. To conclude otherwise would not be based upon Scripture but upon theological presuppositions.

Jesus Christ is our great God and Savior (the same phrase was often used in the papyri and by the Greek Fathers as referring to Christ Jesus). Paul described "the appearing of the glory" of one person, that is, "our great God and Savior, Christ Jesus." The identification of the Lord Jesus by the phrase "great God" is certainly the thought of the context because it was the Lord Jesus who gave Himself for redeeming the believer. Therefore, with this hope in the mind of his readers, the Apostle Paul reminded believers in verse 14 that the Lord Jesus Christ we will meet someday is the one who redeemed us from all wickedness for the intent of purifying a people of His own who are "zealous for good deeds" (an expression appearing several times in this letter to Titus).

The Appearing of the Glory of the Lord Jesus Christ

The Greek word translated "appearing" is *epiphaneian* (ἐπιφάνειαν), and is used in three different New Testament contexts. The *first* context is 2 Timothy 1:10 ("but now has been revealed by the appearing of our Savior Christ Jesus, who abolished death and brought life and immortality to light through the gospel"). The "appearing" in 2 Timothy 1:10 is in reference to the Lord's first coming. The *second* context is identified in 1 Timothy 6:14 and Titus 2:13. First Timothy 6:14 reads, "That you keep the commandment without stain or reproach until the appearing of our Lord Jesus Christ." The "appearing" in 1 Timothy 6:14 and Titus 2:13 is in reference to the pretribulational rapture. The *third* context is 2 Thessalonians 2:8 ("Then that lawless one will be revealed whom the Lord will slay with the breath of His mouth and bring to an end by the appearance of His coming"). The "appearance" in 2 Thessalonians 2:8 is in reference to the Lord's premillennial reign.

With regard to the second context, the Greek word translated "appearing" is followed by a descriptive genitive, *tēs doxēs* (τῆς δόξης), "of the glory." The descriptive genitive may be translated occasionally as an adjective, which would be read as "glorious" in Titus 2:13. The Granville Sharp Rule, which again states that when two nouns of the same case, which are not proper names and are describing a person, and the two nouns of the same case are connected by the copulative "and" (*kai*), if the first noun has the definite article ("the") and the second does not, then both nouns refer to the same person. Therefore, things that are more or less distinct are regarded as one for the immediate purpose, which is reason for the use of only one definite article ("the"). In Titus 2:13, this would mean that "the blessed hope" is the "glorious appearing." The definite article then is explanatory, and introduces the more distinct definition of the character for the blessed hope. Christians are "looking for" the person of hope, our great God and Savior, Christ Jesus, who is the glorious appearing. The reference is to one event (the rapture), which is emphasized by two aspects: anticipation and appearing.

The Doctrine of the Blessed Hope

The imminence of the Lord's return means that He could return at any moment; it is a sudden coming. The rapture may occur today, perhaps tomorrow, or even years from now, but one does not know when Christ will rapture the church. One prevalent danger with regard to the rapture is to mock this imminency of the Lord's gathering of the church (cf. 2 Pet. 3:3-4). There are no specific events that must occur prior to the rapture; rather, there is only the instruction for the believer to be ready. The church is not instructed to await the blessed hope of Antichrist; it is the blessed hope of Jesus Christ that the church anticipates. If any events must precede the rapture, it is impossible not to seek those signs as opposed to the Lord's coming, which would, of course, encourage only a general interest in the blessed hope. The doctrine of imminence in relation to the rapture teaches that other things may occur prior to Christ's removal of the church but nothing else must occur prior to His return. If some event must occur prior to the rapture, it would be a component of the Christian's hope because then one would know assuredly when Christ will return, but such an event would contradict the concept of imminency.

Those who attempt to determine dates for the Lord's return foolishly ignore the fact that no time must transpire prior to the rapture. If time must transpire, then the event is not imminent. Some will argue for Christ's "soon" coming, yet neglect the fact that if an event is soon it must occur within a short period of time; consequently, it would be better to understand "soon" adverbs as indicating the manner of the Lord's return, not time. When the Lord returns it will be swiftly and quickly. The fact that Christ could return for His church at any moment is taught throughout the New Testament (1 Cor. 1:7; 16:22; Phil. 3:20; 4:5; 1 Thess. 1:10; Heb. 9:28; Jas. 5:7-9; 1 Pet. 1:13; Jude 21; Rev. 3:11; 22:7, 12, 17, 20); therefore, only a coming of Christ pretribulationally can be consistently and literally taught from the entirety of Scripture. The pretribulational teaching of the Lord's return is the only manner in which one can honesty assert that Christ could return at any moment because this doctrine alone teaches that the Lord will rapture the church prior to the 70th week of Daniel 9 (or any tribulational events occurring), and therefore nothing must occur prior to His return for the church.

The blessed hope of the church is the appearing in glory of our great God and Savior, Christ Jesus, at the rapture. The doctrine of the rapture should motivate the church to pursue godly living by God's grace, and therefore, to glorify God in this present life. The present tense of the verb *prosdechomenoi* (προσδεχόμενοι), which is translated "looking for," indicates that anticipation of the Lord's return should be the characteristic attitude of the church. The "looking" is a continual process of being always

ready to welcome the appearing Lord. The Greek verb *paideuousa* (παιδευ-
΄ουσα), which is translated "instructing" in verse 12, was also in the present
tense. Therefore, the two participles function harmoniously; it is because
"the grace of God has appeared" (2:11) that believers are instructed "to live
sensibly, righteously and godly in the present age" (2:12) as we are "looking
for the blessed hope" (2:13). The expectation is a continual attitude that
affects one's life in the "looking for" the Lord's return.

One reason for this continual expectation is "so that when He appears,
we may have confidence and not shrink away from Him in shame at His
coming" (1 John 2:28). "And everyone who has this hope *fixed* on Him
purifies himself, just as He is pure" (3:3). The blessed hope of the Lord's
return is not merely an event that is anticipated, but is a promise that gives
assurance to the church; it is a joyous promise of anticipation. There should
never be doubt with regard to the anticipation; the rapture will occur, and
belief in this doctrine results in a joyousness that is looking forward to the
ultimate redemption.

The church has a blessed hope of the glorious appearance of our great
God and Savior, Christ Jesus. The imminency of the rapture is evident in
that the Apostle Paul and the first-century recipients of the epistle to Titus
anticipated the possibility of this event. Of course, all believers may join in
the blessed anticipation of the Lord's return. Verse 12 stresses godly, righteous and sensible living "in the present age" in relation to the anticipation
of the glorious appearing. Doctrine is certainly necessary for living godly.
Verse 11 introduced the first coming of the Lord ("the grace of God has
appeared"), and related this doctrine to living godly (2:12). Christians are
to pursue holy living based upon the doctrine of the Lord's return for the
church at the pretribulational rapture (2:13), and understanding that the
purpose of the Lord's redemption was to "purify for Himself a people for
His own possession, zealous for good deeds" (2:14).

Revelation 3

The message to the church of Philadelphia can be tremendously inspiring when regarded as God's instruction to a faithful church which did not compromise its worship. The recurring theme of this letter is that God is sovereign. Scripture does not advocate trust in anyone else but in God alone (Prov. 3:5-6). He alone can be trusted and humanity's faith must reside in Him. The world is unstable, but God declares I am He "who opens and no one will shut, and who shuts and no one opens" (Rev. 3:7); it is because God is sovereign that He declares there is a door of opportunity, "which no one can shut" (3:8).

Location of the Church

Philadelphia was a city in the Roman province of Asia, that is, in the west of what is known today as Asiatic Turkey. Eumenes, king of Pergamum, is alleged to have founded the city in the second century B.C. Apparently, Eumenes named Philadelphia in honor of his brother Attalus Philadelphus. Therefore, the name Philadelphia came to mean "brotherly love." The city was located near the upper end of a broad valley that passed through Sardis to the sea that was near Smyrna. Philadelphia was on the verge of a quite fertile territory of plateau country, and this geographical area contributed to the commercial prosperity of the city. Philadelphia was noted for its elaborate religious festivals and remarkable temples. Today, the town of Alaşehir occupies the site. The residents of Philadelphia experienced frequent earthquakes, such as one in A.D. 17 that destroyed the city. As earthquakes increased, more of the residents moved their homes to outside the city. An imperial bounty helped the city to recover from the devastation and in gratitude the city changed its name to Neocaesarea. The name of the city was changed again, and the new name, Flavia, indicated another imperial bounty from Vespasian.[348]

---

348 W. M. Ramsay, *The Letters to the Seven Churches* (Peabody, MA: Hendrickson, 1994), pp. 286-302.

Historical Circumstances

"The angel of the church in Philadelphia" (Rev. 3:7-13) was selected among others to receive a message from the Lord. The Philadelphian church appears to have been selected due to the particular issues that it experienced, which would be relevant to churches throughout the church age. Seven churches were chosen since the number indicates completeness. First Corinthians 10:11 indicates that God has elected certain events and the character of individuals to admonish others. The church in Philadelphia was such an example. Summers commented,

> One of the marvelous things about the book is the impression that conditions in churches of every age, including the twentieth century, are illustrated by the conditions of these churches. The message is one of universal application. Wherever the conditions exist, the corrective procedure indicated will find application.[349]

As already stated, the name Philadelphia came to mean "brotherly love" due to the loyalty of Philadelphus to his brother Attalus. The church of Philadelphia was identified with this "brotherly love," which also manifested in the church's loyalty to Jesus Christ. The church was commended because they were faithful to God's Word and was loyal to His name (Rev. 3:8). They also exercised patience toward the Word of God (Rev. 3:10).

Philadelphia was a gateway to the east; it was the farthest city of the Greek civilization in that area.[350] Physically, the city was at the threshold of a fertile geographical area from which it could derive its wealth. From a spiritual standpoint, there were numerous barbarous tribes beyond the city of Philadelphia that granted the church "an open door" of opportunity for missionary activity (Rev. 3:8). The church was loyal to Christ in the past, but two doors lay before them. One door offered physical blessing whereas

---

349   Ray Summers, *Worthy Is the Lamb* (Nashville: Broadman Press, 1951), p. 107.
350   Ramsay, *Seven Churches*, pp. 296-97.

the other offered spiritual blessing. Perhaps the letter to this church serves to remind God's people of their responsibility to the Lord and to examine which "open door" is more important. The mention of a "crown" and the "pillar" in the following verses indicate an eternal point of contrast with the recurring instability of a city plagued with never ending earthquakes (Rev. 3:11-12). Those who overcome were promised eternal blessings.

The church in Smyrna and Philadelphia experienced intense opposition from religious leaders (Rev. 2:9; 3:9). The Philadelphian church was exhorted to "hold fast what you have" amidst the ongoing rejection because they would receive acceptance from their Lord (Rev. 3:8, 11). Again, a contrast is made between the temporal and the eternal. The historical background of this church provides unique insights as to why the church received this message. The church encountered earthquakes, heathenism and religious rejection in a continual manner. Nevertheless, the church remained loyal to Christ. They were encouraged to continue in their separation from "the synagogue of Satan" and heathenism (Rev. 3:9-11). Although the church often journeyed outside the city (due to the earthquakes), a day would come when they would be pillars in the temple of God (Rev. 3:12). The exhortation to this church was continual faithfulness to Christ with their hope in the eternal.

Chronological Aspects

Many competent Bible teachers believe that the seven historical churches in Revelation of the first century provide a sample of the types of churches that will be present throughout the history of the church. Revelation 1:19 does provide a chronological outline for understanding the book of Revelation. For instance, there are "the things which you have seen" (Rev. 1), "the things which are" (Rev. 2—3), and "the things which will take place after these things" (Rev. 4—22).

"The things which are" does relate to the current church age, which is evident in the Lord's recurring command: "He who has an ear, let him hear what the Spirit says to the churches" (Rev. 2:7, 11, 17, 29; 3:6, 13, 22). However, this does not mean that the seven historical churches provide a pattern of the various types of churches throughout history. The historical-prophetic interpretation of the seven churches not only finds application from each of the letters, but also believes that one type of church will be dominant in a particular period of church history. Fruchtenbaum provided an outline representative of this interpretation.

1. Ephesus [30-100] Apostolic Church

2. Smyrna [100-313] Roman Persecution

3. Pergamum [313-600] Age of Constantine

4. Thyatira [600-1517] Dark Ages

5. Sardis [1517-1648] Reformation

6. Philadelphia [1648-1900] Missionary Movement

7. Laodicea [1900-Present] Apostasy[351]

The historical-prophetic interpretation seems to read more into Scripture than what is actually the original intent. For instance, the seven churches would not have understood the letters in such a manner as proposed by the historical-prophetic interpretation. Rejecting such an interpretation, Summers wrote,

> . . . these were actually seven churches in Asia Minor. It stays by the principle announced that the book must be interpreted in a way that would have been meaningful and helpful to those Christians who first received the message. Hence, it rejects the frequently confronted approach that the seven churches represent seven stages in the development of apostasy of the church.[352]

---

351 Arnold Fruchtenbaum, *The Footsteps of the Messiah* (Tustin, CA: Ariel Ministries Press, 1983), p. 36.

352 Summers, *Worthy*, p. 107.

Although none of the seven churches remain today, there are applications for the churches throughout the centuries. The churches selected were chosen due to their representative character. Every church can find some circumstance, trial or temptation within these letters that will provide admonishment to live holy in a godless world, in light of the Lord's imminent return.

God's Message to the Church

The message begins with Christ's presentation of Himself as "holy" and "true." He is the one who holds "the key of David" (Rev. 3:7), which is a reference to Isaiah 22:22 and thus indicates the authority of Christ. He alone is the sovereign. God opens and closes according to His Divine will. There is none that can thwart His eternal decrees. The church in Philadelphia was commended in a fourfold manner (Rev. 3:8): (1) taking advantage of the opportunities granted them by God ("I know your deeds"); (2) display some spiritual maturity ("you have a little power"); (3) keeping the Word of the Lord; and, (4) faithfulness to God's calling ("have not denied My name"). The devotion of the church to Christ resulted in five promises given to them.

The *first promise* given to the church was that their Jewish enemies ("synagogue of Satan") would be humbled before them (Rev. 3:9). Moreover, they would be kept "from the hour of testing" (or "tribulation;" cf. Matt. 13:21; Mark 4:17; Luke 8:13). The *second promise* is noteworthy since many Bible students commonly cite it to teach the pretribulational rapture. While it is common to hear Revelation 3:10 cited as proof of a pretribulational rapture, there are problems with such references. Thomas concluded,

> The statement does not refer directly to the rapture. What it guarantees is protection from the scene of the 'hour of trial' while that hour is in progress. This effect of placing the faithful in Philadelphia (and hence, the faithful in all the churches; cf. 3:13) in a

position of safety presupposes that they will have been removed to another location (i.e., heaven) at the period's beginning.[353]

Therefore, it would be best to understand Revelation 3:10 as promising the church in Philadelphia a first-century deliverance from the tribulation period, but also extending that promise in a general manner to the church throughout the centuries (cf. Rev. 3:13). Thomas was correct that the passage does not *directly* teach the pretribulational rapture. However, this is not to say that the passage does not relate to the rapture of the church. Walvoord stated, "If the rapture had occurred in the first century preceding the tribulation which the book of Revelation described, they were assured of deliverance."[354]

The phrase kept "from the hour of testing" is significant for several reasons. For instance, the word "hour" (Gk. *horas*) designates deliverance not only from the "trial," but also deliverance from the period of time in which the trial exists. Ryrie noted, "In the Septuagint translation the *ek* indicates an external, not internal preservation. *Ek* also is used in the same way of external protection in Joshua 2:13 and in Psalm 33:19; 56:13."[355] If the writer had intended to teach preservation through (rather than from) the tribulation the correct grammar to use would be *en te hora* ("in the hour"). Significantly, John stated, *ek tes haras* ("from the hour"). The same Greek preposition is used in 1 Thessalonians 1:10 wherein Paul communicated the same teaching: "*that is* Jesus, who rescues us from the wrath to come."

The *third promise* is that the Lord will come quickly (Rev. 3:11). Walvoord aptly noted that the "expression 'quickly' is to be understood as something which is sudden and unexpected, not necessarily immediate."[356] *Fourthly*, the church in Philadelphia would be honored in the temple of God (Rev. 3:12a); and, it

---

353   Robert Thomas, *Revelation 1-7* (Chicago: Moody Press, 1992), p. 288.

354   John Walvoord, *The Revelation of Jesus Christ* (Chicago: Moody Press, 1966), p. 87.

355   Charles Ryrie, *Come Quickly, Lord Jesus* (Eugene, OR: Harvest House, 1996), p. 133.

356   Walvoord, *Revelation*, p. 87.

is significant that they "will not go out from it anymore." In other words, that which is eternal and unmovable would replace the unstable earthly dwelling in which they were accustomed. *Lastly*, the church would receive a new name (Rev. 3:12b), which will indicate their eternal identification with God.

Pastoral Application

If the majority of pastors were asked which of the seven churches describes their congregation, it would be honest of most to respond that at times all of them correspond to their local church. The most prominent churches to be mentioned would probably include Ephesus ("you have left your first love" [Rev. 2:4]), Philadelphia ("kept My word, and have not denied My name" [Rev. 3:8]), and Laodicea ("you are neither cold nor hot" [Rev. 3:15]). There are several applications that should be adopted in response to the Lord's evaluation of these historical and representative churches.

First, the church needs a greater awareness of God's holiness and humanity's sinfulness. If the people of God truly understand the wrath from which they have been delivered, they would not become accustomed to living independent of the living and written Word. The church needs to understand the sovereign choice of God in election and also accountability to God. The late Dr. Walvoord stated a great point when he wrote, "It remains true, however, that many casual worshipers in Christian churches today who are quite familiar with the Sermon on the Mount are not aware of the existence of these seven messages of Christ."[357] Even many teachers of prophetic passages in Scripture will emphasize chapter 1 and then chapters 4—22 of Revelation, and only provide a survey analysis of the letters to the seven churches. The exhortations of these letters need to be an emphasis in the church.

The church in Philadelphia was given precious promises from the Lord. However, the exhortation to "hold fast what you have" is also

---

357   Ibid., p. 51.

applicable to the church today. The world today can be profoundly disheartening, without any appearance of hope. However, this is when Christians can be marvelous testimonies of grace in the Lord Jesus Christ by living with the blessed hope of the Lord's imminent return (Rev. 3:11; cf. Tit. 2:13). The suddenness ("I am coming quickly") in which Christ will return is also an incentive for holiness and evangelism that Christians should not be caught unaware when the Lord returns for His church.

RELEVANCY OF THE RAPTURE DOCTRINE

The Christian has a great hope in Jesus Christ. All humanity is condemned before God as sinners, but victory over the wages of sin is by grace through faith in Jesus Christ alone as one's Savior. Christ alone can provide the victory through either resurrection or translation. The rapture of the church is to have a purifying effect upon the body of Christ since at any moment the church saints could be in the Lord's presence. The rapture of the church should also cause Christians to be active in obeying all the Lord's commands and responsible with the privileges of the gospel message, since Christ could return at any moment. Certainly, the church should be active in the work of the Lord and Savior so that when He returns to gather His church there will not be shame, but rather confidence in His coming because one has lived a life of obedience in service of Jesus Christ.

CHAPTER 12

PROPHETIC TIMING AND THE RAPTURE: PRETRIBULATIONISM, PART II

The Pauline epistles may be classified according to chronology and content. In this chapter (and the next) addressing the Thessalonian epistles and the rapture, a modified chronological-content classification will be applied to these writings, which means 1—2 Thessalonians are understood to be eschatological epistles. Eschatology, of course, is not the only content or instruction within the epistles; rather, the classification of "eschatological" with regard to the epistles indicates the primary emphasis.

First and Second Thessalonians were written in response to Timothy's report of affliction of the church in Thessalonica (1 Thess. 3:1-10). Paul was concerned that the church "would be disturbed by these afflictions" (3:3). He sent Timothy to visit the believers "to strengthen and encourage" them, and to provide a report with regard to the nature of their faith (3:2, 5). Timothy provided Paul "good news" of the church's perseverance; consequently, Paul wrote his letter with thanksgiving (3:6, 9).

The majority of the difficulties that the Thessalonians experienced were the consequence of envious Jews inciting a wicked mob, crowd and city officials (Acts 17:5, 8). Since the Thessalonian church was both Jewish and Gentile, some other difficulties that necessitated Paul's instruction were the consequence of those backgrounds. Paul's instruction addressed sexual morality (1 Thess. 4:3-8), social conduct (4:9-10), manual labor (4:11-12), fearing death with despair and as final separation from those in Christ (4:13-18), false teachings with regard to "the day of the Lord" (5:1-11; 2 Thess. 1:3—2:12), and avoiding idleness (2 Thess. 3:10-12). Confusion in regard to these matters necessitated instruction that would explain the nature of new life in the Lord Jesus Christ, and the corresponding respon-sibilities of the Christian.

The Thessalonian epistles instruct believers to affirm the Lordship of Jesus Christ, and therefore submit intelligently to the will of God. Therefore, the issues addressed were practical as opposed to being merely theoretical. The Thessalonian epistles provide practical instruction for life in the present, and yet anticipate the coming day when the Lord Jesus Christ returns in power and glory.

HISTORICAL BACKGROUND

The Apostle Paul wrote the epistles of 1—2 Thessalonians from Corinth on his second missionary journey, approximately A.D. 51 (cf. 1 Thess. 1:7-9; 2:17; 3:1, 6; Acts 18:5, 11). The mission to Thessalonica is reported in Acts 17:1-9. As a self-governing community, Thessalonica enjoyed the status of a free city. The Romans did not occupy local offices and government in Thessalonica; therefore, the city had its own laws and officials called "politarchs" (Acts 17:6, 8). Thessalonica was capital of the Roman province of Macedonia, and therefore an ideal location for mission work.

According to Luke, the missionary endeavor occurred in the synagogue of Thessalonica "for three Sabbaths" (17:1-2). Of course, Luke was probably indicating the duration of Paul's ministry in the synagogue, and not that the church only received a month or less of instruction. Even after a resistance to their ministry arose, Paul and Silas continued the mission work (perhaps for several months) and the church increased to include "a large number of the God-fearing Greeks and a number of the leading women" (17:4). Although the church in Thessalonica began with Jewish Christians, it increased rapidly in number to include Gentiles predominantly, as a consequence of the power of the gospel (1 Thess. 1:5-6, 9-10).

Even with God's blessing in the missionary work, there arose "much tribulation with the joy of the Holy Spirit" (1:6). The jealousy of the unbelieving Jews culminated into "an uproar" (Acts 17:5). Moreover, the accusation against Paul and Silas to the politarchs was that the missionaries were acting "contrary to the decrees of Caesar, saying that there is another king, Jesus" (Acts 17:7). The accusation would have troubled the populace since they would have regarded their favored status as a free city being jeopardized. As a consequence of the affliction the Thessalonian believers were experiencing, Paul was concerned that the temptations would overwhelm them and his "labor would be in vain" (1 Thess. 3:5). He was also distressed by false teaching that the intense difficulties that the Thessalonians were experiencing was part of the fulfillment of the prophecies of the "day of the Lord," and this would diminish their hopes for the Lord's imminent return for His church (1 Thess. 1:9-10; 2:17-19; 3:13; 4:13—5:11; 2 Thess. 2:1-12). For this reason, he sent Timothy to encourage and instruct the church (3:1-5).

The "good news" that Timothy provided to Paul assisted the Apostle in writing the epistles to the Thessalonians. One of the primary doctrines communicated in Paul's epistle is the doctrine of the Lord Jesus' return. With references to Jesus as "Lord" and to His second coming occurring at least once in every chapter of the epistles, this instruction is indeed a primary emphasis.

TRIBULATION AMONG THE THESSALONIANS

The Thessalonians were experiencing tribulation just as the Lord Jesus had promised would encounter all His disciples in any age (John 16:33). The Thessalonians were experiencing tribulation, but "the wrath to come" would not affect them (1 Thess. 1:10; 2:14-16). Noting 12 words that Paul used in the Thessalonian epistles to indicate intense difficulties and experiences is worthwhile.

Nouns

thlipsis (θλῖψις)
  tribulations, affliction(s)
  1 Thessalonians 1:6; 3:3; 3:7; 2 Thessalonians 1:4, 6
agōn (ἀγών)
  opposition
  1 Thessalonians 2:2
kopos (κόπος)
  labor (toil, work)
  1 Thessalonians 1:3; 2:9; 3:5; 2 Thessalonians 3:8
mochthos (μόχθος)
  hardship (labor, exertion)
  1 Thessalonians 2:9; 2 Thessalonians 3:8
diōgmos (διωγμός)
  persecutions
  2 Thessalonians 1:4

Verbs

thlibō (θλίβω)
> *to suffer, afflict, afflicted*
> 1 Thessalonians 3:4; 2 Thessalonians 1:6-7

propaschō (προπάσχω)
> *already suffered*
> 1 Thessalonians 2:2

hubrizō (ὑβρίζω)
> *mistreated (insult)*
> 1 Thessalonians 2:2

kopiaō (κοπιάω)
> *to work hard (toil)*
> 1 Thessalonians 5:12

paschō (πάσχω)
> *to suffer, experience*
> 1 Thessalonians 2:14; 2 Thessalonians 1:5

kōluō (κωλύω)
> to hinder (*prevent, forbid*)
> 1 Thessalonians 2:16

egkoptō (ἐγκόπτω)
> *to hinder (thwart)*
> 1 Thessalonians 2:18

Each of the 12 words employed by Paul are in either the aorist or present tense. The present tense is readily understandable, in contrast to the aorist tense; therefore, the reader is encouraged to understand the grammatical elements of the aorist (as provided in the following sentence). The aorist tense normally indicates verbal action as simply past or without reference to its progress.

There are other grammatical elements that are also significant. The indicative mood is used with both the present and aorist tenses. The aorist indicative normally denotes an experience as past. The present indicative indicates the verbal action as being actual or real (as opposed to possibility). The participles denote the characteristics of both verb and adjective (i.e., "verbal adjective"). The active voice indicates a subject causing or accomplishing a verbal action, and the passive voice conveys a subject as being affected or receiving the verbal action. Understanding these grammatical elements will provide a better understanding of the English translations and the intent of the Biblical author. The tense of the verbs that Paul used in the Thessalonian epistles to indicate intense difficulties and experiences are indeed significant.

> *thlibō* (θλίβω)
>> *to suffer* (1 Thess. 3:4)
>> present passive infinitive
>> *afflict* (2 Thess. 1:6)
>> present active participle
>> *afflicted* (2 Thess. 1:7)
>> present passive participle
>
> *propaschō* (προπάσχω)
>> *already suffered* (1 Thess. 2:2)
>> aorist active participle
>
> *hubrizō* (ὑβρίζω)
>> *mistreated* (1 Thess. 2:2)
>> aorist passive participle
>
> *kopiaō* (κοπιάω)
>> *labor* [toil even though weary] (1 Thess. 5:12)
>> present active participle
>
> *paschō* (πάσχω)
>> *endured* (1 Thess. 2:14)
>> aorist active indicative
>> *are suffering* (2 Thess. 1:5)
>> present active indicative
>
> *kōluō* (κωλύω)
>> *hindering* (1 Thess. 2:16)
>> present active participle
>
> *egkoptō* (ἐγκόπτω)
>> *hindered* (1 Thess. 2:18)
>> aorist active indicative

Please take the time to understand the Biblical grammar as it will enrichen and enliven the Biblical text. Significant to note is that Paul did not use the future tense, but only the aorist and present tenses. The Thessalonians rightly believed that "birth pangs" (Matt. 24:8) would precede the establishment of the kingdom of the Lord Jesus Christ. As a consequence of the present afflictions and difficulties they were experiencing, in addition to false teachings, the Thessalonian church thought they may be experiencing the seven-year tribulation (the 70th week of Daniel). The believers were assured that they were not experiencing the wrath of God characteristic of that future time (nor will the church throughout the ages experience *the* specific tribulation that culminates in the return of the Lord to Earth). Although their persecutions were real, they were to live as if the Lord may return in their own lifetimes and rescue them "from the wrath to come" (1 Thess. 1:9-10) by means of the rapture (cf. 1 Thess. 2:17-19; 3:13; 4:13—5:11; 2 Thess. 2:1-12).

FIRST THESSALONIANS 1:8-10

Paul commended the Thessalonians because "the word of the Lord . . . sounded forth from" them. Since the Thessalonian church was young at the time of Paul's writing, it is improbable that there was any widespread sending of evangelists or missionaries, as was true of the more mature church of Antioch, Syria (cf. Acts 13). For this reason, it is best to understand the sounding forth of the Word of the Lord as related to the extensive commerce that was characteristic of the city, in addition to the likely travels of believers to whom the Thessalonians would have certainly shown hospitality. The idea seems to be that a lively faith reverberates with energy or activity from one person to another. Of course, this is not the model for obeying the great commission, but it is one means that God will use to fulfill the command upon the church. Paul also stated, "but also in every place your faith toward God has gone forth, so that we have no need to say anything." What was the reason for this marvelous testimony? Paul explained in verses 9 and 10.

Paul stated, "you turned to God from idols to serve a living and true God." Idols today may differ in form, but they still epitomize all that people believe constitutes a good life in the absence of God. In modern terms, this would indicate a completely different purpose of life from those who set the world as their example, and as a result of this difference, the church would have the glorifying of the Lord by His grace and power as the express purpose in this world.

As expression of this new purpose in life, Paul commended the church as waiting for God's Son, Jesus Christ, from heaven. He did not say that the church was idle and simply looking into the sky. "To wait" (*anamenō*, ἀναμένω) is a present infinitive and conveys the idea of expectation. Moreover, the Thessalonians were also busy serving God. As Paul instructed elsewhere, "make it your ambition to lead a quiet life and attend to your own business and work with your hands, just as we commanded you" (1 Thess. 4:11). Attending to one's own business and working with one's hands is with a mindset that is hopeful concerning the future. Another meaning of "wait" is to realize that all work done for the Lord will be rewarded or rejected by the Lord Jesus Christ when He returns for His church. Such realization provides the highest purpose for all things accomplished in life. Nothing is wasted or useless in terms of eternity. Everything done in life is significant regardless of how tedious a task may seem. Therefore, live with an eternal perspective!

Summary of 1 Thessalonians 1

The early church expected Jesus to return for them in their lifetimes. Of course, Christ did not return, but they had every reason to expect His return, which is made obvious by Paul's words in 4:17 ("Then we [Paul and his readers] who are alive and remain will be caught up together with them in the clouds to meet the Lord in the air, and so we shall always be with the Lord"). For more than 2,000 years of church history, Christians have been able to say that the return of the Lord may be today, it may be tomorrow, or it may occur years from now. Therefore, plan as if the Lord were not returning for many years, but live this life thinking, "Perhaps today."

FIRST THESSALONIANS 2

In 1 Thessalonians 2:19-20, the Apostle Paul expressed the heart of a shepherd for his sheep. The pastoral concern of the apostle demonstrates that the wellbeing of the sheep is the first priority of the shepherd. Paul communicated his shepherd's heart for the sheep in verse 19 when he referred to the church as his "hope or joy or crown of exultation." Paul emphatically demonstrated the great priority of the spiritual wellbeing of the church "in the presence of our Lord Jesus at His coming." With regard to eschatological events, two questions arise concerning the identity of the "crown" and the timing of the "coming."

The Crown of Glory and Joy

Scripture reveals various crowns that will be given to believers, which appear to be based upon service to the Lord. In 1 Thessalonians 2:19, the focus is a "crown of exultation," which is perhaps a crown received for faithfulness in evangelism and discipleship (given the context of Paul's words to the Thessalonian church). Other passages of Scripture may confirm this understanding. For instance, 1 Corinthians 9:25 reads, "Everyone who competes in the games exercises self-control in all things." The teaching is that the believer who lives a disciplined life will receive an imperishable crown. Paul alluded to the Isthmian games wherein athletes would discipline themselves to receive a perishable reward, but Scripture reveals that those who are disciplined unto the Lord receive an incorruptible, imperishable crown.

In 2 Timothy 4:8, Paul stated, "In the future there is laid up for me the crown of righteousness, which the Lord, the righteous Judge, will award to me on that day; and not only to me, but also to all who have loved His appearing." Apparently, this crown will be given to those who anticipate the Lord's return, that is, yearn for His appearing. All Christians should confess yearning for the Lord's return, but when conversation progresses with one another, it is sometimes evident that some believers are quite comfortable in the present world and should repent of such foolish notions. The idea that Christ could return at any moment ought to result in great rejoicing. Even now in the present world, one should not view the completion of a degree, or desiring to be first married and have children and be successful, as more important or desirable than the return of the Lord Jesus Christ. Sadly, there are some Christians who may prioritize life in the present as opposed to the Lord's appearing, which is the reason for the focus in 2 Timothy 4:8 upon the crown of righteousness for those who truly yearn for the return of the Lord.

Revelation 2:10 refers to another reward, the crown of life, which would be granted to those believers who endure trials, such as suffering a martyr's death. First Peter 5:4 reveals, "And when the Chief Shepherd appears, you will receive the unfading crown of glory." The reference to the crown of glory should be understood as a reward given to those pastors/elders who shepherd God's flock faithfully. Scripture clearly reveals several different crowns that will be granted to believers. Some may say piously that these rewards do not matter, and the only significance is to experience eternity with Jesus Christ. Scripture, of course, responds to these sentiments in 1 Corinthians 9 wherein believers are commanded, "Run in such a way that you may win" (v. 24). Paul said that such rewards are important and stated that he ran "in such a way, as not without aim" (v. 26). He did not state such words of his flesh, but made such sentiments by the inspiration of the Holy Spirit. Therefore, all Christians should adopt the same conclusion that these crowns are important.

Consequently, the Word of God reveals different crowns granted to believers for faithfulness, and that those crowns will be given at what Scripture terms the judgment seat of Christ. Second Corinthians 5:10, for instance, states "For we must all appear before the judgment seat of Christ, so that each one may be recompensed for his deeds in the body, according to what he has done, whether good or bad." The Greek word for "judgment seat" is *bēma*. In the ancient world, the *bēma* was an elevated platform whereupon a judge would be seated to evaluate and reward contestants in the Greek athletic games for their performance. When Paul said he disciplined himself so that he would "not be disqualified" (v. 27), he was not indicating the unlikely possibility that he would lose his salvation. He was stating an analogy to the Christian life because in the Grecian games an athlete could be disqualified for not competing according to the rules, and therefore would not receive a reward. Paul was stating that he did not want to be disqualified for receiving a reward at the judgment seat of Christ. He was storing for himself "treasures [rewards] in heaven" (Matt. 6:20), which is the reason for Paul's declaration that he would live in such a manner as to obtain "the prize" (1 Cor. 9:24). Scripture is not revealing that eternal life is the focus of judgment; rather, at the judgment seat of Christ, the Christian is judged in terms of the opportunities and privileges received in Christ Jesus.

In 1 Thessalonians 2:19-20, Paul referred to the believers at Thessalonica as a crown of glory to him. His sentiment is understandable because the glory of a mentor/teacher is in their students. There is certainly little comparable glory than to be used by God to help others mature in their relationship with the Lord Jesus Christ. The event that Paul described in these verses is identical with the Biblical revelation concerning the judgment seat of Christ. As a result of his convert's spiritual maturity, Paul could regard the time when his works will be evaluated as an occasion of glory and joy. Therefore, it would be best to understand that the reference is with regard to the presence of the Lord Jesus Christ at His coming for the church, for it is then that believers will stand before the Lord Jesus Christ at the judgment seat, and will be granted crowns and rewards.

The Coming of the Lord Jesus

The Greek word translated "coming" in 1 Thessalonians 2:19 is *parousia*, which may refer to "the arrival of a king in classical and biblical times," and is one of three words that reference the second coming of Christ. The other two words that may reference the second coming of Christ are *apocalupsis* ("revelation") and *epiphaneia* ("appearing"). Perhaps readers are familiar with epiphany—the liturgical season that focuses upon the coming of Christ—which is derived from *epiphaneia*. Understanding that there are different words used for the second coming of Christ is important. With regard to *parousia* in particular, it is essential to examine the context to determine whether it is referring to Christ coming for the church in the rapture or is it Christ coming at the end of the seven-year tribulation in judgment to establish His kingdom. Sometimes the focus of the word *parousia* can be the moment of arrival, and other times the focus may be upon the state that is initiated by that arrival, and therefore it is crucial to examine the context to understand the reference because it can refer to a person arriving, simple presence, or even the appearance of Antichrist. Context indicates whether *parousia* is used in reference to the coming of the king, the establishment of the kingdom, or in reference to the rapture. Some Bible teachers combine all the usages, and believe that *parousia* only means one thing, such as the coming of Christ to earth to establish His kingdom, which it does not. (More is written regarding the context of *parousia* in addressing 1 Thessalonians 4—5, in addition to 2 Thessalonians, to determine whether such references are with regard to the rapture or second coming.)

Summary of 1 Thessalonians 2

Paul expressed his desire to visit the church at Thessalonica but was hindered by Satan (1 Thess. 2:17-18). Even though a physical visit was not possible, Paul was concerned for the believers. He was "all the more eager with great desire to see [their] face," and therefore longed for the presence of the Lord Jesus when a joyous face-to-face meeting would occur. At the coming of Christ for His church, the Thessalonian believers would be his "crown of exultation" in the presence of the Lord Jesus. At the rapture, the believers will be presented as his hope and joy, which indicates a different context than the coming of Christ in judgment to establish His kingdom.

FIRST THESSALONIANS 3

As stated already in regards to 1 Thessalonians 2, the Apostle Paul expressed pastoral concern for the wellbeing of the church. Specifically, Paul regarded the church as his "hope or joy or crown of exultation," and indicated his pastoral priority for the spiritual wellbeing of the church "in the presence of our Lord Jesus at His coming." Paul expressed this same attitude again in 1 Thessalonians 3:13.

Anticipating the Coming of the Lord Jesus

With regard to the coming of the Lord Jesus, it was Paul's desire "that He may establish your hearts without blame in holiness before our God and Father at the coming of our Lord Jesus with all His saints." Paul expressed pastoral concern that the believers would be prepared to give a blameless account of their lives to God, and therefore would be ready for the coming of the Lord Jesus. The reason for his concern is that all Christians will appear before the judgment seat (*bēma*) of Christ (cf. 2 Cor. 5:10; 2 Thess. 1:10).

One should note that the coming of the Lord Jesus referenced in both 1 Thessalonians 2:19 and 3:13 is imminent, which is evidence of a pretribulational rapture. If the midtribulational view that the church will experience half of the seven-year tribulation is correct, or the pre-wrath rapture view that the church will experience three-quarters of the tribulation, or even the posttribulational view, as noted in a somewhat recent book that Baker Books released addressing historic premillennialism[358] (which is essentially posttribulationalism), then the longing expressed in 1 Thessalonians 2:19 and 3:13 would be different. The longing would be for the appearance of the Antichrist because then Christ will return at the end of the tribulation.[359] However, nothing is stated to occur prior to the rapture. Events may occur prior to the rapture but there are not any prophesied events that must occur, whereas it is different for the second coming of the Lord Jesus to earth because a multitude of prophesied events must occur (cf. Rev. 6—19). Jesus even said that there are signs to indicate His return to earth, and yet there are no such indications for the rapture. Obviously, the Bible is referring to distinctions between the rapture and Christ's earthly coming, that is, once for the church to rapture her[360] to heaven, and then at the end of the tribulation with His glorified saints to rule and reign. In 1 Thessalonians 2:19 and 3:13, the expectation is an imminent return of Jesus Christ. Difficulties will manifest in interpretation if these two passages are interpreted as Christ's coming subsequent to the wrath of the seven-year tribulation.

The primary difficulty would be disregard for the contextual emphasis upon the *bēma* of Christ for believers. The judgment that Paul referenced in

---

358 Craig L. Blomberg and Sung Wook Chung, eds., *A Case for Historic Premillennialism: An Alternative to "Left Behind" Eschatology* (Grand Rapids: Baker Books, 2009).

359 In recognition of this truth, posttribulationist Bob Gundry titled his book correctly (to be consistent with his belief) as *First the Antichrist* (Grand Rapids: Baker Books, 1997).

360 The feminine pronoun, "her," is used with regard to the church because the Greek word, *ekklēsia*, is a feminine noun. The grammatical gender, of course, should not be confused with sexual gender (i.e., femininity as opposed to masculinity, or vice-versa).

1 Thessalonians 2:19 and 3:13 will occur "in the presence of our Lord Jesus at His coming" and "before our God and Father at the coming of our Lord Jesus with all His saints." The function of the improper preposition, *emprosthen* ("before," "in the presence of," "in the face of"[361]), is adverbal.[362] As Jelf noted, "The original force however of the cases may in most of the combinations with a preposition be discerned. The preposition often either brings out the original force of the case yet more emphatically, or modifies it. . . ."[363] The force of *emprosthen* is local, which provides the notion of place and time, and would therefore lose its local force if it were "regarded as casual."[364]

The local force of *emprosthen* indicates "appearing before a judge" (Matt. 27:11; 25:32; Luke 21:36; 2 Cor. 5:10; cf. the contrast in 1 Thess. 1:3; 3:9; 1 John 3:19).[365] In 1 Thessalonians 2:19, the Lord Jesus is identified as the judge at the place and time of the *bēma*, and there is not a contradiction in 1 Thessalonians 3:13 by indicating judgment by "our God and Father." The unity of the Father and the Son at the place and time of the *bēma* is a mutual judgeship, as stated in verse 11: "Now may our God and Father Himself and Jesus our Lord direct our way to you." Only God knows the time of the *bēma*, but the place of the judgment is revealed to be with the Father on His heavenly throne (Rev. 3:21; cf. Rom. 8:34; Eph. 1:20; Col. 3:1; Heb. 1:3; 10:12; Rev. 4—5) and will occur "at the coming of our Lord Jesus."

The place of judgment is unmistakable, and therefore the time of the judgment cannot follow the wrath of the seven-year tribulation because the *bēma* will have already occurred in heaven. The coming of the Lord

---

361   William D. Mounce, *The Analytical Lexicon to the Greek New Testament* (Grand Rapids: Zondervan, 1993), p. 184.

362   Herbert Weir Smyth, *A Greek Grammar for College* (New York: American Book Company, 1920), p. 366.

363   William Edward Jelf, *A Grammar of the Greek Language*, 3rd ed., 2 vols. (Oxford and London: John Henry and James Parker, 1861), 2:283.

364   Ibid.

365   William F. Bauer, William F. Arndt, and F. Wilbur Gingrich, *A Greek-English Lexicon of the New Testament and Other Early Christian Literature*, 2nd ed., rev. F. Wilbur Gingrich and Frederick W. Danker (Chicago: University of Chicago Press, 1979), p. 257.

Jesus in both 1 Thessalonians 2:19 and 3:13 must anticipate Paul's words in chapter 4 with regard to Christ's return "in the clouds." Both these verses, therefore, have reference to the *bēma* and not the return of Christ to earth. The coming of Christ in the air at the rapture is not His arrival to judge and reign upon the Earth.

Two Prophecies and the Doctrine of Imminency

With regard to the doctrine of imminency, questions arise occasionally concerning the statement in John 21:18 ("Truly, truly, I say to you, when you were younger, you used to gird yourself and walk wherever you wished; but when you grow old, you will stretch out your hands and someone else will gird you, and bring you where you do not wish to *go*."). The Johannine statement is a reference to Peter's death. The question that arises is with regard to the possibility for Scripture to teach an imminent return of Christ, and yet Jesus said Peter would die in old age. According to church tradition,[366] John 21:18 may be a prediction of how Peter died because he was crucified downward as a consequence of his confession of unworthiness to die similarly to his Lord and Savior.

Certainly, the ancient tradition indicates an amazing transformation in the life of Peter, which is a marvelous argument for the historicity that the resurrection actually occurred. For instance, Peter was an absolute coward before "one of the slaves of the high priest" (John 18:26), even cursing that he did not know the Lord Jesus (Matt. 26:69-75; John 18:25-27), and when the opportunity arrived for him to appear before the Roman leaders his response was with boldness that he was not worthy to die in the same manner as the Lord Jesus and therefore was crucified downward at his own request. The only manner in which one can explain the transformation of

---

366 According to church historian Eusebius, the Apostle Peter "was crucified with his head downward, having requested of himself to suffer in this way" (*Ecclesiastical History*, trans. Christian Frederick Cruse [Grand Rapids: Baker Book House, 1994], 3.1).

the cowardly disciples[367] into a bold and courageous group is that Jesus truly did rise from the grave. People do foolish things in their lives that they believe to be true, but when people know that something is false, they are not bold and courageous for a lie (such actions are contrary to human nature, and are therefore remarkable evidence with regard to the historicity of the resurrection of Christ). Nevertheless, these remarkable truths are a digression from the primary issue with regard to the prophecy that Peter would die in old age.

Prior to answering the question of John 21:18, it is also prudent to mention Acts 23:11 which states, "But on the night *immediately* following, the Lord stood at His side and said, 'Take courage; for as you have solemnly witnessed to My cause at Jerusalem, so you must witness at Rome also.'" Not only was there a prophecy with regard to Peter, but also for the Apostle Paul. God said that Peter would die in old age, and also in Acts 23:11, there is the prophecy that Paul would visit Rome. The question arises with regard to reconciling the notion that Christ may return imminently, yet there were prophesied events in the history of the early church to occur. Peter was to experience old age, and Paul was to visit Rome before the Lord could return.

The answer is that the Johannine prophecy concerning Peter could have been fulfilled shortly after Christ's ascension, if Peter had been confined. For instance, Peter could have undergone confinement in prison, which would satisfy the language of the prophecy that he had grown old in prison by being confined. With regard to the promise to Paul, it seems assumed that unless the Lord returned this would occur. If the Lord returned then Paul would not visit Rome, but if the Lord delayed, then indeed Paul would be able to visit Rome. John 21:18 and Acts 23:11 are not two texts that argue in defense of the imminent return of Jesus Christ, but the texts would be consistent with contemporary expression. For instance, in writing this chapter, the editor may be told that it will be received on Monday . . . unless. The editor will

---

367 John was the only disciple to have been an eyewitness of the crucifixion (John 19:17-37).

receive this chapter on Monday unless the Lord Jesus returns. Therefore, it would appear that the two Biblical texts were spoken in the same manner, that is, the prophecies in John and Acts stated that unless the Lord would return in the first century this is what would occur for both Peter and Paul. The practice of speaking in this manner is quite common. For example, a group of believers have been told, "See you in a couple days for Bible study, Lord willing," which would be consistent with the spoken intent of John 21:18 and Acts 23:11. Therefore, these texts do not contradict the doctrine of imminency with regard to the coming of the Lord Jesus.

Perseverance until the Lord Returns

Paul also expressed pastoral concern in 1 Thessalonians 3:5 "that the tempter might have tempted you, and our labor would be in vain." Verse 5 is typically understood in two different manners. Some interpret Paul as expressing fear that the Thessalonians would actually apostatize from the faith, which would result in their loss of salvation. However, it is simply incongruent with the doctrine of justification by grace through faith in Christ alone to affirm such an interpretation. One cannot locate Biblical evidence *in context* that would affirm that a regenerate believer could lose his or her salvation.[368]

"*For I am* confident of this very thing, that He who began a good work in you will perfect it until the day of Christ Jesus" (Phil. 1:6). Christians are not saved as a result of the flesh or self will (Eph. 2:8-10; Tit. 3:5). Those who are in Christ experience that eternal relationship (John 17:3) as a result of the sovereign outworking of God. Salvation is not "of yourselves" or the "result of works" (Eph. 2:8-9), which means there is no possibility of losing one's salvation (justification). The teaching of Scripture is once justified,

---

368 One would be more Biblical in stating "once justified, always justified," in contrast to "once saved, always saved" because salvation may be regarded *Biblically* as past (justification), present (sanctification) and future (glorification). The experience of one's sanctification may change, but justification is and glorification will be unalterable by the very power and decree of God.

always justified. Certainly, believers may sadly lose their sanctification, but justification is not something that is ever lost. Moreover, it is beyond this author's comprehension to understood how one may experience *eternal life* and then receive *eternal damnation* as a result of works or self. If salvation (justification) is eternal then it cannot be lost.

The motivation for Paul's words in 1 Thessalonians 3:5 was fear that the labor of the Christians would be in vain in the sense of an impediment in their spiritual life, that is, a setback in their spiritual growth, but not actually losing their salvation. Paul's concern was that sometimes there is setback in the life of a true believer. Sometimes true believers do indeed backslide and they must repent inevitably and persevere in faith. According to Scripture, the setbacks are never permanent, and if ever such would be the experience of one who professes faith in Christ, the Biblical revelation would teach, "They went out from us, but they were not *really* of us; for if they had been of us, they would have remained with us; but *they went out*, so that it would be shown that they all are not of us" (1 John 2:19).

Sadly, a true believer may experience a setback in spiritual growth. True believers sometimes drift from God. Nevertheless, as the writer of Hebrews said in chapter 2 of his epistle, there will be spiritual scars. There can be restoration to fellowship, but there are spiritual scars that often result. Paul's fear was that the difficulties the church was experiencing would overwhelm them to the point of a setback, and then there would be spiritual scars that would develop as a consequence. Therefore, the closing words of 1 Thessalonians 3 would be an exhortation to persevere in faith—despite the circumstances—because all believers will stand before God for judgment and evaluation of works accomplished in the service of the Lord. As heavenly citizens who will yet face the heavenly authority at the rapture of the church, both 1 Thessalonians 2:19 and 3:13 provide good motivation to examine one's life with an eternal perspective.

Summary of 1 Thessalonians 3

Paul expressed his desire for the church at Thessalonica specifically and for the church throughout the ages generally to preserve in faithfulness to the Lord Jesus Christ. Prior to Christ's return to Earth for judgment and to establish His kingdom, there will be the seven-year tribulation, and prior to that prophesied event will be the rapture of the church and appearance before the judgment seat "in the presence of our Lord Jesus" and "our God and Father." The contextual emphasis indicates the place of the *bēma* is heaven, which is consistent with the doctrine of the pretribulational rapture. Although only God knows the timing of the rapture, the church may live with an imminent expectation of the return of Christ "in the clouds" of heaven to rapture His beloved elect from the Earth. With such a hope for the present may every believer yearn for the work of the Holy Spirit in establishing his or her heart "without blame in holiness . . . at the coming of our Lord Jesus with all His saints."

FIRST THESSALONIANS 4

If one were to request only one passage of Scripture as proof for a pretribulational rapture, the majority of pretribulationists would likely cite 1 Thessalonians 4:13-18 as Biblical proof of this blessed doctrine. Since it is a foundational passage, it is pertinent to understand rightly what God has revealed (cf. 2 Tim. 2:15). The primary issue to be addressed here is the words used with regard to the coming of the Lord Jesus. The Greek word translated "coming" in 1 Thessalonians 4:15 is *parousia* (παρουσία). One would be wise to become familiar with the word *parousia* since it is referenced often by those seeking to understand and interpret Biblical eschatology.

The Timing of the Parousia

There are three views with regard to the timing of the Lord's coming, and those are pretribulationism, midtribulationism and then posttribulationism.[369] The timing issue with regard to the Lord's coming (i.e., the doctrine of the rapture as distinct from the second coming) is the result of premillennial theology. For instance, amillennialists and postmillennialists do not believe Scripture to teach any kind of rapture because those theologies believe there is only one return of the Lord Jesus, which is accompanied by a general resurrection and general judgment.[370] Consequently, amillennial and postmillennial eschatology is simplistic (and therefore easy to understand) because all prophecies with regard to judgment and resurrection are combined.

Premillennial eschatology is very complex because there are many diverse events. Scripture prophesies of a rapture, seven-year tribulation, second coming, a 75-day interval prior to the millennium, the final rebellion of Satan at the end of the millennium; moreover, there is not a general resurrection and general judgment, but there is the judgment seat of Christ, the first resurrection, the second resurrection, and the great white throne judgment. What is noteworthy with regard to premillennialism is to compare it to diagrams of the book of Kings or the book of Chronicles, which are also incredibly complex because those Old Testament books are accounts of real history. Likewise, premillennial eschatology is complex because it systematizes what will be historical, and therefore literal, details of the Bible.

Furthermore, it is also worth noting that there is nearly universal agreement that if one interprets Scripture literally, the outcome will be a

---

369 Pre-wrath rapturism would be best identified as a variation of midtribulationism.

370 Scripture distinguishes the rapture of the church and coming of the Lord Jesus Christ to Earth, in addition to differentiating the first resurrection (which includes the judgment seat of Christ for the church, the judgment of Old Testament saints, the judgment of tribulation saints, the judgment of millennial saints) from the second resurrection (the judgment of unbelievers at the great white throne).

premillennial eschatology. For instance, (amillennialist) Oswald T. Allis wrote, "The Old Testament prophecies if literally interpreted cannot be regarded as having been fulfilled or as being capable of fulfillment in this present age."[371] Floyd E. Hamilton, who was also opposed to premillennialism, wrote similarly, "Now we must frankly admit that a literal interpretation of the Old Testament prophecies gives us just such a picture of an earthly reign of the Messiah as the premillennialist pictures. That was the kind of a Messianic kingdom that the Jews of the time of Christ were looking for, on the basis of a literal interpretation of the Old Testament."[372] Of course, amillennialists and postmillennialists attempt to provide explanations as to why one should not regard specific prophetic texts literally and why one should not interpret Biblical prophecy literally. Certain passages in 1 Thessalonians, or in Daniel (chs. 7—12) and Revelation are regarded as an apocalyptic genre (sc. symbolic primarily) and/or interpreted spiritually (allegorically) so that the literal meaning is not desired.[373] Therefore, addressing the issue of the distinction between the rapture and the second coming is not a concern for amillennialists and postmillennialists.

---

371 Oswald T. Allis, *Prophecy and the Church* (Philadelphia: Presbyterian and Reformed, 1945), p. 238.

372 Floyd E. Hamilton, *The Basis of Millennial Faith* (Grand Rapids: Eerdmans, 1942), p. 38.

373 For example, Allis wrote, "obedience is the precondition of blessing under all circumstances" (*Prophecy and the Church*, p. 33). One would be correct in stating that some blessings of God in both the Old Testament and New Testament are conditioned upon obedience. However, it is equally true that the sovereign decrees of God will be fulfilled exactly as He promised. Moreover, while Israel was disciplined severely for disobedience, the fulfillment of God's promises to the believing remnant is unconditional (as in election). Hamilton provided another alleged reason for rejecting premillennial doctrine, "Jesus Himself, in speaking of that whole idea said, 'The kingdom of God is within (or, in the midst of) you' (Luke 17:21), thus contradicting the idea that it was an earthly, literal Jewish kingdom" (*Basis of Millennial Faith*, p. 39). Jesus, however, did not declare a spiritual form of the kingdom had arrived, but was indicating that the kingdom was near because He was present on earth, and a genuine offer of the kingdom was proffered to the nation of Israel (see Ron J. Bigalke Jr. and George Gunn, "Contingency of the Davidic Reign," in *Progressive Dispensationalism: An Analysis of the Movement and Defense of Traditional Dispensationalism*, ed. Ron J. Bigalke Jr. (Lanham, MD: University Press of America, 2005), pp. 181-82.

Pretribulationism and Midtribulationism

The issue with regard to the rapture of the church is a premillennial discussion dealing with the timing of that coming, and whether it is pretribulational, midtribulational or posttribulational. The pretribulational view that the rapture will precede the seven years of tribulation is what Scripture teaches. The midtribulational view is actually a variation of the pretribulational because midtribulationists simply regard the church as being exempt from tribulation, or the wrath of God, which begins at the midpoint of the tribulation, that is, the last three-and-a-half years. Both pretribulationists and midtribulationists would agree the church is not destined to experience the wrath of the tribulation, but pretribulationists and midtribulationists disagree as to when that wrath begins.

The pretribulationist understands the wrath of God to begin at the beginning of the tribulation, and the midtribulationist believes that God's wrath occurs at the tribulational midpoint, which is their method for affirming that the church it raptured prior to the outpouring of God's wrath. Midtribulationists refer typically to Revelation 11 wherein the Biblical text refers to the snatching upward of the two witnesses who have been martyred. Midtribulationists believe the prophesied event to be symbolic of the church. Consequently, the midtribulationist does not believe the rapture is imminent; it cannot occur at any moment because certain events must occur, which is a primary distinction from pretribulationism because the rapture can occur at any moment (i.e., although events *may* precede the rapture, there are no prophesied events that *must* occur).

Midtribulationism does not receive much attention, as there are not many midtribulationists presently, and there have not been many midtribulationists throughout the history of the church. Marvin Rosenthal, the founder of Zion's Hope Ministries and the Holy Land Experience in

Orlando, Fla.,[374] has attempted to revive midtribulational thinking with what he calls the "pre-wrath rapture of the church." Rosenthal does not regard his view as midtribulational and does not make any reference to midtribulationism. However, his argumentation is entirely similar to midtribulationism, and should be understood as a combination of both pretribulational and posttribulational assertions. The majority of rapture discussions involve the pretribulational or posttribulational views.

Posttribulationalists are attempting to reassert their position because adherents of that position recognize that primarily with regard to the rapture, the majority of the focus has been upon pretribulationism. According to the posttribulational view, the church will experience the entire seven years of tribulation, and the rapture and the second coming are regarded as one event. George Eldon Ladd (1911-82), who was professor of New Testament exegesis and theology at Fuller Theological Seminary, is a primary reference for posttribulational studies. There is also much attention upon Ladd's eschatology and its relationship to the miraculous gifts of the Holy Spirit.[375]

The theology of Ladd was a major influence upon John Wimber (1934-97), founder of the Vineyard Christian Fellowship, who was convinced that demonstration and validation of the power of the gospel was through miracles. Ladd is a noteworthy individual not only for eschatological studies, but also for pneumatology (doctrine of the Holy Spirit) among those who argue that signs and wonders of the New Testament times should be common practices in the contemporary church. Ladd's writings remain influential in the current time.

As a futurist posttribulationist, Ladd wrote, "The parousia, the apokalypse, and the epiphany appear to be a single event. Any division of

---

374 As a result of increasing debt, the Holy Land Experience was purchased by Trinity Broadcasting Network in June 2007.

375 Bruce A. Baker, "Progressive Dispensationalism and Cessationism: Why They Are Incompatible," "Is Progressive Dispensationalism Really Dispensational?," in *Progressive Dispensationalism*, pp. 257-84, 346-60.

Christ's coming into two parts is an unproven inference."[376] Ladd believed the words "parousia, the apokalypse, and the epiphany" refer to the same, single event, and therefore are not to be differentiated. Ladd is incorrect, however, in his assertion. The first word, *parousia*, is translated "coming" in 1 Thessalonians 4:15, and in that passage refers rather specifically to the rapture of the church. The same Greek word, *parousia*, is used in Matthew 24:27 and is accurately translated "coming" with regard to the Lord's return to Earth. Since the same Greek word is used in Matthew 24:27 and 1 Thessalonians 4:15, posttribulationists believe the texts refer to the same, single event. Pretribulationists disagree, and understand *parousia* to describe two separate events: the rapture and the second coming.

Parousia is properly translated as coming, and literally bears the idea of presence associated with the coming. An illustration may help to clarify the literal meaning. Grandparents may say they are expecting the presence (the *parousia*) of their grandchildren for a special occasion. The statement may be understood in a twofold manner. The *first meaning* may be that the grandparents are expecting the presence of their grandchildren soon, and they will be present for the special occasion. In other words, the grandchildren will come soon, which will be evident in them being present and experiencing the special occasion of their grandparents. Therefore, the soon coming and the actual celebration occur at one time. The *second meaning* of the statement could be that the grandparents will be experiencing the presence of their grandchildren soon, and they will also be present for the special occasion. Therefore, two events are understood. The grandchildren could come soon, leave the grandparent's home, and return again for the special occasion. The coming of the grandchildren may refer to one event, or it could refer to two events.

The illustration serves to demonstrate that the coming of the grandchildren does not necessarily infer one, single event; it is similar with the

---

376 George E. Ladd, *The Blessed Hope* (Grand Rapids: Eerdmans, 1956), p. 69; cf. Douglas J. Moo, "The Case for the Posttribulation Rapture Position," in *The Rapture: Pre-, Mid-, or Post-Tribulational?* (Grand Rapids: Zondervan, 1984), pp. 176-78.

presence (coming) of the Lord Jesus. When the Greek word, *parousia*, is used, it does not have to mean that the rapture and the second coming are one event. *Parousia* could quite simply be a word that describes two separate events. Ladd's statement is wrong because the mere use of *parousia* does not indicate whether the coming is the rapture of the church or the Lord's return to Earth. Only the context of the Biblical passage will indicate which coming is being referenced.

The other word used with regard to the Lord's coming is *apokalupsis* (ἀποκάλυψις). The three uses of this word in 1 Corinthians 1:7 and 1 Peter 1:7 and 4:13 are references to the rapture. *Apokalupsis* simply means "revelation." In the Corinthians passage and the two references in 1 Peter, the Greek word is referring to when Christ comes for His church, He will reveal Himself to her. At the second coming, of course, Christ will also reveal Himself, but in a different manner; He will reveal Himself as He returns to Earth at the close of the tribulation (i.e., He will reveal Himself as Lord of lords and King of kings to the entire world). One must examine context to determine which coming is being referenced. Context will indicate whether the usage is with regard to Christ coming to reveal Himself for who He is, or whether it is His second coming when He reveals Himself to the entire world.

The third word mentioned by Ladd is *epiphaneia* (ἐπιφάνεια), which simply means "manifestation." Christ will certainly manifest Himself to His church. *Epiphaneia* is used in 2 Timothy 4:8 and Titus 2:13 with reference to Christ manifesting Himself to the church at the rapture. The same word is used in 2 Thessalonians 2:8, which refers to the time when Christ destroys Antichrist; the Lord Jesus manifests Himself by His coming, which is an epiphany that destroys Antichrist. Context determines whether the rapture or the second coming is intended.

If posttribulationists are correct (which they are not), the Greek words—*parousia, apokalupsis* and *epiphaneia*—must catalog the time of the Lord's return whenever they are used. In other words, anytime one reads the three Greek words (or their translation), they must be cataloged into one single event. The Biblical response would be not to catalog but to recognize that the three Greek words characterize the coming of Lord Jesus. *Parousia, apokalupsis* and *epiphaneia* do not catalog the Lord's return as a single event; rather, they characterize His return at the rapture and at the second coming. For instance, the word *parousia* characterizes the presence of the Lord at the rapture and also at the second coming. The *apokalupsis* characterizes the revelation of Christ; there will be a revelation of who He is at the rapture and also at the second coming. Moreover, at the rapture, there will be a manifestation of the Lord to His church; therefore, the Greek word *epiphaneia* is used.

Grief and Hope in 1 Thessalonians 4

With regard to the coming of the Lord Jesus, there is much emphasis upon the Greek words *parousia, apokalupsis* and *epiphaneia*. As already demonstrated, those words do not catalog one single event; rather, these words are used throughout the New Testament to characterize both the rapture and the second coming. Since it is the Biblical context that will determine which coming is referenced, the context of 1 Thessalonians 4:13-18 will demonstrate that the comfort of this passage is the reunion of the deceased and living saints in Christ at the pretribulational rapture.

Pretribulationism and posttribulationism are the two primary premillennial views with regard to the rapture of the church; therefore, it is prudent to consider only those two doctrines. When examining 1 Thessalonians 4, both pretribulationists and posttribulationists agree that there truly was a grieving of the church at Thessalonica, but believe that they were grieving for different reasons. Verse 13 reads, "But we do not want you to be uninformed, brethren, about those who are asleep, so that you will not grieve as do the rest who have no hope."

Pretribulationists understand the grief of 1 Thessalonians 4:13 as a consequence of believing that the rapture of the church would culminate with all the church receiving glorified bodies, and that this coming of the Lord could occur in their own lifetimes. Possibly the early church would not experience death but would be raptured as those who were alive and remained until the coming of the Lord Jesus. The Apostle Paul even included himself as one who could have experienced the rapture in his own lifetime (cf. his usage of the inclusive first person plural "we"). Following the initial teaching with regard to the rapture, some Christians had died, and the Thessalonian church had become intensely concerned because they were inquiring what would occur to the dead in Christ at the rapture. The question it seems was whether the dead in Christ would participate in the rapture, or would they have to wait until the end of the seven-year tribulation.

Some posttribulationists understand the grief of 1 Thessalonians 4:13 as a consequence of believing that the resurrection of the dead in Christ would occur at the end of the millennium.[377] According to such an interpretation, the Thessalonian believers understood the rapture as granting new, glorified bodies to those living, but then having to wait until the end of the millennium for the dead in Christ to receive their glorified bodies. Therefore, the concern was regarding a long separation between those believers alive at the time of the rapture from those who had already died, and would have to wait for receiving their new bodies.

The primary focus of the Thessalonian believers was the thought that to experience the rapture one had to be alive. Therefore, the grief was the consequence of believing (incorrectly) that the dead in Christ would not participate in the rapture.[378] If one considers the posttribulational view, it would seem that the focus of the posttribulationist should be upon

---

377   Robert H. Gundry, *The Church and the Tribulation* (Grand Rapids: Zondervan, 1973), p. 101.
378   Charles A. Wanamaker, *The Epistle to the Thessalonians* (Grand Rapids: Eerdmans, 1990), pp. 169, 172.

the tribulation. If the church were taught that they would experience the seven years of tribulation, it would not be logical for them to be concerned regarding those who had died in Christ. Moreover, it is extremely doubtful that the church would be grieving in relation to those who were dead in Christ, but would rather be happy for them. For example, when a family member died, the memorial card stated how he was now experiencing peace and rest. My relative experienced difficult medical conditions, and the card was focused upon the fact that his suffering had ended. His earthly pain had ceased and the family was focused upon the end of painful medical conditions. (Of course, only those in Christ will experience peace and rest upon death.) Consider this example with regard to 1 Thessalonians 4.

If the Thessalonian believers thought the church was going to experience the tribulation, they should be relieved that those who had died in Christ would not experience any of those seven years. The emphasis would be upon persevering through the tribulation, and not focused upon the dead in Christ. The focus does not coalesce with a non-pretribulational understanding of the rapture. The focus of the believers was upon those who were not living because they imagined one had to be alive at the time of the rapture to experience it, which is consistent with a pretribulational perspective.

The concern of the Thessalonian believers simply does not coalesce with non-pretribulational views. Verse 14 reads, "For if we believe [or literally, "*since* we believe"] that Jesus died and rose again, even so God will bring with Him those who have fallen asleep [died[379]] in Jesus." The reality of the rapture in 1 Thessalonians 4:14 is related to the historicity of the death and resurrection of Jesus Christ. The reality of Christ's death and resurrection is evidence that the rapture will occur; the focus of verse

---

379 The Old French word *cimetiere* ("graveyard") is derived from the Late Latin *coemeterium*, which is derived from the Greek word here, *koimaō*, which means "*to sleep* in death." The Greek word, *koimeterion* ("cemetery"), is derived from *koimaō*, and designated a place of burial (sleep). Ancient writers used "sleep" as a common euphemism for "death" (e.g., 1 Kings 2:10).

14 is upon the assurance that those in Christ will experience the rapture, and references with emphasis upon "those who have fallen asleep in Jesus" (i.e., those who have died in Christ).

The Church Will Be Raptured

The language used in 1 Thessalonians 4:14 indicates that the prophecy of the rapture is with regard to Christians (the church) as opposed to the saved of all the ages. For example, when Jesus raised Lazarus from the dead, He did not merely say, "come forth"; rather, He said "Lazarus, come forth" because if He said "come forth" only, then all the dead would rise. Jesus spoke specifically, and said only "Lazarus, come forth" (John 11:43). The rapture of the church will occur similarly because it is only the dead "in Christ" that will be resurrected.

If the saints of all the ages who have died are resurrected at the time specified in 1 Thessalonians 4, it would conflict with other Scriptural passages that place the resurrection of Old Testament saints subsequent to the tribulation, and therefore receiving their glorified bodies in preparation for the millennium (Dan. 12:2). The resurrection (rapture) of 1 Thessalonians 4 is prophesied for the church. There are multiple times of resurrection that constitute the first resurrection of Revelation 20:1-6, which in context is referring to details following the second coming of Christ. Thereafter, verses 11-15 refer to the second death, or resurrection of the wicked. The first resurrection involves multiple times. "First" does not mean only one resurrection, but refers to a certain kind of resurrection (i.e., "blessed and holy").

Continuing in 1 Thessalonians 4, verse 15 reads, "For this we say to you by the word of the Lord, that we who are alive and remain until the coming of the Lord, will not precede those who have fallen asleep." When Paul wrote, "we say to you by the word of the Lord," apparently he was indicating that he received this teaching directly from the Lord.

The prophesy of the rapture was a doctrine previously unrevealed, which is why he emphasized that the teaching was by the authority of the Lord. The emphasis of thought upon the dead in Christ continues in this verse.

Apparently, the believers thought the living would only experience the rapture, that is, only the living can participate in the rapture. First Thessalonians 4:13-18 addresses this concern. The teaching of Scripture is that neither the dead in Christ nor those "who are alive and remain until the coming of the Lord" will be in better position than the other because all will be raised together with the Lord in the air. The dead in Christ and those who are "alive and remain" will be translated at the same coming of the Lord so there will not be any advantage in that sense. Regenerate members of the church—whether deceased or living—will receive their new resurrection bodies at that rapture.

Verses 16-18 state clearly, "For the Lord Himself will descend from heaven with a shout, with the voice of *the* archangel and with the trumpet of God, and the dead in Christ will rise first. Then we who are alive and remain will be caught up together with them in the clouds to meet the Lord in the air, and so we shall always be with the Lord. Therefore comfort one another with these words." The teaching of these verses is the exact opposite if one were taught that he or she would experience any of the seven-year tribulation. As many believers will be martyred in the tribulation, it would not be a comforting thought.

The promise of the church's exemption from the tribulation is not a reward for the church, but it is simply something that God in His purposes has not destined to occur. The reason is that God has a specific purpose for the tribulation. He is focusing his attention primarily on Israel in preparation for the millennial kingdom. Therefore, another name for the tribulation is the "70th week" of Daniel (Dan. 9:24-27). Sixty-nine weeks of Daniel's prophecy have already been fulfilled with the nation of Israel, and it is a prophecy dealing with events that occurred to them historically.

The remaining 70th week of that prophecy is focused upon Israel, and it is therefore incongruent contextually to relate the church to those prophecies.

The Tribulation with Regard to Israel

The focus of the tribulation—the 70th week of Daniel—is upon God purging the rebel from among Israel. God will purge the rebels exactly as the prophet Zechariah indicated; namely that two-thirds of the Jewish people will perish in the tribulation, and only a third will persevere in faith to the end (Zech. 13:8-9), which will be a fulfillment of Romans 11:25-27 that "all Israel will be saved" at the time of the second coming. At the end of the tribulation, all living Jews will be saved and will enter into the millennial kingdom on the basis of faith in King Jesus. The focus of the tribulation is preparing Israel to receive Messiah in fulfillment of the unconditional covenants that God made with the nation. God will also use the tribulation to judge the wicked among the Gentiles, the world. The latter purpose is interesting currently because when one considers the world of Christendom today there are tremendous Biblical failures. The extent of apostates and heresies that are tolerated today would exasperate the early church, which was entirely dedicated to the preservation and promotion of sound doctrine (Jude 3).

Among the Jewish people, the Messianic movement continues to grow, which seems to indicate that God is removing their blindness to the gospel. He blinded Israel to bring many Gentiles into salvation, and blinded His own people for the benefit of the nations (Rom. 11:7-11). Apparently, today, God is returning the blindness to the Gentiles, that is, the nations are returning to their paganism and something distinctive is occurring with the Jewish people as they search the prophecies in understanding (cf. Dan. 12:4). The Jewish people are witnessing enormous activity in their homeland with discussion regarding the Temple Mount, the Arab-Israeli conflict and alleged peace agreements. Whereas as the Jewish people are asking questions concerning these things, many of the Gentiles are oblivious with regard to God's eternal purposes for Israel.

The Heralding of the Lord's Return

What is not readily apparent in the Biblical text is whether the "shout," "the voice of *the* archangel" and "the trumpet of God" are one event or three events. They are obviously literal and what they accomplish is to herald the Lord's return from heaven, and to focus attention upon the fact that God will raise the dead and translate the living to receive glorified bodies. Beginning with Revelation 8, there is much focus upon the seven trumpets, and some attempt to relate "the trumpet of God" in 1 Thessalonians 4:16 with those trumpets of Revelation. However, there is no indication in 1 Thessalonians 4:16 that the Lord Himself will be descending in any manner subsequent to the seal and trumpet judgments of the tribulation.

The emphasis of 1 Thessalonians 4:13-18 is that the rapture of the church is imminent, that is, it could occur at any moment without any events preceding it. Certainly, in the ancient world, trumpets were used to herald many things. There is a problem with saying that every trumpet has to be the same. For instance, the trumpet in 1 Thessalonians 4 heralds the rapture of the church, whereas the trumpets of Revelation herald the bowl judgments and that Christ will be returning to Earth. There is not any reason to prevent one from concluding that 1 Thessalonians 4 and the book of Revelation refer to multiple soundings of trumpets; it is similar to how the Greek words *parousia*, *apokalupsis* and *epiphaneia* do not refer to one event but characterize two separate events.

Rapturing the Church to Meet the Lord

In verse 17, the Greek word translated "caught up" is *harpazō*, which in the Latin Vulgate was translated by Jerome as *rapiemer* from which the term "rapture" is derived. Rapture is a Biblical term for the event when God resurrects and translates the church to meet the Lord in the air. The reason for this event is so that the church may go with Christ to heaven where she will abide with Him in the place that Christ has prepared in fulfillment of John 14:1-3. The language of both these passages is remarkably similar.

JOHN 14:1-3	1 THESSALONIANS 4:13-18
do not let your heart be troubled (v. 1)	so that you will not grieve (v. 13)
believe in God (v. 1)	even so God (v. 14)
believe also in Me (v. 1)	believe that Jesus died and rose again (v. 14)
I would have told you (v. 2)	for this we say to you (v. 15)
come again (v. 3)	coming of the Lord (v. 15)
receive you (v. 3)	caught up (v. 17)
receive you to Myself (v. 3)	to meet the Lord (v. 17)
where I am, *there* you may be also (v. 3)	we shall always be with the Lord (v. 17)

Other passages will focus upon receiving rewards at the judgment seat of Christ, and the need to await return with the Lord Jesus at the second coming to Earth to rule and reign. Nevertheless, the teaching of 1 Thessalonians 4:13-18 is that the entire seven-year tribulation for the church will be in heaven, not on the Earth, which is a tremendous comfort, and certainly even more so because it could occur at any moment. The doctrine of the rapture is a tremendous emphasis upon living one's life in holy and diligent expectation of the Lord's return.

At any moment, the church could be in the presence of our God and Savior, which should motivate believers to live holy and pure lives because that is always the emphasis of the doctrine of the rapture in Scripture. The doctrine is always used with the sense of living a holy and a godly life, because at any moment the church could appear in the Lord's presence; believers, therefore, are to maintain an active ministry for the Lord's glory and honor, not wasting time and opportunity. At any moment, the church could be in the Lord's presence and will need to give an account of one's life.

How did one use the gifts the Holy Spirit gave? How did one serve the Lord as His bondslaves? Was one just merely attending worship on a weekly basis, and satisfied with "warming a pew," as opposed to being active in serving the Lord? The doctrine of the rapture has a tremendous emphasis upon how believers live their lives, how the church proclaims the gospel, and it is a tremendous comfort, as verse 18 states—"comfort one another with these words"—because at any moment the believer could be with the Lord and in His presence. Therefore, do not waste time and opportunity, but live holy and diligently unto the Lord.

Summary of 1 Thessalonians 4

In its original language (Koine ["common"] Greek), the New Testament used different words to describe the rapture and the second coming. The usages do not catalog the Greek words, nor indicate that the coming of Lord Jesus is a single event; rather, the usages characterize the return of Lord Jesus at the rapture and at the second coming (i.e., two events—not one). Perhaps another illustration may help. One could say that an air conditioning unit has a motor, but it is also true to state that cameras and vehicles have motors. If the three references to motor are catalogued this would mean that a motor is always the same (within an air conditioning unit, a camera, a vehicle, etc.), but this would not be the intended meaning of the word usage because what is meant is just what a motor does. One understands the function of a motor, and therefore the usage of that word is characterizing; it is not intended to mean that every reference to a motor refers to the exact same motor, and it is similar with the words used for the rapture and the second coming.

Therefore, *parousia, apokalupsis* and *epiphaneia* do not catalog the Lord's return into a single event; rather, one must examine context to determine what the words characterize. One must ask, Does the word characterize the rapture, or does the word characterize the second coming? To be rather direct, there are too many irreconcilable differences between the Biblical passages with regard to the rapture and the second coming for them to be cataloguing the same event. Revelation 19, for instance, prophecies Christ's coming, and the emphasis is upon His judgment of the wicked. Whereas, in 1 Thessalonians 4, there is only a depiction of the righteous in Christ, and the emphasis upon the dead being raised to life. The dead are raised to life and the living are immediately translated (i.e., they receive new, glorified bodies).

In Revelation 19, however, the living are judged: either the living are judged to experience death, or the living are judged to enter the kingdom. In 1 Thessalonians 4, the living meet the Lord Jesus in the air; whereas, in Revelation 19, there is the prophecy of Christ coming with the armies of heaven, that is, coming with His saints. The emphasis in 1 Thessalonians 4 is upon the guests at the marriage supper of the Lamb; whereas, in Revelation 19, the "bride" is distinct from those assembled "for the great supper of God." In 1 Thessalonians 4, the emphasis is upon the coming of Lord Jesus for those who will be with Him forever. Conversely, in Revelation 19, the emphasis is upon those forever separated from Christ Jesus. Incredibly distinct events are being described in 1 Thessalonians 4 and Revelation 19.

John 14:1-3 and 1 Thessalonians 4 use remarkably similar language. In John 14, Jesus said "do not . . . be troubled," and in 1 Thessalonians 4:13, Paul said "you will not grieve" because the emphasis is upon the fact that if one trusts in Jesus as Lord and Savior, and therefore believes in God, then when Christ comes, He will take those individuals to be with Him. John

14 states that Lord Jesus will receive them, whereas 1 Thessalonians 4 says they will be raptured, taken to be with the Lord, and will always be with Him. Of course, these are tremendous differences from what one reads in Matthew 24—25 and Revelation 19; in those passages, the emphasis is upon events when Christ returns to earth. Therefore, the Biblical text causes this writer to disagree with his posttribulational brethren, and he does not believe that *parousia*, *apokalupsis* and *epiphaneia* catalog one single event. When context is examined more carefully, it is evident that those words may refer to two different events: the rapture of the church and the Lord's return to earth. The believer in Jesus may Biblically anticipate the return of the Lord prior to the beginning of the seven-year tribulation.

The teaching of 1 Thessalonians 4:13-18 is a comfort to believers. Scripture teaches that the dead in Christ will not be excluded from participation in the rapture with those "who are alive and remain until the coming of the Lord" Jesus (cf. 1 Cor. 15:50-58). "The dead in Christ will rise first, then we who are alive and remain will be caught up together with them . . . to meet the Lord in the air." The rapture is indeed imminent (preceding the seven-year tribulation) and therefore a great comfort to believers. Therefore, as 1 Thessalonians 4:13—5:11 teaches, the church is to be ready always to meet the Lord and be with Him forever.

FIRST THESSALONIANS 5

First Thessalonians 5:1-11 is the second of three primary eschatological passages in the letters to the Thessalonians. The first, of course, was 1 Thessalonians 4:13-18. The next principal passage will be in 2 Thessalonians 2:1-12, which addresses issues relating to the rapture of the church. The consideration of 1 Thessalonians 4 in the previous sections addressed the invalid attempts to merge the rapture and the second coming into a single event, and demonstrated that the comfort of that passage will be the reunion of the deceased and living saints in Christ at the pretribulational rapture. First Thessalonians 5:1-11 provides a different focus with emphasis upon the Day of the Lord, and this passage also has relevance for the doctrine of the rapture.

Distinguishing the Coming of Lord Jesus

Scripture does not employ the actual language "first coming" and "second coming," but this does not imply that the doctrinal terminology is unbiblical. The Bible, for example, does not use the term "Trinity," nor in a solitary verse does it state that God is three equally eternal persons, who are the same substance but distinct in subsistence. Biblical theology is the systematic formulation of the doctrinal (propositional) statements of Scripture. Therefore, simply because the specific language that modern readers of Scripture desire—such as "first coming" and "second coming"—is not employed does not mean that *the teaching* represented in the doctrinal and theological classifications is not explicit.

Often questions are asked concerning why Scripture does not state explicitly that Christ will return once in the rapture followed by His return to the Earth at least seven years later. To answer that question, one may also consider the first and second comings of Messiah. The Old Testament certainly prophesied that Christ would suffer on behalf of His people, that is, to give His life as a substitute, and that Messiah would rule and reign upon the Earth. In reading the New Testament, it is evident that there will be two comings of Messiah. However, if one were to talk with the Biblical scholars of Jesus' time (and the general populace), the notion of a first coming to suffer followed by a second coming to reign seemed preposterous. Even the disciples struggled with the concept.

Acts 1:6 records the disciples' question to the Lord with regard to the kingdom. Believing correctly that Jesus is the Messiah, the disciples expected Him to "restore the kingdom to Israel." The disciples struggled to think in terms of Messiah leaving for any period of time and then returning to establish the Davidic (millennial) kingdom.[380] With the vantage of hindsight, it is evident that an intercalation (i.e., the introduction of an unseen time element) between the first and second comings is occurring.[381] The time element between the first and second comings establishes a Biblical precedent that what may appear to be an indication of only one future event may actually require two separate events. Not only is the intercalation true between the first coming of Christ to suffer, and His second coming to rule and reign, but also with regard to the rapture and the second coming.

A Different Emphasis in 1 Thessalonians 5

Whereas the emphasis of 1 Thessalonians 4 is upon the awe and hope associated with the coming of the Lord, the focus of 1 Thessalonians 5 is somewhat gloom. The change in emphasis is evident in the two Greek words, *peri de* ("but [now] concerning [as]"), that begin the chapter.[382] Whenever the Apostle Paul used these words in 1 Corinthians and 1 Thessalonians, it was to introduce a new subject.[383] Therefore, the Greek

---

380 In Matthew 24:1-2, the thinking of the disciples was based upon Zechariah 14, wherein verses 1–2 describe Jerusalem's deliverance, verses 3–8 prophesy the destruction of Jerusalem's enemies by Messiah, and verses 9–11 record the establishment of the kingdom. Therefore, the disciples thought the A.D. 70 destruction of Jerusalem would culminate in the reign of Messiah. In the Olivet Discourse, however, Jesus warned against thinking that the destruction of Jerusalem and cataclysmic events would signify the end (Matt. 24:6). He warned the disciples with regard to deception concerning false messiahs, wars and other events.

381 *All* amillennialists and *some* premillennialists and postmillennialists believe the kingdom of God was inaugurated (initiated) at the first coming of Christ. One should note that the prophecies concerning the Roman Empire in Daniel 2 and 7 were fulfilled precisely at the time of the first coming of Christ, yet the prophecy concerning the final destruction of that empire has never been fulfilled. For instance, Rome did not fall as a result of Christianity but fell primarily due to corruption that decayed the empire internally. The influence of the Roman Empire—the legs and toes of the image of Daniel 2—continued for several centuries after the first coming of Christ. Moreover, it was the Visigoths, with Alaric in command, in the year 408, who besieged Rome and defeated it. However, in reading Daniel 2:35, it is evident that all effects of the fourth kingdom and the preceding kingdoms are destroyed and disappear at the second coming of Christ so that it is said, "The wind carried them away so that not a trace of them was found."

382 The practice is distinct to Paul, although some seek to apply the action to other Biblical authors, such as in Matthew 24:36, but this is incorrect.

383 James D. G. Dunn, *The Theology of Paul the Apostle* (Grand Rapids: Eerdmans, 1998), p. 611;

preposition and conjunction in 1 Thessalonians 5:1 indicates a transition from the emphasis upon the rapture in 1 Thessalonians 4:13-18; therefore, the emphasis of verses 1-11 in 1 Thessalonians 5 is judgment. For instance, one reads, "For you yourselves know full well that the day of the Lord will come just like a thief in the night."

Paul indicated that the Thessalonian believers were quite knowledgeable with regard to the Day of the Lord, but such language may not be as familiar to modern readers. Consequently, the reader will benefit from seeking definition and explanation of this Old Testament event by consulting three Old Testament passages. The Day of the Lord is a well-developed prophetic concept in the Old Testament prophetical books. Since this concept was known well, it was only prudent for Paul to address the rapture first since this is a distinct New Testament doctrine.

There are references to the second coming in the Old Testament, but none with regard to the rapture, which was the source of confusion. The church was well acquainted with Old Testament history, and then Paul introduced a mystery teaching, which was something that was not mysterious in the sense of being some kind of esoteric teaching, or some pagan, occultic teaching—not a mystery in that sense—but a mystery in the sense that it was not revealed in the Old Testament, and so it was a source of confusion.

With regard to the Day of the Lord, however, the early church was quite familiar. Isaiah 13:9-11 reads:

> Behold, the day of the LORD is coming,
> Cruel, with fury and burning anger,
> To make the land a desolation;
> And He will exterminate its sinners from it.

Margaret M. Mitchell, "Concerning PERI DE in 1 Corinthians," *Novum Testamentum* 31 (1989): 229-56; Huub van de Sandt and Jürgen Zangenberg, eds., *Matthew, James, and Didache: Three Related Documents in Their Jewish and Christian Setting* (Atlanta: Society of Biblical Literature, 2008), p. 157.

For the stars of heaven and their constellations
Will not flash forth their light;
The sun will be dark when it rises
And the moon will not shed its light.

Thus I will punish the world for its evil
And the wicked for their iniquity;
I will also put an end to the arrogance of the proud
And abase the haughtiness of the ruthless.

The prophet Isaiah revealed that the Day of the Lord would be a time of very specific judgment that God will bring upon the Earth for the wickedness of humanity. Of course, the language used in verse 10, is also language that is prevalent in the book of Revelation. The same type of language is also very dominant in Matthew 24—25, the Olivet Discourse.

Zephaniah 1:14-17 reads:

Near is the great day of the LORD,
Near and coming very quickly;
Listen, the day of the LORD!
In it the warrior cries out bitterly.
A day of wrath is that day,
A day of trouble and distress,
A day of destruction and desolation,
A day of darkness and gloom,
A day of clouds and thick darkness,
A day of trumpet and battle cry
Against the fortified cities
And the high corner towers.
I will bring distress on men
So that they will walk like the blind,
Because they have sinned against the LORD;
And their blood will be poured out like dust
And their flesh like dung.

The focus in Zephaniah is again upon the fact that the Day of the Lord is a judgment that God will instigate against the wicked. There is also the idea in the Old Testament that the Day of the Lord is not only a judgment on the wicked nations and depraved humanity, but also the Day of the Lord is a judgment upon unbelieving Israel.

Zephaniah 1:14 states specifically, "Near is the great day of the LORD," which is a combination of near and far elements in the warnings regarding the Day of the Lord. In some of the prophecies, there is a more immediate judgment of the exile that God will accomplish, but in other prophecies, there is the warning of an end-time judgment with the more immediate exile as something of a preview. The easy manner to think of these near and far judgments is that of types and antitypes.

Types and Antitypes

There are certain types that are specified in the Bible, like Abraham offering his son, Isaac, which is a type of the Father offering His Son, the Lord and Savior, Jesus Christ. Abraham and Isaac are the type, whereas the antitype—the non-type—is the Father and Jesus Christ. Hebrews is filled with explanations of all sorts of types and shadows, and how they all pointed to Jesus Christ, the antitype. Just as there are types and antitypes with regard to individuals, so there are with regard to events, such as the judgment passages of the Day of the Lord. Zephaniah provided a preview of some kind of a near fulfillment, but there will also be a complete fulfillment in the future, in a prophetic time.

A type gap is when an Old Testament prophet described an event, person, or institution ("type") and progressive revelation in the New Testament indicates the prophetic significance of this event, person or institution ("antitype").

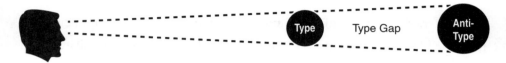

A time gap is when an Old Testament prophet spoke with regard to two different events, which are separated by a wide space of time, as thought they were one event. Generally, the two different events, separated by the time gap, have reference to the first coming and second coming of Messiah. The Old Testament prophets were unaware of such gaps when they were inspired with the prophecy (1 Pet. 1:10-12), in order that the prophet communicated a message for his own day in addition to a future time.[384]

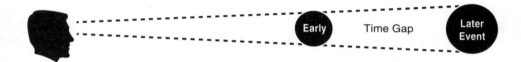

The manner in which one may distinguish the near and far fulfillment is to answer whether everything prophesied was fulfilled historically and literally. If an event was fulfilled entirely in the past, one should not expect any future fulfillment; however, if there are things stated that did not occur in the historical timeframe, then that leads one to conclude that such events are yet future because God said that He will fulfill all His Word (Matt. 5:17-18). Often connected with the judgment passages is blessing associated with it, and therefore, the Day of the Lord ultimately manifests the omnibenevolence and omnipotence of God.

What is curious is that those who reject a premillennial understanding of the Bible will interpret the judgment upon Israel very literally. God has

---

384   Sometimes there is even a combination of a type gap and time gap. In this double reference, the Old Testament prophet would speak of two similar events, people or institutions (type) although they are widely separated from the antitype in time. The first event is a prefiguring of a later event. For example, the invasion of locusts in Joel 1-3 is the type and the invasion of human armies in Matthew 24:15-22 is the antitype.

judged Israel in such a mindset, and He has fulfilled those prophecies, but then the blessings that are so connected with the judgment are spiritualized (i.e., the blessings now refer to blessings in Jesus Christ and the blessings of heaven). However, the judgments are literal and so will the blessings be literal. When the Word of God reveals specific details with regard to judgment for Israel, it almost always addresses blessings associated with the judgment that has not been fulfilled. Consequently, one should conclude that God will fulfill His Word entirely and literally, and one should expect that a prophecy is still future if it has not been historically fulfilled in its entirety.

In the Old Testament prophecies there are references to a near fulfillment, and then sometimes a far fulfillment. Amos 5:18-20 reads:

> Alas, you who are longing for the day of the LORD,
> For what purpose *will* the day of the LORD *be* to you?
> It *will be* darkness and not light;
> As when a man flees from a lion
> And a bear meets him,
> Or goes home, leans his hand against the wall
> And a snake bites him.
> *Will* not the day of the LORD *be* darkness instead of light,
> Even gloom with no brightness in it?

In Amos 5:18-20, there is another reference to the future Day of the Lord—a time of great judgment that God will inaugurate—the Day of the Lord being something that awaits the conclusion of the end times in establishing the millennial kingdom. Verses 23-24 are interesting within the same chapter of Amos 5.

> Take away from Me the noise of your songs;
> I will not even listen to the sound of your harps.
> But let justice roll down like waters
> And righteousness like an ever-flowing stream.

Amos prophesied a judgment upon the nations and upon Israel, but then also there is the reference to justice and righteousness being established throughout the Earth subsequent to that judgment. There is a brief reference to the millennial kingdom as something that is future.

The Day of the Lord was a well-known concept, and would be understood as a time of tremendous judgment that God would bring not only Israel, but also upon the nations for their wickedness. Some comment and teach that the Day of the Lord should be associated with the tribulation period—the entire seven years of judgment—but then also say that the Day of the Lord should include the millennium. *The Day of the Lord is simply the tribulation period.* Whenever prophecies reference the millennium, the language is always "in that day;" therefore, "that day" seems to be generic language which could refer to either times of judgment, the tribulation or the millennium. Conversely, the Day of the Lord seems to refer very specifically to the time of judgment that God will bring upon Israel and the nations. The Day of the Lord should be defined primarily as an Old Testament term referring to the seven years of tribulation. Moreover, the term is never used in reference to the millennial kingdom, but "that day" is an Old Testament term that may reference either the tribulation or millennium.

Of course, when Scripture uses the idea of the Day of the Lord, it is not speaking of a 24-hour period, a calendar day. For example, in 2 Thessalonians 2:2, Paul wrote, "That you not be quickly shaken from your composure or be disturbed either by a spirit or a message or a letter as if from us, to the effect that the day of the Lord has come." The idea in the Greek (*enestēken*) is that the Day of the Lord has already come. The Greek is in the perfect tense, which would literally mean "has already come and continues," which demonstrates that a day can be longer than just simply 24 hours, and so it is with the Day of the Lord.

Posttribulationalists (in addition to amillennialists) disagree that the Day of the Lord is longer than a calendar day for they believe that it is the second coming. However, such an understanding does not adequately consider the Greek perfect tense because the indication is that the Day of the Lord comes and then continues. Sometimes in life one day leads into another, especially if one is busy, but Biblically the Day of the Lord should be something regarded as a longer framework of time that would include the prophesied judgments of the Bible. Of course, in the creation account of Genesis, the word "day" means something entirely different, because there it uses *evening* and *morning*, *day one* and *day two*, etc., so that the reader knows that those are not longer than 24-hour periods, and therefore revealing that creation occurred in six 24-hour days.[385]

The Day of the Lord as a Night Thief

According to 1 Thessalonians 5:1-2, the church was not uninformed with regard to the prophesies of the Day of the Lord. Their confusion was concerning the rapture because it was a new teaching, that is, something not known from the Old Testament. Additional instruction was not needed regarding the Day of the Lord because the believers knew "full well that the day of the Lord will come just like a thief in the night." Conversely, when the unbelievers will be saying, "'Peace and safety!' then destruction will come upon them suddenly like labor pains upon a woman with child, and they will not escape" (5:3).

Matthew, in his gospel (Matt. 24:8), referred to the same period and called it "birth pangs." Even in Jewish commentaries, this concept of birth pains preceding the time of Messiah's return is established. Relying upon extra-biblical sources, Raphael Patai devoted an entire chapter to "The Pangs of Time."

The pangs of the Messianic times are imagined as heavenly as well as earthly sources and expressions. From Above, awesome

---

385   For more information on this subject, see Ron J. Bigalke Jr., "The Preeminence of Biblical Creationism," in *The Genesis Factor*, ed. idem (Green Forest, AR: Master Books, 2008), pp. 95-122.

cosmic cataclysms will be visited upon the earth. . . . All this will lead to internal decay, demoralization, and even apostasy. Things will come to such a head that people will despair of Redemption. This will last seven years. And then, unexpectedly, the Messiah will come.

Because of this gloomy picture of the beginning of the Messianic era, which by Talmudic times was firmly believed in, some sages expressed the wish not to see the Messiah. . . . In any case, both the people and its religious leaders continued to hope for the coming of the Messiah.[386]

The Jewish understanding of the birth pangs associated with the Day of the Lord and Messianic era is certainly consistent with the sequence of the book of Revelation and the eschatological discourses in the synoptic gospels (Matt. 24; Mark 13; Luke 17).[387]

In 1 Thessalonians 5:4-11, the characteristics of the Day of the Lord are described with focus upon the fact that believers are well informed with regard to that period, and then compared its coming to a thief in the night. No one knows when a thief will come, but when a thief does come, then it becomes patently obvious, and so Paul used that language with regard to the unbelievers' surprise. The Jewish tradition is that the Messiah will come in the middle of the night, in the same manner as the destroyer came to the Egyptians.[388] There are some early traditions that relate the coming of Christ to the midnight of Easter, which does not seem accurate. However, the midnight hour is evident in passages such as Psalms 119:62 and Matthew 25:1-13 (of course, midnight occurs at different times throughout the world). Comparing the book of Revelation and other Old Testament prophesies, it would seem that the Day of the

---

386 Raphael Patai, *The Messiah Texts* (Detroit: Wayne State University Press, 1979), pp. 95-96.

387 Ron J. Bigalke Jr., "A Comparison of the Synoptic Eschatological Discourses and Revelation 6—20," *Chafer Theological Seminary Journal* 13 (Spring 2008): 68-70.

388 Clemens Leonhard, *The Jewish Pesach and the Origins of the Christian Easter: Open Questions in Current Research* (Berlin: Walter de Gruyter, 2006), p. 417.

Lord begins with the opening of the first seal of Revelation. The rapture will precede the tribulation, and then the Day of the Lord may be regarded as coming in an unexpected manner.

For the second coming to occur and the establishment of the millennium, there are specific events that must occur. Consequently, it is not possible to say that the rapture is the same as the second coming, or that the Day of the Lord (as posttribulationists believe) is the second coming because it would not occur as a thief in the night. One would know how to count to the very end of the seven-year tribulation, and expect the second coming. The fact that Paul used language of unexpectedness in relation to his teaching of the rapture in 1 Thessalonians 4 supports pretribulational doctrine that the rapture will precede this period.

According to 1 Thessalonians 5:1-11, those who enter the tribulation will know that the period has come (cf. Rev. 6:12-17), which would eliminate any kind of false teaching such as the Day of the Lord was being experienced by the Thessalonians. The false teaching being circulated among the church at Thessalonica was that they had somehow missed the rapture of 1 Thessalonians 4, and were now experiencing the Day of the Lord. Paul said the period is a time of judgment—a well-established fact of the Old Testament—and when it does occur, it will be obvious. The Day of the Lord will occur when people "are saying, 'Peace and safety!'" (1 Thess. 5:3). The unexpected beginning of the period would seem to parallel the first half of the tribulation from Daniel 9:24-27, and the emphasis therein upon the signing of a peace treaty with Israel. Even in the current time, there is continual discussion regarding peace in the Middle East, and demands for a two-state solution in "Palestine."

Scripture prophecies that Israel will become "a cup that causes reeling to all" the world (Zech. 12:2), which indicates a focus upon Israel, and a type of individual coming and enforcing peace upon them. Isaiah referred to the false peace treaty as "a covenant with death" (28:15, 18), because it is not Messiah providing peace for them, rather they will have been deceived by Antichrist. The book of Revelation also pictures the first three-and-a-half years of the tribulation as relatively peaceful in Israel, for it is not until halfway through that period that Antichrist breaks his covenant with the Jewish people, and then they understand who he is, and they flee for their lives. First Thessalonians 5:3 is stating that those people who enter the tribulation—the people that are saying peace and safety—are the ones who are also going to experience the judgment of God: "They will not escape." They will experience God's due wrath and judgment, which leads into another teaching of 1 Thessalonians 5.

Not Destined for Wrath

Verse 9 reads, "For God has not destined us for wrath, but for obtaining salvation through our Lord Jesus Christ." The concept of wrath is a term that, whenever it is used, is reserved strictly for Divine punishment upon those for whom there is no longer any hope of salvation. The wrath of the tribulation is punishment for wickedness, and so it will be expended upon the wicked. First Thessalonians 1:9-10 already expressed the teaching here in 1 Thessalonians 5:9. In comparing the two parallel statements, the teaching is that God has not appointed the church unto receiving His wrath. According to these texts, God has said very clearly that He has not appointed the church unto receiving His wrath, but unto salvation. Such a statement would support a pretribulational understanding of these things because the wrath is the entire period of the tribulation, and it is not God's purpose to take the church through that period.

The rapture is not a reward for faithfulness, but correlates with God's plans for Israel in relation to the kingdom. The tribulation is a period that is prophesied for Israel; it is a judgment upon them for things in the past and a time of purging the rebel from among Israel in preparation for Messiah's return. Furthermore, it is evident from this text and others that the church will not experience the tribulation. Of course, not all details are answered here in this first letter to the Thessalonians, but will be explained more fully in 2 Thessalonians 2, which does provide a very specific rapture statement.

Awake or Sleeping

First Thessalonians 5:1-11 continues the teaching with regard to prophetic events. The doctrine of the rapture was introduced exhaustively in 1 Thessalonians 4:13-18. First Thessalonians 5:1-11 continues the discussion of prophetic events; therefore, in verses 1-3, Scripture states that the church had "no need of anything to be written to" them with regard to "the times and epochs." The reason for this statement is given in verse 2: "The day of the Lord will come just like a thief in the night," which means it will result in sudden destruction upon unbelievers (5:3).

Only two of the first 11 verses of 1 Thessalonians 5 were written concerning unbelievers. The two verses were recorded to emphasize the contrast between the blessed hope of the believer as compared to the destruction that is to come upon the unbeliever. The contrast is especially encouraging in verse 9: "For God has not destined us for wrath, but for obtaining salvation through our Lord Jesus Christ." The majority of the focus of 1 Thessalonians 5:1-11, therefore, is upon believers and specifically how the blessed hope of the Lord's coming is contrasted with the destiny of unbelievers.

First Thessalonians 5:10 reads, "Who died for us, so that whether we are awake or asleep, we will live together with Him." Perhaps most commentators, including theological dictionaries and lexicons, will state that Paul's words in verse 10 ("whether we are awake or asleep") is a reference to sleep as death, but such meaning does not correspond to the context. The entire context of 1 Thessalonians 5:1-11 is focused upon watching so that the Day of the Lord does not come as a thief in the night. For the unbeliever, the Day of the Lord brings destruction; it comes unexpectedly upon them, as a thief in the night. The believer is to be watching and waiting for the return of the Lord.

A different Greek word was used in verse 10 than the word used in 1 Thessalonians 4:13. The Greek word, *koimaō*, used in 1 Thessalonians 4:13 always means physical death. The verb, *katheudō*, used in 1 Thessalonians 5:10, is seldom used for death in Biblical Greek. The correct interpretation should not be focused upon whether one is awake or dead—whether one is living or dead—it should be whether one is awake or not awake. The Greek verb, *katheudō*, is used almost consistently to have the idea of watchfulness. Of course, the context of verse 10 is indeed an exhortation to watch. In other words, it concerns living believers, not those deceased, because only living believers can be watching and waiting.

Moreover, such an understanding would correspond with the statement in verse 6 ("so then let us not sleep as others do, but let us be alert and sober"). The same Greek word, *katheudō*, is used in verse 6 and verse 10 (and also verse 7). Paul's contrast in this verse was not between the living and the dead. He stated, "Let us not sleep as others do." The exhortation is to be alert, sober-minded and watching for the coming of the Lord Jesus Christ. Therefore, it is necessary to distinguish between the rapture and the second coming. The rapture is an event that could occur at any moment; therefore, the church is to be waiting and watching. The second coming, however, is preceded by seven years of tribulation. There are numerous signs and wonders that occur on the earth, and it is impossible to catalog the rapture and second coming as one single event. When referring to the second coming, it is necessary to distinguish the rapture of the church from the Lord's earthly coming at the end of the tribulation. In the context of 1 Thessalonians 5, the Apostle Paul was teaching the rapture of the church.

The statement in 1 Thessalonians 5:10 parallels that of 4:14 ("For if we believe that Jesus died and rose again, even so God will bring with

Him those who have fallen asleep in Jesus"). How does one experience the rapture? One must be "in Jesus." The exhortation is alertness. According to 1 Thessalonians 4:14 and 5:4-10, whether one is watching or not as a member of the church, they will be taken in the rapture. Brethren and sisters in Christ who are not waiting and watching for the rapture will still be taken. The church will be transformed in a moment in the twinkling of an eye, and receive glorified bodies. If one compares the same thought to 1 Thessalonians 5, the exhortation is to be watching, but even if not, the believer will be taken because he or she is "in Jesus." Does that mean it does not matter? Scripture would indicate that it does because one may experience loss of reward (cf. 1 Cor. 3:15). There is "the crown of righteousness" given "to all who have loved His appearing" (2 Tim. 4:8).

Watching and Waiting

The imperative in verse 6 is to "be alert and sober," which would be consistent with the teaching of a pretribulational rapture. Such an imperative is the precise aspect of salvation that Paul stated in verse 9, "For God has not destined us for wrath, but for obtaining salvation through our Lord Jesus Christ." In these verses, the rapture is related to the time in the context. The context is the Day of the Lord, which is a time of judgment. Paul said that God has not appointed the church for that wrath. In Revelation 6, the very beginning of the tribulation witnesses the outpouring of God's wrath. God, however, has not appointed the church for the wrath of the Day of the Lord. He has appointed the church unto salvation.

A both/and statement is not used. God has not appointed the church unto salvation and wrath—it is not both, rather a contrast. He has not appointed the church to wrath, the wrath of the Day of the Lord; He has appointed the church unto salvation, the Lord Jesus Christ. There is an evident contrast. Therefore, verse 3 reads, "While they are saying, 'Peace and safety!' then destruction will come upon them suddenly like labor pains upon a woman with child, and they will not escape." When would unbelievers be saying, "Peace and safety"? Would they speak such words at the midpoint of the tribulation? Would they speak such words at the end of the tribulation? Even in the beginning of the tribulation, Matthew's gospel prophecies there will be "wars and rumors of wars" (Matt. 24:6). The book of Revelation prophesies the four horsemen as the opening of the first four seals (Rev. 6:1-8). Would this be the time that unbelievers are saying, "Peace and safety"? When would the unbelieving world speak such words?

The fact that the rapture and the beginning of the Day of the Lord could occur at any moment must be understood pretribulationally. First Thessalonians 5 is teaching to be watching for the rapture because it could occur at any moment, and then, when the rapture occurs, what happens next is the Day of the Lord comes upon the unbelievers when they are saying, "Peace and safety." The G-20 Summit, for example, experienced excitement with regards to a world currency as the means to solve all financial problems. The unbelieving world is convinced that globalism is the answer to terrorism, peace in the Middle East and financial stability. In other words, the world leaders are seeking the time of peace and safety. They shout "hurray," "peace and safety," and then, according to Scripture, the Day of the Lord comes upon them; it comes swiftly with destruction; wrath comes upon them. If one remembers Y2K, there were Christians who believed in the need to stockpile, which never made sense. Many believers were confused during that time. However, there were many Bible teachers who believed the prognosticators were not correct, as a consequence of studying 1 Thessalonians 5. If one looks prophetically, it is not that the world collapses and then the Day of the Lord begins; it begins during a time of peace and safety.

Those who were more careful in their teaching did not believe that Y2K would be much of an issue because the statements of speaking "peace and safety" contradicted those sentiments. Sudden destruction comes during a time of peace and safety, then according to 2 Thessalonians 2, those in unbelief cry for a world leader to solve the crisis and look to him as God. Of course, then he proclaims to be God, and requires all humanity to bear his mark and to worship his image. Scriptures seems to be indicating that things will not become worse in the world, but better; it does not mean that there is not going to be challenges, such as currently, but things will generally progress to a time of delusional peace and safety. Prior to the coming of the Lord is a time of peace and safety; the world believes they do not need God. When the church is raptured, it does not seem that the majority of the world, at least at the beginning of the tribulation, will be concerned, and it is then that God outpours His wrath.

Therefore, 1 First Thessalonians 5:1-11 is referring to the rapture as preceding the tribulation. God has not obtained the church to that time of wrath, but to salvation in the Lord Jesus Christ. The church is to be watching and waiting, which only makes sense if the pretribulational rapture is true. If one is a posttribulationalist, he or she would be watching and waiting for the Antichrist, and then experience the seven years of tribulation, and the rapture and second coming would occur as a single event. However, this is not the teaching of Scripture. The only means of making sense of 1 Thessalonians 5:1-11 is a pretribulational rapture, prior to the Day of the Lord, which is the outpouring of God's wrath. Therefore, the church is to be watching and waiting because the rapture could occur at any moment because, "God has … destined [the church] … for obtaining salvation." Consequently, verse 11 reads, "Therefore encourage one another and build up one another, just as you also are doing."

Comfort One Another

If Paul taught that the church would endure seven years of tribulation, it does not seem possible to encourage one another, as 1 Thessalonians 4:18

also states. How could there be comfort? Most of those reading this book and their believing family members and friends would die at the hands of Antichrist. Therefore, one must understand two different comings of the Lord: *for* His church, and then coming in judgment *with* His church; it is similar as with the first and second coming of Christ. One could not understand everything prophesied with regard to a suffering and reigning Messiah as one event. The disciples and apostles struggled to understand the comings because they believed correctly that Jesus is truly Messiah, but were confused because He did not establish His reign at the first coming.

Now that more than 2,000 years of church history have elapsed, it is understandable that Christ came once and will return again to establish His kingdom. All the prophecies concerning Messiah would have been impossible to fulfill in one coming. However, the disciples struggled to understand the distinctions between the first and second comings of Messiah. The distinction between the first and second comings establishes an example for the rapture and second coming because is impossible to catalog all the prophecies with regard to the second coming of Christ as one event. Therefore, one must make a distinction between Christ coming for His church, and then He outpours His wrath (the Day of the Lord), and finally returns with His saints to establish His kingdom on earth. The doctrine of the rapture is to be encouraging and taught to edify one another. At any moment, the Lord Jesus Christ could return for His church, and it does not matter that the first-century church read these prophecies and also expected the any-moment coming of the Lord. The rapture is as imminent then as it is currently.

The rapture will occur for one generation, as Paul taught in 1 Corinthians 15. There will be a generation which will not experience death. Apparently, the Thessalonians were encouraging and edifying one another. Paul wrote in verse 11, "just as you also are doing"; therefore, continue doing this, continue to encourage one another. The context of this letter demonstrates that the Thessalonians were confused; they thought that because of the persecution they were experiencing, they were in the Day of the Lord, and Paul taught them otherwise. Indeed, they were experiencing afflictions, difficulties, persecutions, but they were not in the tribulation period. Paul then provided very explicit details teaching the church would not enter into that period, but would be taken by the Lord Jesus Christ prior to the beginning of the tribulation and the outpouring of God's wrath.

Doctrine and Practice

Scripture almost always provides doctrine first, and then gives the exhortation and application of that doctrine. In other words, if one seeks the application first, he or she will be confused. The first application that Paul addressed was the attitude of the Thessalonians towards their leaders. Verses 12-13 read, "But we request of you, brethren, that you appreciate those who diligently labor among you, and have charge over you in the Lord and give you instruction, and that you esteem them very highly in love because of their work. Live in peace with one another."

The leaders mentioned in those verses were the elders in the Thessalonian church—possibly deacons also, and maybe some others in positions, but certainly elders. Paul taught that his readers were to appreciate these leaders. The epistles are almost always written to the church leaders—to the elders, the pastors, the shepherds—which would reinforce the doctrine of plurality of eldership; there is not a single-elder-led church, but the witness of Scripture is always a plurality of elders. The listing here is not exhaustive, but representative, wherein Paul charged these believers to esteem their leaders very highly in love (5:13). Certainly, it is easier to love some leaders more than others, but Paul said not to make that distinction, but to demonstrate self-sacrificing love to all spiritual leadership.

In verses 14-15, Paul indicated how believers should relate to one another. "We urge you, brethren, admonish the unruly, encourage the faint-hearted, help the weak, be patient with everyone. See that no one repays evil for evil, but always seek after that which is good for one another and for all people." All the believers were responsible to minister to one another. Those who would neglect their daily duties needed to be encouraged to have action. There may be some who, as stated in 5:14, were fainthearted, and tended to become discouraged or despondent more easily. Scripture teaches that they need encouragement to stimulate them to persevere. Those who had not yet learned to rely upon the Lord for their needs, as they should, needed special encouragement. Scripture teaches that above all, the church should be patient with one another and with all people. The church is to use their gifts to edify one another for the mutual benefit of the body, not to retaliate, but do positive things to all people, which is a wonderful encouragement of how believers relate in peace not only with those who lead, but then also how to respond in peace toward one another.

Jesus said, "By this all men will know that you are My disciples, if you have love for one another" (John 13:35). What is entirely dynamic is to have a group of people of various income levels, races and nationalities, who all come together. They all come together to worship the Lord, which is a powerful testimony to the Lord. The unity that the church has in Christ Jesus is to be evident in the peace, care and concern that believers have toward one another. The exhortation is not divorced from the eschatological teaching. The exhortations focus upon living in such a manner that when the Lord returns, it will be a time of rejoicing—for one has been obedient to the exhortations, and will be rewarded.

Summary of 1 Thessalonians 5

The emphasis of 1 Thessalonians 5:1-11 is upon the suddenness of the Day of the Lord, which is a well-developed Old Testament teaching. The Day of the Lord is not only a time judgment upon the Earth for the wickedness of humanity, but also will be a time of purging the rebel within Israel in preparation for the Messianic kingdom. The Day of the Lord is the same as the seven-year tribulation, or Daniel's 70th week. Although the church may benefit from persecution (and much of the church throughout the world is experiencing tribulation*s*), it is not God's purpose to have the church enter this period of wrath and judgment. God's purpose for the church is distinct from Israel, and therefore the rapture of the church will precede *the* tribulation. What a wonderful privilege to possess God's revelation of the future, which is certainly worth a lifetime of study, in addition to all the truths of Scripture. The church has a responsibility in this world until the time of the rapture, and should be diligent in service of the Lord by His grace and for His glory. The instruction to pray for the true peace of Jerusalem is always binding (Ps. 122:6), yet believers know that it will be the return of the Lord to establish His kingdom of righteousness that will culminate in peace being experienced throughout the world.

CHAPTER 13

PROPHETIC TIMING AND THE RAPTURE: PRETRIBULATIONISM, PART III

Since the content of 1 and 2 Thessalonians is similar, it is prudent to reconsider the primary teachings of the first epistle written to the church at Thessalonica. Paul commended the church for three necessary virtues: faith, hope and love (1 Thess. 1:3; cf. 1 Cor. 13:13). Without these qualities, a good pastor, good organization, good discipleship and a good evangelistic outreach are worthless. In verses 4-9, Paul reminded the Thessalonians of the radical transformation they experienced because of the proclamation of the gospel (which would have included essential teachings as regards the person, death and resurrection of Jesus Christ). In verse 10, he taught the church "to wait for His Son from heaven, whom he raised from the dead, *that is* Jesus, who rescues us from the wrath to come." A major component of the Christian's spiritual growth and purity of life is the result of anticipating the return of Christ.

SECOND THESSALONIANS 1

Living in anticipation of the return of Jesus Christ certainly serves as an impetus for spiritual growth. The words "wait for His Son from heaven" (1:10) establish the tone for the remainder of the first epistle to the Thessalonians and, indeed, establish the major theme. The conversion of the Thessalonians was expressed by turning to God from idols, and their life transformation was by serving the living and true God. Waiting for God's Son from heaven appears to have expressed itself in an attitude of anticipation that tended to be a significant inspiring factor in their new life. Apparently, he identified this factor among several other possible factors, because Paul desired to build upon it and relate to it throughout his epistle.

The spiritual growth of these new believers is described in two paragraphs: 1 Thessalonians 1:2-3 describe their "work of faith and labor of love and steadfastness of hope;" and, 1 Thessalonians 1:4-10 describe their increasing reputation for faith in God. Throughout the first epistle, living in anticipation of the return of the Lord is the theme. Both 1 and 2 Thessalonians are thematically similar. Paul's reference to the persecution of the church and God's judgment upon unbelievers in 2 Thessalonians 1:4-10 establishes the theme of encouragement in the second epistle (because the Lord Jesus Christ will return for His people). In 2 Thessalonians 1, the reader is instructed with regard to difficult times becoming encouraging experiences.

The word "tribulation" is not a technical term, which means it can have more than one meaning. Context will help determine whether the word is used with regard to general suffering (John 16:33; Acts 14:22; Rom. 5:3; 12:12), to the seven years of Daniel's 70th week (Jer. 30:7-9; Dan. 9:24-27; 12:1), or to the second half of that week, the "great tribulation." (Matt. 24:21 refers to the last half of Daniel's 70th week as the "great tribulation," whereas Matt. 24:8 uses "beginning of birth pangs" for the first half.) Daniel's 70th week (the seven-year tribulation) does not relate to God's purpose for the church. *The* tribulation will come upon a world that is in rebellion against God (Rev. 15:1; 16:1-21; 19:15) and will reveal Satan's nature (12:7-12). During *the* tribulation, national Israel will come to repentance and faith in the Messiah in preparation for the millennium (Jer. 30:7-9; Zech. 12:9–14:5; Rev. 19:1-6); it will also be a time of evangelism (Matt. 24:14; Rev. 6:9-11; 7:1-17; 11:2-14; 12:13-17; 13:7; 14:1-5, 12-13). Although the church may experience trials and tribulations, the tribulation is not in the future for Christians. Nevertheless, when believers suffer as a result of faith in God or simply experience the troubles of this life, difficult times reveal the character of Christians, and it is in that sense that one can welcome difficulties as a means by which faith in God is revealed.

Spiritual Growth through Difficulty

Second Thessalonians 1:1-2 is a typical salutation for a first-century letter to a local church. Therefore, the development of thought begins with verse 3. The Thessalonians were growing spiritually in spite of (or perhaps because of) persecution. Nevertheless, they needed encouragement. In verses 3-4, Paul expressed gratitude for their spiritual growth. All believers should be encouraged when their faith is increasing. The language that Paul used indicates a faith that was increasing "more and more." The Greek word, *huperauxanei*, used in verse 3 indicates wonderfully vigorous growth, which was probably the result of the suffering. Indeed, faith often increases as the result of suffering.

Additionally, all believers should be encouraged when their love increases. The same word that Paul used in 1 Thessalonians 3:12 as his prayer is seen here as reflecting God's answer. Believers should also be encouraged because they endure (persevere) in faith. "Perseverance" means believers endure their trials and persecution in a godly manner, that is, without complaint. The word "persevere" (Gk. *hupomonēs*) in 2 Thessalonians 1:4 may be accurately translated "patience" and literally means "to remain or abide under."The preposition "under" (Gk. *hupo*), of course, is a prefix (i.e., attached to the beginning of the word to modify its meaning) to the word "abide." A common word picture to convey this idea is one in which an individual is standing under an ominous threat or danger but not moving.

The church may be encouraged because of their faith, love, and endurance. However, a rather unexpected form of belief also encouraged these first-century believers: God's righteous judgment. Someday, those who persecuted them will be "persecuted" by God in the form of eternal punishment. Apparently, Paul considered the possibility that this generation could experience the return of Christ and this judgment would then occur to unbelievers who were living at the time. Verses 5-10 contain the next element of encouragement by way of vindication (sc. clearing someone of any wrong by showing they are justified or correct) of believers through the destruction of their enemies.

Confident Endurance Because God Is Just

God will vindicate Himself and believers. The vindication is evidence of God's righteous judgment that honors the confident endurance and patience of the church. God will vindicate Himself and those trusting in Him. The idea here is to declare the believer's worth to be a partaker of the kingdom of God. The verb for "worthy" (Gk. *kataxiōthēnai*) means "to declare or count worthy," not to "make worthy" (such as to justify or declare righteous). Therefore, believers are urged to regard their endurance as evidence of God working in them and assurance that He would keep His promises concerning their future place in the coming kingdom.

God will also repay every injustice. Paul wrote, "it is *only* just for God to repay with affliction those who afflict you" (1:6). Since God is just (righteous), He cannot allow evil to be unpunished. Those who persecuted the believers would experience the judgment of God. The Hall of Names at Yad Vashem (Holocaust Martyrs' and Heroes' Remembrance Authority) is a tribute to the victims of the Holocaust by remembering them not as anonymous numbers but as individual human beings. To date Yad Vashem has computerized 3.2 million names of Holocaust victims, compiled from approximately two million pages of testimony and various other lists. The Hall of Names is Israel's way of saying that none of the victims of the Holocaust will be forgotten. Not one act of injustice will ever be forgotten. Scripture teaches the same in verse 6.

Not one act of injustice upon believers will be forgotten. The righteous God of justice will repay every injustice with affliction. Certainly, this verse is teaching Christians something with regard to the nature of God for it is not just first-century injustices that will be repaid. According to the Christian ministry Voice of the Martyrs, more Christians are being persecuted today than any other time in history. God will make every one of those injustices right someday because it is consistent with His character to do so.

God will judge those who reject Him and rebel against His authority. The Lord Jesus will administer retribution to those who do not trust in Him alone for eternal salvation. In other words, the Lord Jesus will personally judge those who reject the gospel message. All who do not have a faith relationship with God will receive His retribution. Some translations may read "vengeance." The word does not mean revenge (which would be the satisfaction of a personal grudge). The word for "retribution" or vengeance (Gk. *ekdikēsin*) means God will satisfy His holy law.

According to Romans 1:20, all humanity is accountable to God and without excuse for rejecting Him, "for since the creation of the world His invisible attributes, His eternal power and divine nature, have been clearly seen, being understood through what has been made." The problem with those who reject God is not that they are innocent, but they "suppress the truth in unrighteousness" (Rom. 1:18). If someone rejects the revelation of God, he or she will receive His retribution, that is, the Lord's judgment;

and, it is for this reason that all local churches should support missions at home and abroad because all humanity is accountable to God, and therefore, all believers should desire to proclaim the full revelation of God's grace, so those who hear may believe and receive the gift of eternal life.

The Lord Jesus will also administer retribution to those who rebel against Him. The first group rejected what revelation they had received, while the second group heard the truth of God's Word and rebelled against it. All who reject the gospel and rebel against God will be accountable. Verse 9 reads, "These will pay the penalty of eternal destruction, away from the presence of the Lord and from the glory of His power." If by grace through faith, Christ alone does not pay the penalty for your sin, then you will "pay the penalty of eternal destruction."

The relief here is not a reference to the rapture of the church, but the second coming of Christ subsequent to the seven-year tribulation. The Lord Jesus being revealed "from heaven with His mighty angels in flaming fire" is against the unbeliever on earth. The "relief" (rest) is "relief from affliction" (tension). The knowledge that God will judge wickedness should give believers relief in trials and even in persecution. Justice and righteousness will right all wrongs when God judges. God will also enforce eternal punishment. The Bible does not teach that when the wicked die they are annihilated. The retribution of the wicked and unbelieving and the reward of the righteous are everlasting, and as the reward is conscious, so is the retribution. God breathed the breath of life into the nostrils of mankind, and thus all humanity is a living being, with a spirit that will endure forever in the presence of the Lord or in the lake of fire separated from the presence of the Lord. Indeed, according to 2 Corinthians 6:2, "now is 'THE DAY OF SALVATION.'"

Destruction in verse 9 means separation "from the presence of the Lord and from the glory of His power," which means an eternity of woe or ruin. The thing ruined is the opportunity to ever be restored to fellowship with the Creator for eternity; it is the eternal ruin of everything worthwhile, including the purpose for which humanity was created. Asked the question of the purpose of mankind, the authors of the Westminster Confession responded, "to glorify God and enjoy Him forever." The opportunity for those who God will judge will be ruined and lost forever.

Moreover, "the presence of the Lord and . . . the glory of His power" will be displayed. What this means is that no one alive *at this moment in time* has experienced eternal separation from "the presence of the Lord and . . . the glory of His power." Those who reject and rebel against God have no idea of what they are destined to experience for eternity. The Bible refers to this destiny as the second death in the book of Revelation. The first death is the separation of one's spirit to heaven or hell from his or her body. The second death is the eternal separation from "the presence of the Lord and . . . the glory of His power." The truths of the afterlife are sobering. However, there is a positive and encouraging aspect to God's righteous judgment.

God will grant victory and glory to believers. As terrible as the judgment will be for the unbeliever, there is a positive side for the believer. Of course, it is not pleasurable to think of the ruin of the wicked, but it will be a reality and it is an incentive to do the work of an evangelist and be a witness of God's saving grace. For the believer though, there will be victory and glory. The second coming of the Lord Jesus Christ is the subject of verse 10. While the unbeliever will experience judgment and retribution, the believer will experience glory and victory. The church will have been removed from Earth to heaven prior to God's wrath beginning, and will return with Him to Earth when His wrath is concluded. In heaven, reigning with Christ during the millennium, and into eternity, the saints of God will forever be trophies of God's grace, and the glory of Christ will be revealed in the redeemed of all ages. The glory of the Creator is revealed in the disciples He produces, and so Christ's glory will be revealed in the victorious believers who accompany Him when He returns to Earth to rule and reign, and it will be a glorious sight to behold those Christ has redeemed and who radiate His eternal glory.

Conduct Yourself Worthily

The next element of encouragement is to conduct oneself worthily during difficulties. The final manner in which Paul encourages believers is through his prayers. Christians should pray to be worthy. Persecution did not produce godly believers *per se*, nor do trials determine the character of believers. Instead, persecution of believers and the troubles that Christians endure demonstrate one's character. Paul did not pray for the persecution to cease, but instead prayed that the believers would be counted worthy to endure suffering for Christ! Those who are worthy of the calling of Christ will persevere for His glory, and their faith is revealed as committed and resolute when difficulties arise. Paul's prayer was that the Christians would be worthy to endure reproach in Christ's name. How do you respond in the trials of life? Is your faith worthy to endure hardships for Christ? Do you see trials as opportunities to show forth your calling in your moral and spiritual life, and that God would empower you in this important function? Trials and temptations are certain to come if one belongs to God, but believers should demonstrate perseverance in response to difficulties and thereby manifest God's effective calling.

Paul also prayed for the church to "fulfill every desire for goodness and the work of faith with power." His prayer was that the church would be fruitful during trials. Often when troubles arise, Christians retreat from service to the Lord, and pray the difficulties disappear. However, there are many in the church today who do not yield to that temptation, but serve God willingly in the midst of many demanding circumstances. The trials and temptations of life may tempt the believer to retreat from service to the

Lord, but where would be the evidence of "the work of faith with power" (2 Thess. 1:11)? Paul's prayer was that believers would be fruitful in the midst of troubles.

Lastly, Paul prayed that the church would be faithful, and that the grace of God would cause their lives to glorify the Lord Jesus Christ. God has designed a plan whereby He uses limited and weak earthen vessels to accomplish His work. Second Corinthians 4:7-11 is an example of the kind of faith of which Paul prayed. Paul's words in 2 Corinthians and 2 Thessalonians remind believers that even in the most difficult situation that one can imagine, God is working to bring glory to His name through the faithfulness Christians demonstrate as His people. The believer's response should be as this first-century church: a life of faith, increasing love and hope that glorifies Christ. By being in Jesus, the Christian is also glorified, and set forth to receive an honor not self-generated, but given by virtue of one's relationship with the Savior.

Count Yourself Worthy

As will be evident in the next chapter of 2 Thessalonians, the church received a letter from someone claiming to be the Apostle Paul. The letter stated that the seven-year tribulation had arrived, and that the church was living in that period. The trials and tribulations of the church were said to be evidence that the tribulation had already begun, and therefore the Christians had not been taken in the rapture. Paul corrected such thinking by indicating events that must occur prior to the beginning of the tribulation. Second Thessalonians was written to correct this erroneous teaching among the church. The church was indeed experiencing difficult times, but this was not because the rapture had already occurred and they somehow missed the event. Therefore, the opening chapter of 2 Thessalonians provides encouragement to the church. Their difficulties were not the prophesied events of the tribulation, and therefore, they should thank God for the opportunity to be counted worthy to suffer for His glory.

Faith, love and hope are essential virtues in the life of every believer. Considering the example given to Christians today, the faith of believers should be working and ever strengthening. The love of God's people should be increasing. When suffering or witnessing others in distress, it is an opportunity to give empathy and understanding, and to increase in love. Hope should be persevering. Trials provide opportunities to endure with hope of future victory and glory at Christ's return. Though one's trials as the church will not include the coming wrath of God in the tribulation, believers still need to thank God that He counts them worthy to suffer for Him. The prayer of the church should model the Apostle Paul's, and ask God that He would count us worthy through our trials, to bring forth fruit in the midst of the trial, and to increase our personal faith and the faith of the church around us.

In this opening chapter of 2 Thessalonians, there is a two-fold source of God's grace and peace: from the Father and the Lord Jesus Christ. The fountain of grace is God the Father and His grace is mediated through the Lord Jesus Christ, and it may also be said to come from Him. Certainly, every believer should pray each and every day that God would fully glorify Christ in them, as they in turn receive glory from Him in accordance with the gracious calling of God and the Lord Jesus Christ.

SECOND THESSALONIANS 2

The majority of 2 Thessalonians 2 is prophetically significant; therefore, much concentration will be devoted to explaining the teaching of these verses. Certain verses are fundamental for doctrinal issues relating to the rapture and the coming of Christ, and therefore deserve special attention to understand the Biblical revelation with regard to those doctrines. The emphasis of the second chapter is evident in verses 1-2, which read, "Now we request you, brethren, with regard to the coming of our Lord Jesus Christ and our gathering together to Him, that you not be quickly shaken from your composure or be disturbed either by a spirit or a message or a letter as if from us, to the effect that the day of the Lord has come."

The Coming of Lord Jesus

There are several things worthy of comment with regard to verses one and two. Paul wrote to the Thessalonians to teach them clearly with regard to the rapture. Consequently, it would be proper to consider such teaching as the primary focus when the text mentions the coming of the Lord Jesus Christ and being gathered together to Him. Some Bible teachers attempt to distinguish the coming of the Lord Jesus and the gathering together to Him as two events, but the manner in which it is written in the Greek would be better understood as "the coming of our Lord Jesus Christ, *even our gathering together to Him.*" When the text states, "with regard to," it is referring to one event. The "gathering together" is with regard to the rapture, which is the emphasis of 1 Thessalonians 4:13-18, wherein Scripture reveals how the Lord will descend from heaven to gather His church unto Himself.

Apparently, according to verse 2, there were individuals in danger of being troubled, who were being shaken and disturbed. What is interesting is that in John 14, which is the only reference to the rapture in the four gospels, the very same language is employed when it says do not let your heart be troubled. John 14:1 uses the same language of 2 Thessalonians 2:2, instructing believers not to be quickly shaken from their composure, and not to be disturbed. The word "disturbed "is the same as found in John 14:1, so there are some parallel thoughts between the passages. Jesus explained in John 14 that He was going to prepare a place for His church. Wherever this place would be, which seems to be the new Jerusalem of

Revelation 21, Jesus would take the church unto Himself to be with Him forever. Unfortunately, there were individuals in danger of being troubled with regard to this teaching.

Three things may have caused the disturbance: a spirit, a message or a letter (2 Thess. 2:2). First John 4:1 exhorts believers to examine the spirits; examine them all to know if they are truly of God. Simply because somebody claims to be a "Christian" or to communicate "Christian teaching," or even if something is printed by a "Christian" publisher, believers are still to examine all things in light of God's Word. Even if something is in the Christian bookstore and one of the top 10 bestsellers, it still needs to be examined to determine if it is truly Biblical. Many times those things that are the bestsellers tend to be the most unbiblical. Not always, but they tend to be, at least in the 20th and 21st centuries.

There were individuals who were troubled by a spirit, and it states also troubled by a word, by a message (so perhaps a false preacher or teacher), which proclaimed things that were contrary to what Paul had taught the Thessalonians. Moreover, a third form of disturbance was the letter. Paul said "a letter as if from us," so apparently, there was a letter that was being distributed that was forged, which was actually said to be written by the apostle. Of course, there are many evidences of these so-called "gospels" that are actually forgeries of an apostle.

The three things—the spirit, the message and letter—were troubling some individuals. The idea, the troubling aspect of it, is stated at the end of verse two; the disconcerting facet was that the spirit, the message, the letter, was saying, "the day of the Lord has come." (Although there are some translations that read, "the day of Christ" [i.e., NKJV], there is not good manuscript evidence for that reading; the best manuscripts favor the reading, "day of the Lord.") The day of the Lord is a prophesied event in the Old Testament; it is a time of judgment that God will bring upon the world that will culminate in the establishing of His kingdom, a literal monarchy, which will be a realm of peace and righteousness. The false teaching from the three sources was that the day of the Lord had arrived.

When the text reads, "the day of the Lord has come," in the Greek, the teaching was that the day of the Lord is at hand. The verb is in the perfect tense in the Greek, which would signify past action with present results. In other words, the false teaching was that the day of the Lord was being accomplished, it was occurring to these first-century believers; it had past action with present results. The teaching was that the Thessalonian believers were actually in the tribulation period, the day of the Lord. According to the perspective of this author, it does not seem possible to explain their concern unless Paul had taught them a pretribulational rapture, a rapture to occur prior to the day of the Lord, prior to the tribulation. Why else would they be concerned? If they were to go through any aspect of the tribulation period, then why be concerned, why be troubled? The troubling aspect only makes sense with a pretribulational rapture. Paul had taught them that they would be taken prior to the beginning of that period, but there was false teaching that they were actually in the day of the Lord.

The fact that they were experiencing intense persecution led them to assume they were, indeed, in that period. The same phenomenon occurred during the Protestant Reformation; many of the Reformers believed they were in the tribulation. They believed the pope was Antichrist because of the persecution that they were enduring. Apparently, the Thessalonian church believed something similar as a consequence of the influence of false teachers saying that they were actually in that period. Of course, again, that only makes sense with a pretribulational rapture.

Understanding that rapture issues are only related to premillennialism is beneficial. Often when the doctrine of the rapture is mentioned, individuals want to discuss premillennial or amillennial issues. However, the doctrine of the rapture of the church is only a premillennial issue. In other words, only those who believe in premillennialism read the eschatological passages and say, When will the coming occur? Will it be prior to the day of the Lord, in the middle, three-fourths of the way, at the end? The doctrine of the rapture is only a premillennial issue.

When one reads the book of Revelation, it is fairly evident (according to ch. 19) that Christ is coming to this Earth. What is the very next event stated subsequent to His coming? Chapter 20 emphasizes the millennial reign—six times it uses the Greek word for *thousand*, so it should be interpreted literally. Six times it uses the Greek word for *thousand* (*chiliades*), which informs the reader that the duration is a literal 1,000 years, in comparing that to all the Old Testament prophesies. Understanding fundamentally that premillennialism is true, then, one can confidently discuss issues with regard to the rapture. The foundational teaching is premillennialism, and from that understanding, one is able to Biblically and intelligently address issues with regard to the rapture and the second coming.

The Apostasy: Physical or Religious?

The focus of verses 3-10 is to demonstrate to the believers that they were not experiencing the tribulation, the day of the Lord. Verse 3 indicates that two things have to occur prior to the tribulation period beginning: "Let no one in any way deceive you, for *it will not come*"—in other words, the day of the Lord will not come—"unless the apostasy comes first, and the man of lawlessness is revealed, the son of destruction." Two things have to occur: there has to be apostasy first, and then the man of lawlessness is revealed, the son of destruction.

According to Daniel 9:26, "the prince who is to come" will confirm a covenant with many for seven years, and then break that covenant in the midst of that week. Therefore, the revealing of the man of lawlessness—the son of destruction—is not when he breaks the covenant; according to

Daniel 9:26, it is actually when he enforces the seven-year covenant. Paul wrote that the seven-year covenant could not occur "unless the apostasy comes first, and the man of lawlessness is revealed, the son of destruction" (2 Thess. 2:3).

The Greek word for apostasy, in verse 3, is *apostasia*. There are generally two solutions given for understanding the Greek word *apostasia*. The first, and the traditional and probably the most popular view (or it is the popular view adopted by commentators) is that the *apostasia* should be identified as a "falling away;" in other words, it is a religious apostasy. Even the King James Version translates the Greek in that manner. The most common view in commentaries is to understand 2 Thessalonians 2:3 as teaching not to be deceived because the "falling away" will come first—religious apostasy will appear initially—and then the man of lawlessness will be revealed.

"Departure" as Physical

Another view is that the departure is actually a reference to the rapture of the church. There are valid reasons for accepting the interpretation that *apostasia* should be regarded as referencing the pretribulational rapture of the church. One of the first reasons to understand this Greek word, *apostasia*, as a physical departure, is that the word can truly have the meaning of a physical departure. Whether it is a religious departure or a physical departure depends upon the context. In their *Greek-English Lexicon*, Liddell and Scott listed "departure, disappearance" as the second meaning of *apostasia*.[389] According to one of the standard Greek lexicons, *apostasia* can have reference to an actual, physical departure, not just religious.

Part of the interpretative problem is that the word *apostasia* is used only twice in the New Testament. Forms of it—noun forms and verbal forms—have other uses in the New Testament, but the actual word, *apostasia*, is only used

---

389 Henry George Liddell and Robert Scott, comps., *A Greek-English Lexicon*, 9th ed. (1843; reprint, Oxford: Clarendon Press, 1940, 1996), p. 218.

in two places in the New Testament—here in 2 Thessalonians 2, and then a second reference in Acts 21:21, where Paul was accused of teaching a departure from Moses. According to the context of Acts 21, the accusation against Paul was clearly in the sense of religious departure. He was accused of teaching religious *apostasia* from the law of Moses; therefore, the context lets the reader know how to understand the Greek word. In the Greek translation of the Old Testament (Septuagint), one will find the word used in various passages, and the idea is religious departure in all those usages (Josh. 22:22; 1 Kings 21:13; 2 Chron. 29:19; 33:19; Isa. 30:1; Jer. 2:19; cf. 1 Macc. 2:15). In reading through all these verses, the context indicates religious departure. Sometimes there will be a descriptive phrase used in addition to this Greek word *apostasia* to inform the reader that religious apostasy is the meaning. Either context or a descriptive phrase is needed to indicate the meaning, which means *apostasia* has a more general rather than specific (technical) meaning.

The verbal form of *apostasia* is used 15 times in the New Testament (Luke 2:37; 4:13; 8:13; 13:27; Acts 5:37-38; 12:10; 15:38; 19:9; 22:29; 2 Cor. 12:8; 1 Tim. 4:1; 6:5; 2 Tim. 2:19; Heb. 3:12). Of those 15 references, only three have reference to a religious departure, and those three are always qualified by the context, because *apostasia* seems to be a general word that requires contextual consideration to indicate the meaning. For example, the context in Luke 8:13 indicates religious apostasy in reference to the rocky soil: "there are those who when they hear, they receive the word with joy; and these have no firm root; they believe for a while, and in time of temptation"—they apostasize—they "fall away." First Timothy 4:1 is another example of religious apostasy: the *apostasia* is departure from the cardinal doctrines of Christianity. The descriptive phrase, "from the faith," explains the manner of departure. Hebrews 3:12 is another example wherein the descriptive phrase indicates religious apostasy from the living God.

Another reference, Acts 12:10, states: "When they had passed the first and second guard, they came to the iron gate that leads into the city, which opened for them by itself; and they went out and went along one street, and immediately the angel departed from him." The verbal usage of *apostasia* in Acts 12:10 is a physical departure. Therefore, *apostasia* can sometimes have the meaning of a religious apostasy from the living God (as in Heb. 3:12), from the faith (as in 1 Tim. 4:1), an apostasy from salvation itself (as in Luke 8), or it can have the idea of physical departure (as in Acts 12:10). In 2 Corinthians 12:8, Paul prayed that the thorn in the flesh might apostasize (depart) from him. Obviously, the intent of *apostasia* is used generally, and not technically (i.e., only one meaning). Interestingly enough, William Tyndale, Thomas Cranmer, Theodore Beza and the *Geneva Bible* translated *apostasia* in 2 Thessalonians 2:3 as departure.

"Departure" and Use of the Definite Article

Another issue that helps in determining whether *apostasia* should be understood as a physical or religious departure in 2 Thessalonians 2:3 is the use of the Greek definite article. The definite article, "the," is *hē* in the Greek, so that the text reads, *hē apostasia*. The use of the definite article seems to indicate that *apostasia* is a reference to the rapture. The use of the article with a word makes that word conspicuously distinctive because the basic function of the definitive article is to identify an object or to bring attention to it.[390] So, again, the use of the article with a word (i.e., *hē apostasia*) makes that word conspicuously distinctive. What that means is that Paul was not referring to an *apostasia*; he was referring to *the apostasia*—something very specific. The definite article indicates that *the apostasia* will be a very specific event, that is, something the apostle had discussed previously with the Thessalonian believers.

Although he seemed to understand apostasia (ἀποστασία) as "a religious revolt," Robertson stated, "the use of the definite article (*hē*) seems

---

390 H. E. Dana and Julius R. Mantey, *A Manual Grammar of the Greek New Testament* (New York: Macmillan, 1927), p. 137

to mean that Paul had spoken to the Thessalonians about it."[391] The highly esteemed Greek grammarian, A. T. Robertson, indicated that the use of the definite article points to something that Paul had previously discussed with the Thessalonian believers. He spoke to them previously with regard to *the apostasia*. If *apostasia* is understood as religious apostasy (apostasy from the Christian faith), where is the prior reference? The reference cannot be found in 1 Thessalonians, and there is no reference to a religious apostasy thus far in 2 Thessalonians. Nevertheless, the use of the definite article indicates that Paul was referring to something very specific. He wrote with regard to *the apostasia*, "the departure."

Consider the emphasis of 1 Thessalonians 4 to answer the question with regard to prior reference. In his first epistle, Paul taught the church with regard to Christ coming for His church and taking His church from the Earth, and gathering all church saints to heaven to always be with the Lord. He did not make any reference to a religious apostasy. Certainly, in the "Pastoral Epistles" (1-2 Tim.; Tit.) there is reference to religious apostasy, but not here in Thessalonians. If he was referring to something that he had already discussed with the Thessalonian believers, the only previous reference would be the rapture of the church in 1 Thessalonians 4, or as he said in 2 Thessalonians 2:1, "the coming of [the] Lord Jesus Christ and our gathering together unto Him."

"Departure" is First

There is also evidence in Paul's style of writing that lends support to the idea that *apostasia* is the rapture, because in verse 3, Paul stated that two events have to occur first. He used the Greek word *proton* (πρῶτον) and taught that one event has to come first. Paul taught that *the apostasia* must come first, which is followed by the revealing of the

---

391 Archibald Thomas Robertson, *Word Pictures in the New Testament*, 6 vols. (Nashville: Broadman Press, 1931), 4:49

man of sin. In the next section, verses 6-7 will be examined, which read, "And you know what restrains him now, so that in his time he will be revealed. For the mystery of lawlessness is already at work; only he who now restrains *will do so* until he is taken out of the way." In those verses, Paul apparently referenced *the apostasia* more fully in referring to a physical departure of the church.

When all the various factors with regard to the use of *apostasia* in 2 Thessalonians 2:3 are considered together, the traditional interpretation of this Greek word as religious apostasy seems to be not wholly accurate. Apparently, there is an unmistakable pretribulational rapture statement in verse 3 when one considers the different lexicons and contexts, verbal forms in the New Testament, the use of the definite article, the idea that verse 3 states the departure has to come first, and the context of Thessalonians. Paul referred to a physical departure, and said that physical departure has to come first, and then after that physical departure, there is the revealing of the man of lawlessness. Paul referred to a physical departure in 2 Thessalonians 2:3, and said that physical departure must occur first, and then following that physical departure, there would be the revealing of the man of lawlessness.

Identifying the Restrainer

Second Thessalonians 2:6-7 refers to a restrainer that continues to restrain "until he is taken out of the way." There are generally five different views as to identifying the restrainer, with the first being that it is the Roman Empire. The restrainer cannot be the Roman Empire because such a view limits the restrainer to the past, and Paul indicated that the one being restrained, the man of sin, will live in the future during the day of the Lord. One other view is that the restrainer is human government, which cannot be correct because human government will continue to exist even after the man of sin is revealed.

The man of sin will establish his own government and will enforce it as his government and his administration only, and his government will even require believers to deny the living God but unbelievers will obey; therefore, a government still exists even when the man of lawlessness, the man of sin, is revealed, so it cannot be human government. Another idea is that the restrainer is Satan. Scripture teaches that a "house divided against itself will not stand" (Matt. 12:25); therefore, the restrainer cannot be Satan, either. Is the restrainer the church? According to 2 Thessalonians 2:9, the restrainer will prevent "the activity of Satan, with all power and signs and false wonders." Certainly, it is nice to think that the church could restrain the activity of Satan, his power, his signs and false wonders. In a sense, the church can with the gospel, with the preaching of the Word of God, but not in the fullest sense because only God can do that.

As Martin Luther said in agreement with Scripture, "Satan is God's devil;"[392] he is not a rival, but he is God's devil and the Lord God just uses Satan to accomplish his purposes, but the church does not have that power. According to Jude 9, dispute with the devil must be on the basis of the Lord's rebuke. Even Michael the archangel recognized that only God could oppose Satan. What is stated with regard to the restrainer in 2 Thessalonians 2 is the fact that this restrainer prevents one who has powers, signs and lying wonders; therefore, it cannot be the church.

Indication as to the identity of the restrainer can be determined because the gender for the word actually changes. The Greek word for "restrains" changes from the neuter, which is just generic as opposed to being masculine or feminine, in verse 6, to the masculine in verse 7. What is noteworthy is that the gender changes from one verse to the

---

392 Paul Althaus, *The Theology of Martin Luther*, 2nd ed., trans. Robert C. Schultz (Gütersloh, Germany: Gütersloher Verlagshaus Gerd Mohn, 1963; reprint, Philadelphia: Fortress Press, 1966), p. 165; Craig Ott and Stephen J. Strauss, with Timothy C. Tennent, *Encountering Theology of Mission* (Grand Rapids: Baker, 2010), p. 245.

next. Why would verse 6 state, "what restrains him now," and do so in a general sense, and then change to a masculine form in verse 7, when stating, "he who now restrains"?

Apparently, the only manner one can understand the change from the neuter present active participle (*to katechon*, τὸ κατέχον) in verse 6 to the masculine present active participle (*ho katechōn*, ὁ κατέχων) in verse 7 is that the latter should be understood as referring to the Holy Spirit. The restrainer will restrain until removed, and it is the Holy Spirit accomplishing the action. The restrainer will restrain until He is removed (*genētai*, γένηται). *Genētai* (γένηται) is an aorist middle subjunctive from the deponent verb *ginomai* (γίνομαι). Deponent verbs have middle or passive endings but are translated as active in meaning. In 2 Thessalonians 2:7, the verb would mean that the subject is acting. *Genētai* (γένηται) does not denote removal by an outside agent but indicates a voluntary action of the restrainer. The Greek indicates that the restrainer is actively performing the act of restraining. The restraining is not some kind of a passive thing, but the restrainer is doing this actively.

Some have said that the idea of the restrainer being "taken out of the way" cannot refer to a spatial removal. In other words, it cannot refer to a physical removal, but only some form of resignation. Page 159 of *A Greek-English Lexicon of the New Testament and Other Early Christian Literature* (1979) references 2 Thessalonians 2:7 as an example of deponent verb usage "to denote change of location" (i.e., "leave the scene").[393] The deponent verb usage in 2 Thessalonians 2:7 does indeed indicate a change in location. The 2000 (third) edition of this standard Greek lexicon (pp. 198-99) refers to the same verse as an example of deponent verb usage to indicate "[making] a change of location in space."[394] Therefore, when one examines the context

393   William F. Bauer, William F. Arndt and F. Wilbur Gingrich, *A Greek-English Lexicon of the New Testament and Other Early Christian Literature*, 2nd ed., rev. F. Wilbur Gingrich and Frederick W. Danker (Chicago: University of Chicago Press, 1979), p. 159.

394   William F. Bauer, Frederick W. Danker, William F. Arndt and F. Wilbur Gingrich, *A Greek-English*

of the Greek word *apostasia*, and examines what is stated in verses 6-7, it is easy to discern that the focus is upon a spatial departure, a physical departure. The entire context favors such an interpretation.

Removal of the Restrainer

Based upon context and grammar, it is best to understand that the Holy Spirit is specifically doing the restraining. Is the Holy Spirit taken from the Earth? The Holy Spirit cannot be taken from the Earth because He is omnipresent. He is the one who effects salvation. Consequently, if the Holy Spirit were removed, then nobody could be saved during the tribulation, if that were a possibility. One reads in Revelation with regard to multitudes coming from the period having received salvation, believing in God, as a result.

What is the restraining influence? Upon examining the New Testament and understanding what the Bible reveals concerning the Holy Spirit indwelling believers (which is something that never occurred in the Old Testament in the sense that the Holy Spirit actually dwelt within the believer *and remained permanently*), it would be natural to understand the removal of the restrainer as referring to the pretribulational rapture of the church. In the Old Testament, the Holy Spirit would empower for ministry and come upon someone, and sometimes there would be a filling, but it was not permanent. The experience with the church is enduring; it is a permanent filling of the Holy Spirit. He does not depart from the church. Such a doctrine is both comforting and humbling to recognize that God sees everything, but also it is comforting in the sense that believers know that God is always with them, to strengthen, to guide and to empower. The doctrine has a sobering aspect, but it also has a comforting aspect. What does it mean? In verses 6-7 of 2 Thessalonians 2, what currently restrains?

Lexicon of the New Testament and Other Early Christian Literature, 3rd ed. (Chicago: University of Chicago Press, 2000), pp. 198-99.

The Holy Spirit, as He indwells the church, is actually used by God to restrain evil.

The church cannot complain and say how bad the world is without first looking inward and understanding that the church is a restraining influence. If the church is doing what she has been commissioned to accomplish, if the church is being obedient to God, there is a restraining influence of evil as the church is being faithful. The church has much opportunity to be faithful to God and have a tremendous impact upon the culture. The restraining influence is the Holy Spirit within the church. Examination of the context and all the other factors (identified in this section and the previous) indicate a pretribulational rapture, such as statements in verse 3 that unless the apostasy, that is, the departure (rapture) comes first, the man of lawlessness cannot be revealed, which is then the tribulation, the day of the Lord beginning. Paul said the departure, the physical departure of the church, has to come first. The church is that restraining influence, when the church departs and leaves this earth, then that restraining influence is taken, and the man of lawlessness can then be revealed.

The man of lawlessness cannot be revealed now while the church is here. Why? The answer is that the church would oppose him by citing the Scriptures and indicating that he is the prophesied man of sin. The church would oppose the man of sin; therefore, the church has to be removed for the man of lawlessness to be revealed, and then the events of Revelation will be fulfilled. Second Thessalonians 2 has two very obvious references to the rapture of the church.

The removal of the restrainer is a reference to the departure of the Holy Spirit in the pretribulational rapture of the church. The church has been granted a tremendous opportunity to restrain evil in this world through faithfulness to God, through proclamation of the gospel, and through the making of disciples. May the church pray for God's help to be faithful until the very moment, the very second, that God calls His people home to glory.

Second Thessalonians 2 corrected the thinking of the church with regard to the day of the Lord, which someone had taught them was already occurring. Paul articulated reasons why the day of the Lord had not begun because he was concerned that their error in this regard would compromise their hope to experience the "gathering together" he had described in 1 Thessalonians 4:13-18. Second Thessalonians 2 is a pivotal chapter in teaching eschatological doctrines; therefore, the concluding sections herein will review the primary teachings of that chapter.

The Coming of Christ and the Gathering Together

The coming of the Lord Jesus Christ and gathering together to Him is referenced in verse 1. The Greek word for coming is *parousia*, which is a very common word. Some think it has a technical meaning, which would mean that anytime the word is used, it only refers to the second coming, but such a notion is incorrect. However, context always determines whether the reference is with regard to either the rapture or second coming. The "gathering together to Him" is parallel to the promise of 1 Thessalonians 4:13-18 with regard to the Lord coming, descending in the clouds and gathering His church from this world. Of course, the 1 Thessalonians passage is where the language is derived for the rapture because the Greek was translated *rapier* (i.e., rapture) in the Latin Vulgate. The Western church uses the Latin term for the doctrine of the rapture, but the teaching is certainly taught in Scripture. The reference in 2 Thessalonians 2 with regard to the coming of our Lord Jesus Christ and our gathering together to Him is to the rapture.

According to verse 2, some were concerned with regard to teaching that the day of the Lord had come. Only a pretribulational understanding of the text would make sense, because if Paul had taught the Thessalonians that they had to experience the tribulation, they would just be looking at the calendar and counting how much persecution until they would be delivered at the second coming. The perspective in 2 Thessalonians, however, is that they were in that period and some people were telling them that the day of the Lord had occurred. The day of the Lord is a prophesied time of intense judgment that God brings upon the wicked and is also a period that God brings against Israel, to bring them to salvation, to judge them for their sins, to prepare them for the receiving of Messiah, and for the establishment of His kingdom.

There are certainly some Christians who favor an idealist interpretation of this passage, which means that the text is simply addressing general troubles and difficulties that the church experiences. Therefore, the text is non-literal and spiritualized, and simply instructing the church with regard to the ultimate victory in Jesus Christ. In other words, the text is not chronological in any manner because the chapter must bear a direct relationship to the present day and age. In response to such assertions, it would be wise to consider the Old Testament prophesies of Messiah and the kingdom. The generations that received those prophecies were thousands of years removed from fulfillment. Was it any less important or relevant to them? Certainly not! Simply because events may be future, it does not mean there is not an application or relevancy to the church in the present age. There are some that think conversely, and they attempt to spiritualize these things, or seek to find some first-century fulfillment, which would mean that one is reading historical fulfillment concerning these things.

The problem is that when one reads individuals that embrace these different views, such as preterists, idealists and historicists, they all contradict one another regarding the fulfillment. They simply cannot be unified regarding whether the events of 2 Thessalonians 2:1-12 are already passed, or if the events are being fulfilled in the present age. Those who interpret the text literally have amazing agreement with each other, and generally only have minor points of disagreement.

There may be many possible interpretations with regard to the best sense of the Biblical text, but readers must always seek the best meaning of the text, which would be pretribulationism. Some had taught that the day of the Lord had come, and the church was experiencing this persecution, thinking they had missed the rapture, that is, the coming prior to that period. Therefore, Paul said not to be deceived "for *it will not come* unless the apostasy comes first, and the man of lawlessness is revealed, the son of destruction" (2 Thess. 2:3). He said two things have to occur: there must be apostasy, and the man of lawlessness revealed. Contextual examination of the Greek word, which is translated apostasy, would be better understood as a physical departure. If one were to examine the meaning of the word in Greek lexicons and grammars, it would seem that a physical departure is based upon the context of what Paul had written previously. The church was already experiencing lawlessness, which would hardly qualify as a sign. Lawlessness has been a continual force against the church since its inception. The spirit of Antichrist is ever with the church; therefore, a religious departure from the faith would hardly be a sign that one was not entering the day of the Lord.

Even today, church members discuss the apostasy of the church and how it is increasing progressively, yet it is amazing what people thought was sinful 10 or 20 years ago, and now looking at what doctrines and practices are being embraced. The point is that apostasy can always get worse. During the time of the Protestant Reformation, however, it was a time when it did not seem that things could worsen, and then God appointed individuals to proclaim the truth of Scripture, such as justification by faith alone, and tremendous revival occurred, of which all Christians are recipients. Apostasy or religious departure is not truly a sign, but is something that is always present with the church. The history of Israel and the church is one of frequent apostasies even among themselves and would not be a noteworthy sign.

Paul's exhortation not to be deceived would relate best to Daniel 9, where it prophesies with regard to the prince who will come and make a covenant with the Jewish nation and promise them peace for a seven-year period of time. Second Thessalonians 2 prophesies apostasy, and then the man of lawlessness is revealed, the person who makes the covenant with the Jewish nation. Verse 4 gives further explanation with regard to the man of lawlessness, the one "who opposes and exalts himself above every so-called god or object of worship, so that he takes his seat in the temple of God, displaying himself as being God." Approximately A.D. 40, the Roman emperor Caligula entered the Holy of Holies, and established an image of himself, and declared himself as God. Paul did not say that was fulfillment; rather, he said that the event was still future when writing Thessalonians (probably in the early 50s of the first century). Even the first epistle of John prophesies that there will be a future Antichrist.

Second Thessalonians 2 is prophesying with regard to events that have not yet occurred, and predicting a man of lawlessness who will proclaim himself as God in the Jewish temple. The Romans destroyed the temple in A.D. 70, and there is also mention of a temple in the book of Revelation, which was written A.D. 95. If those things were fulfilled in the first century, then Paul could have cited the case of Caligula as fulfillment; or John, in the book of Revelation, could have referenced the destruction of the temple, which was 25 years prior. The correct understanding is that the prophecies are with regard to a third temple, a rebuilt temple, which is not there today.

Certainly, it is easy to understand—given situations currently in the Middle East—that if an individual can promise peace, and find a way that the Muslims can worship Allah and the Jews can rebuild their temple, that the world would hail this individual as a great leader. America has already witnessed—without addressing the merits or demerits of that presidency—how someone can achieve a celebrity status as president, and how amazingly that people—through use of media—could proclaim an individual to have a messiah-like character. Combine that with the actual sense of accomplishments, solving peace in the Middle East, and then it is easy to understand how all the world will worship an individual as a great leader. Therefore, verse 5 reads, "Do you not remember that while I was still with you, I was telling you these things?" Paul was reminding the church that he had been with them a few weeks, and he had taught them all these things. The apostle taught them all manner of chronological events (with regard to the coming of the Lord, the rapture, the man of sin, a temple, etc.), which demonstrates that he considered these things to be important. Verse 5 is instructive to believers not to neglect the teaching of any aspect of God's Word. Paul was obviously saying that it was important for the Thessalonians to understand these things, and it is important for the church also, to understand prophetic truth. Such teaching is essential to victorious Christian living.

Prior to the Day of the Lord

In verses 6-12, Paul continued his instruction regarding events that must occur prior to the beginning of the day of the Lord, and he did that by placing emphasis upon the lawlessness of that period. In these verses, Paul explained more clearly to the church why the rapture had not occurred and why they had not missed it; therefore, they were not experiencing the day of the Lord, the time of God's judgment, and the time of God's wrath.

Verse 7 mentions he who now restrains, and in the Greek the word is a masculine tense. The church is never referenced in that manner; the Greek New Testament always uses a feminine gender for the church. Therefore, the question is with regard to the masculine gender in verse 7. The reference is to the Holy Spirit, which is why verse 7 contains the masculine gender.[395] The Holy Spirit is removed only as He indwells the

---

395   In response to feminist theology, which is exceedingly critical with regard to masculine gender terminology in naming the persons of the trinity, it is essential to affirm that God has inspired

church. The Holy Spirit is not taken from the Earth because He is God, and therefore omnipresent. The removal must involve the indwelling presence of the Holy Spirit. The Holy Spirit indwells every Christian at the moment of baptism into the body of Christ (1 Cor. 12:13). The indwelling of the Holy Spirit is unique for the church; a *permanent* indwelling of the Holy Spirit never occurred in the Old Testament.

Revelation does not mention any kind of indwelling of the Holy Spirit either; it mentions an indwelling, but it is the indwelling of the man of sin by Satan. The restraining influence in 2 Thessalonians 2 is the Holy Spirit as He indwells the church. The restraining influence is the indwelt church, which will be removed from the Earth at the rapture, and this event is the removal of the restrainer. The rapture and the restrainer being removed are equal in meaning. Subsequent to the removal of the restrainer, the man of lawlessness is revealed by what he does according to Daniel 9, and then that would be the beginning of the day of the Lord.

In 2 Thessalonians 2:8, there is good indication of the wrath of God being mentioned when it addresses the Lord coming and slaying with the breath of His mouth this man of lawlessness. Such teaching very much correlates with Revelation 19; it is the same depiction of Christ descending from heaven, King of kings, Lord of lords, and by the words from His mouth, He destroys the wicked. The very next chapter in Revelation prophesies

---

the masculine imagery in Biblical revelation, and is therefore, not to be regarded minimally. The trinitarian name of God is revealed in Scripture. For instance, Jesus addressed His Father uniquely as "Abba" (Mark 14:36), which was His own self-revelation and self-understanding as the Son of God, even though His favored name throughout His earthly ministry was "Son of Man." By simply requesting of His Father, Jesus promised that the Holy Spirit would be given (John 14:16). When the ministry of the Holy Spirit was promised, Jesus deliberately violated peculiarities of the Greek language in employing the masculine pronoun "He" (16:14). Therefore, the Biblical and historic identity of the trinity would be compromised, if not negated, by obscuring this masculine nomenclature. For instance, see William J. Hill, *The Three-Personed God: The Trinity as a Mystery of Salvation* (Washington, DC: Catholic University of America Press, 1982); Elizabeth A. Johnson, *She Who Is: The Mystery of God in Feminist Theological Discourse* (New York: Crossroad, 1992); Alvin F. Kimel Jr., ed., *Speaking the Christian God: The Holy Trinity and the Challenge of Feminism* (Grand Rapids: Eerdmans, 1992); and, Peter John Widdicombe, "The Fatherhood of God in the Thought of Justin Martyr, Origen and Athanasius." Ph.D. dissertation, University of Oxford, 1990.

concerning the millennial kingdom, which seems to be sequential. The judgment associated with the second coming of Christ to Earth, and then the establishing of the kingdom, is paralleled. Verse 8 of 2 Thessalonians would also be indication of Revelation 19, and the fact that Christ himself will destroy the man of sin, the lawless one. The only indication of a future wrath in the two epistles to the Thessalonians is 1 Thessalonians 1:10, where it notes that the church was "to wait for [God's] son from heaven, whom He raised from the dead, *that is* Jesus, who rescues [the church] from the wrath to come."

The *wrath* mentioned in 1 Thessalonians 1:10 is in reference to a coming of Jesus and how this coming is going to prevent the church from experiencing a future period of wrath. The scenario is of a coming of the Lord Jesus Christ, which provides deliverance from future wrath. One could certainly think that deliverance is the wrath of the tribulation, and it is referencing the second coming. Such a notion, however, would be incorrect because at the second coming, the wrath is completed, and it will be time for establishing the kingdom, so it could not be the second coming mentioned in 1 Thessalonians 1:10, nor in 2 Thessalonians 2. The coming has to be a delivering, a coming of the Lord Jesus Christ, and that coming results in one being delivered, not experiencing a future period of wrath, which would be the tribulation. Such statements are indications of rapture, a gathering of the church, prior to the beginning of the seven years of tribulation.

Expounding upon verse 3, when it referenced the apostasy, Paul addressed all these texts with regard to what restrains the man of lawlessness. Again, the best manner to understand that restrainer is that this is dealing with the indwelling of the Holy Spirit within the church, and that when the church is removed from this Earth in the rapture, that restraining influence is taken so that then the man of lawlessness is revealed. The church is "the pillar and support of the truth" (1 Tim. 3:15); therefore, it is necessary to remove the pillar and support of the truth, and then the man of lawlessness can be revealed, and it is impossible currently for such an event to occur because the church is still present in this earth. As bad as things may be or seem, it is comforting to know that the church has a restraining influence. Anytime society goes bad, the church should always look at itself first and ask what is the church doing or not doing that is contributing to the fall. Sometimes the religious and ungodly persecute, and sometimes difficulties are the righteous judgment of God, and sometimes those experiences are the outcome for those who should be more obedient.

Second Thessalonians 2 is saying that the restraining influence has to be removed before the man of lawlessness can be revealed. Verse 7 states that this mystery of lawlessness is already at work; it was already at work in the first century, which is why it cannot be the Roman Empire or something similar. The restrainer cannot be human government because this is something that existed in the first century and continues even today, and will culminate in one specific individual, a lawless one that the Lord Jesus will destroy with the breath of His mouth. Verse 9 indicates the power that this individual will possess, a power from Satan to deceive many people into following him through signs and false wonders. Of course, this is something that the second beast of Revelation is also able to do; he is able to perform counterfeit miracles—signs and wonders—that deceive people. People are deceived by the so-called miraculous displays because it seems that the individuals possess the power of God.

God's Glory in Salvation and Judgment

Verses 10-12 mention those who are deceived and are perishing. The text indicates that those who "did not receive the love of the truth so as to be saved" received "a deluding influence" from God. There have been some that have taught that if the lost hear the gospel prior to the rapture and do not believe it, they will receive a deluding influence so that they will never have another chance to believe. In other words, anybody who heard the gospel and rejected it prior to the rapture cannot be saved once the rapture has occurred, but this is not the correct interpretation. The motivation is sincere to cause individuals to think seriously with regard to faith in Jesus Christ. The Biblical text, however, is just simply indicating the type of people (i.e., unbelievers) who do "not receive the love of the truth so as to be saved" and take "pleasure in wickedness." They willingly reject the gospel prior to the rapture and subsequent to the rapture, which is an accurate description of all unbelievers who do not receive the truth and willingly reject it; they will be given a deluding influence so as to believe what is false. The conscience is seared.

According to Romans, all humanity possesses knowledge of God's existence. All humanity is without excuse; all have natural revelation (creation); all have a conscience; consequently, all humanity is accountable to God and without excuse for not living in a manner consistent with such knowledge. Romans 1:18-20 teaches that humanity does not rebel because there is insufficient knowledge of God's existence; it is not that the conscience fails to convict; rather, fallen humanity suppresses the truth of God in unrighteousness.

Probably everyone reading this chapter is able to recollect someone who heard the gospel proclaimed, and did not even want to hear the truth or think regarding the demands of the gospel of Jesus Christ. They would rather pretend that God does not exist, or that the gospel is unclear or untruthful, which is the same that is expressed in 2 Thessalonians 2:10-12. God sears the conscience and gives the unbeliever a deluding influence, which leads to eternal punishment. There is a somber application to this text when the church proclaims the gospel, which is to say that if the lost hear the gospel and reject it, there cannot be any confidence that God will not send a deluding influence so that there is not opportunity to trust again.

For those who do not love the truth and reject it, God will give a deluding influence and cause them to believe what is false.

The text clearly demonstrates that God not only is glorified in the salvation of the righteous, but He is also glorified in His judgment of the wicked. The truth that God is glorified in the judgment of the wicked, which is something that all humanity deserves, is a humbling teaching. God would be tremendously glorified if there were no saved people, not a soul—if Adam and Eve, and all their children after them, if none of them ever entered heaven, God would be glorified, the Lord would be praised for all eternity by the angels. The thought is sobering. Why are any saved? The only answer is because God is gracious and merciful. He is glorified in the salvation of the righteous; He is also glorified in demonstrating His justice against those who persist in wickedness, which according to Romans 3 and Ephesians 2 includes all humanity. The only difference in believers, as the church, is that God in His grace drew them to Christ, and He is to be praised for His grace and mercy, but the individuals in 2 Thessalonians 2 are those with whom He does not demonstrate His grace and mercy, and He is glorified for His actions.

Summary of 2 Thessalonians 2

In the closing verses of 2 Thessalonians 2, the emphasis is upon God's calling. Paul gave thanks for his readers' salvation, praise for their perseverance, and that they appreciate the secure position that they have in holding to apostolic teaching. In contrast to the wicked unbelievers that were referenced in verse 12, Paul expressed his gratitude for his readers, those who are part of the church. The reason for his joy, he said in verse 13, is the result of God's choice of them for salvation before He created the world. Consistently throughout the New Testament, "from the beginning" indicates a time prior to the world being created, before the foundation of the world, before creation itself; the emphasis is upon God's choice of individuals for salvation. The initiative for salvation comes from God; it is His choosing; it does not come from fallen humanity; rather, God accomplishes His salvation through the work of the Holy Spirit, which is the reason for Paul's joy (i.e., the fact of God choosing for salvation). Paul gave thanks for those that have received God's salvation.

In verse 14, Paul gave thanks that God called the Thessalonians so they could share splendor with the Lord: "that you may gain the glory of our Lord Jesus Christ." The experience of being made holy (sanctification) occurs in three different realms. Positional sanctification is equivalent to justification. Experiential sanctification is the believer becoming being more and more Christlike. Ultimate sanctification is the glorification of the body when believers are confirmed in holiness. Paul was addressing the latter when he referenced believers receiving splendor and honor, the ultimate glorification of the body.

Praise God for His revelation regarding the present times and what the future entails for believers. God is gracious in calling sinners unto salvation. What longing there should be for the day when believers will be with God, and experience all the splendor and honor of their relationship with the Lord Jesus Christ. Scripture gives a hope unlike any other. Praise God for His grace and salvation! The grace of the Lord should continue to enable His people to "stand firm and hold to the traditions which" are taught in Scripture, and do all things as to His glory and by His grace.

CHAPTER 14

THE IMPORTANCE OF BIBLICAL PROPHECY

lthough there are Christians who seek to undermine the study of Biblical prophecy, the need to understand eschatology is imperative because it is the only manner to know the entire counsel of God's holy and inspired Word. For instance, approximately three of every 10 verses in Scripture is prophetic (meaning 27 percent of all the Bible is predictive of future events). Furthermore, the prophetic Word is important to study for, at least, six reasons. *First*, Bible prophecy demonstrates the veracity of God's Word (Isa. 40—49; 2 Pet. 3:13). There are more than 300 prophecies with regard to Christ's first coming and approximately one quarter of the New Testament is prophetic. *Second*, Bible prophecy demonstrates the sovereignty of God in history. God has declared history before it commences. *Third*, Bible prophecy demonstrates the believer's responsibility in the current age. One's view of the future will determine how he or she lives in the present. *Fourth*, an understanding of

Bible prophecy should be an impetus for evangelism. Christ will judge the world of sin and unrighteousness, thus the gospel message needs to be proclaimed boldly and distinctly. *Fifth*, Bible prophecy should be an impetus for godly living. One does not want to be caught in shame when Christ returns for His church. *Sixth*, Bible prophecy gives comfort in the midst of sorrow and facilitates perseverance with a hope of the future.

The Prophetic Word

The issues in Bible prophecy are vital because the answers provided in study reflect the entire counsel of God's Word, and clarify the eschatological hope of the Christian. The study of Bible prophecy also follows Biblical admonitions (cf. Matt. 16:1-3; 24:3). Hebrews 11:13-16 (cf. Luke 21:34, 36) refers to those who lived in light of God's future promises. Second Peter 3:11-14 emphasizes the urgency of being ready when Christ returns. First Thessalonians 5:1-11 contrasts the "you" (those who are able to understand the times in which they live) and "they" (those who are unaware of God's prophetic decrees). Bible prophecy is important because Jesus commended the study of prophecy.

The world today wants to make sense of the events currently transpiring. In Matthew 24—25, the question is answered with regard to the sign of Messiah's coming and the end of the world. The Jewish understanding of the end of the age and Messiah's subsequent coming are intricately related. The reference to the "coming" in verse 3 (also vv. 27, 37, 39) would have meant the kingdom of God being established by Messiah as a literal, earthly reign. When the Lord Jesus establishes His kingdom on earth it is then that the unconditional promises made to Israel in the Abrahamic covenant will be fulfilled. Prior to that time, Jerusalem will be "a cup that causes reeling to all the peoples around" (Zech. 12:2). The present turmoil in the world today is leading toward the fulfillment of Bible prophecy.

Much confusion occurs with the interpretation of Biblical prophecy due to a failure (or refusal) to distinguish between Israel and the church, and thereby denying any future to national Israel and equating the historical throne of David with God's heavenly throne. The former rule (the throne of David) could be called the single, unified, mediatorial kingdom that existed historically under the Mosaic covenant and was prophesied by the Old Testament prophets to be restored in its former glory at the second coming of Jesus Christ. The latter rule (God's heavenly throne), which is eternal, would be understood as involving aspects of God's universal and spiritual kingdoms.

Christians who are keen to appropriate and assert the future blessings that belong to a redeemed and restored national Israel (throughout the kingdom reign of Christ from David's throne in Jerusalem) are not willing—in any manner—to accept the curses and judgments that are associated with those blessings, and which have been fulfilled literally. For example, consistently throughout the book of Isaiah there is a reference to a future King, and He is consistently depicted as the one who will fulfill the Davidic covenant, in addition to sitting forever upon David's throne, which existence has always been historical.

To assert that the numerous kingdom prophecies of the Old Testament are fulfilled in the present spiritual blessings of the church is to abandon the literal meaning of prophecy and to be without a basis or standard for interpretation. For instance, Isaiah 13—23 contain a series of messages, which are primarily oracles or judgments against various Gentile nations. The emphasis within the prophecies is judgment, and thus the oracles should be given careful attention by all nations. One can be fairly certain that the foreign nations were not intended to read the judgments that God had decreed for them; rather, the intent of the messages was primarily to grant prophetic hope for the people of God. The expectation would be immediate for the original recipients of the Divinely inspired messages (in the days of the prophet Isaiah), and would also inspire future generations as they observed the fulfillment of the prophecies.

Within the 11 burdens (oracles) upon the nations, the prophet Isaiah demonstrated what would occur throughout the ensuing several generations in the Near East, as a consequence of the Assyrian invasion force whose armies were marching westward with a yearning for conquest and vengeance. Isaiah's contemporaries would be able to evaluate the accurateness of his message, and thereby determine whether or not God had indeed revealed the burdens against the nations and was speaking those oracles to His people through the prophet.

The only consistent hermeneutic is one that regards—with utmost literalness and solemnity—the numerous and sometimes extended Old Testament prophecies that reference Israel's eternal possession of land and the Davidic dynasty's eternal occupancy of the historical throne. Indeed, the New Testament commences with the demonstration that Jesus Christ is "the Messiah, the son of David, the son of Abraham," and thus the fulfiller of both the Abrahamic and Davidic covenants (Matt. 1:1). Consequently, when one heeds a literal interpretation that grants the recognition of such distinctions, one may then achieve a reasonable deduction.

CONCLUSION

Bible prophecy is as an impetus for believers to warn the lost. Since the prophesied events have not occurred yet, it proves "*that* the longsuffering of our Lord *is* salvation" (2 Pet. 3:15, NKJV). Peter's words of exhortation are both dramatic and sobering as he prioritized the believer's responsibilities to live a diligent life "in peace, spotless and blameless" in Christ (v. 14). The future is certain for all those in the Lord Christ Jesus, and the duration of all the saints in fellowship with the God of peace, who has reconciled the elect unto Himself, will be eternal. Certainly, with such a great hope for the church, God's people should take comfort that "God has not destined us for wrath, but for obtaining salvation through our Lord Jesus Christ" (1 Thess. 5:9; cf. Tit. 2:13). Christians are to warn those that do not have such hope that the coming of God in judgment will be swift (1 Thess. 5:1-6). The early church would greet each other (in the form of a petition) with the word "Maranatha" (1 Cor. 16:22) meaning "our Lord come;" it was spoken to indicate their eager anticipation for the coming of the Lord Jesus to deliver the church from the coming day of the Lord (1 Thess. 1:10). As Christians, we should live each day with an eternal perspective knowing that our future in Christ is certain. *Maranatha*!

ABOUT THE AUTHOR

Dr. Ron J. Bigalke is the Georgia state minister for Capitol Commission. He has experience in numerous discipleship and evangelistic ministries. Dr. Bigalke has instructed courses for Bible colleges and seminaries, and continues to hold professorship in apologetics and theology. Primarily, he serves as a research associate with the University of Pretoria (missions and ethics project).

His church and leadership experience includes conference speaking, pastoral ministry, pulpit ministry and youth ministry. Bigalke is an ordained minister, and is certified in apologetics evangelism. He pastors a church plant through Biblical Ministries Worldwide. His teaching experience includes service as a secondary teacher and administrator, in addition to serving on several school boards. Bigalke is a frequent contributor to and editor for various publications through Eternal Ministries.

He is also a member of several Christian professional societies. His training includes many years of service through the local church. His formal training includes the following degrees: A.B.S., B.S., Moody Bible Institute; M.Apol., Columbia Evangelical Seminary; M.Div., Luther Rice University; M.T.S., Ph.D., Tyndale Theological Seminary; and Ph.D., University of Pretoria.

He and his wife, Kristin, have two children.

Dispensational Publishing House is striving to become the go-to source for Bible-based materials from the dispensational perspective.

Our goal is to provide high-quality doctrinal and worldview resources that make dispensational theology accessible to people at all levels of understanding.

Visit our blog regularly to read informative articles from both known and new writers.

And please let us know how we can better serve you.

Dispensational Publishing House, Inc.
PO Box 3181
Taos, NM 87571

Call us toll free 844-321-4202